PANIC ENCYCLOPEDIA

*the definitive guide
to the postmodern scene*

Arthur Kroker
Marilouise Kroker   David Cook

M
MACMILLAN

First published 1989

Published by
MACMILLAN EDUCATION LTD
Houndmills, Basingstoke, Hampshire RG21 2XS
and London
Companies and representatives
throughout the world

Printed in Canada

British Library Cataloguing in Publication Data

Kroker, Arthur 1945-
    Panic encyclopedia: the definitive guide to
    the postmodern scene — (Culturetexts)
    1. Culture. Postmodernism
    I. Title   II. Kroker, Marilouise
    III. Cook, David, 1946-
    IV. Series
    306

ISBN 0-333-51075-5 pbk.

Before Elvis ...
there was nothing

John Lennon

CultureTexts

Arthur and Marilouise Kroker General Editors

CultureTexts is a series of creative explorations in theory, politics and culture at the *fin-de-millenium*. Thematically focussed around key theoretical debates in the postmodern condition, the *CultureTexts* series challenges received discourses in art, social and political theory, feminism, psychoanalysis, value inquiry, science and technology, the body, and critical aesthetics. Taken individually, contributions to *CultureTexts* represent the forward breaking-edge of postmodern theory and practice.

Titles

The Postmodern Scene: Excremental Culture and Hyper-Aesthetics
Arthur Kroker/David Cook

Life After Postmodernism: Essays on Value and Culture
edited and introduced by John Fekete

Body Invaders
edited and introduced by Arthur and Marilouise Kroker

Panic Encyclopedia
Arthur Kroker, Marilouise Kroker and David Cook

Forthcoming

Seduction
Jean Baudrillard

CONTENTS

Why Panic?   13

A

Panic Alphabet   15
Panic Art   18
Panic Astronomy and Torture   28
Panic Art in Ruins   31
Panic America the Beautiful   35
Panic (Viral) Advertising   38
Panic Architecture   40
Panic Ads   53

B

Panic Babies (Ollie and Gorby too!)   57
Panic Beaches   60
Panic (Chromatic) Bureaucracy   62

C

Panic Crash   64
Panic Canada   68
Panic (Computer) Capitalism   70
Panic Chip Technology   73
Panic Commies   76
Panic Cyberspace   78
Panic Cowboy   80

D

Panic Doughnuts   82
Panic Drugs in America   83
Panic de Tocqueville   86
Panic Dread   92
Panic Desert   93

E

Panic Elvis   95

F

Panic Fashion   97
Panic Finance   99
Panic Feminism   102
Panic Florida Sunstrokes   107

G

Panic God   112

H

Panic Hollywood   114
Panic History   117
Panic Hamburgers   119

I

Panic Ideology   120
Panic Pleasures of Invention   128

J

Panic Jeans   131

K

Panic Killing   137

L

Panic Lips   141
Panic Lovers   142

M

Panic Magnets   144
Panic Money   146
Panic Mythology   148
Panic Masterpieces   150
Panic Manhattan   152
Panic Music   155
Panic Martians   157

N

Panic Nietzsche's Cat (on Panic Particle Physics)   158

O

Panic Obscenities   163
Panic Ovaries   170
Panic Olympics   172
Panic Ozone   173

P

Panic Pigeons   175
Panic (Virtual) Pilots   177
Panic Penis   180
Panic Plague   182
Panic Perfect Faces   186
Panic Psychoanalysis   188
Panic Politics   190

Q

Panic Quiet   192

R

Panic Reno Romance   193
Panic Racing   201

S

Panic Sex   203
Panic SuperScience   204
Panic Shopping Malls   208
Panic Suburbs   211
Panic Surrealism   215
Panic Seagulls   218

T

Panic TV   220
Panic Toys   223

U

Panic USA   227
Panic Urine   232

V

Panic Viral Computers   235
Panic Viral Theory   238
Panic Vanities   239
Panic Vice Versa   244

W

Panic Worms   248
Panic Waiting   250

X

Panic Xanax   251

Y

Panic Yuppies (East and West)   259

Z

Panic Zombies   261

Acknowledgements   263

Notes on Contributors   265

WHY PANIC?

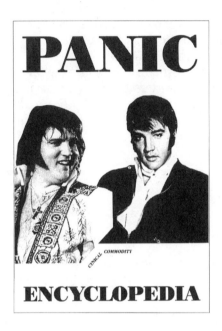

Panic is the key psychological mood of postmodern culture.

In pharmaceuticals, a leading drug company, eager to get the jump on supplying sedatives for the panic population at the end of the millenium, has just announced plans for a "world wide panic project." In television, Vanna White — co-host of the *Wheel of Fortune* — can (finally) confess that she was chosen for her role by Merv Griffin because of her disproportionately large head-size. After all, in the age of the talking heads of television as the real world what counts is the sheer giganticism of media silhouettes.

Panic patriotism too. That is Donald Trump and Lee Iacocca as self-nominated American heroes of the market-place. Breaking with the old robber baron tradition of practicing primitive exploitation in the age of an equally exploitative primitive capitalism, they have discovered the secret formula of postmodern robber barons as that of merging the economic calculus of "let's make a deal" with the political rhetoric of making America stronger.

And finally, even panic Elvis is invited to come on down for one last retro-appearance as a memory residue, made all the more nostalgic because Elvis' disappearing body is like a flashing event-horizon at the edge of the black hole that is America today.

Panic culture, then, as a floating reality, with the actual as a dream world, where we live on the edge of ecstasy and dread. Now it is the age of the TV audience as a chilled superconductor, of the stock market crash as a Paris Commune of all the programed super-computers, of money as an electronic impulse fibrillating across the world, and of the individual as a quantum energy pack tracing/racing across the postmodern field.

Welcome to the *Panic Encyclopedia* where everybody can get in on the feast. Panic readers too! If you have a panic flash, send your account along for Volume II of the *Panic Encyclopedia*, as we are pulled by cultural gravitation into the dark and dense vortex of the Year 2000.

A

PANIC ALPHABET

What is the panic encyclopedia?

It's a frenzied scene of post-facts for the *fin-de-millenium*. Here, even the alphabet implodes under the twin pressures of the ecstasy of catastrophe and the anxiety of fear. From panic art, panic astronomy, panic babies and panic (shopping) malls to panic sex, panic perfect faces and panic victims, that *is* the post-modern alphabet. Not then an alphabetic listing of empirical facts about the modern condition, but a post-alphabetic description of the actual dissolution of facts into the flash of thermonuclear cultural "events" in the postmodern situation.

As the dark, reverse and imploding side of all the modernist encyclopedias, *Panic Encylopedia* begins with the fateful discovery in contemporary physics that ninety percent of the natural universe is missing matter, just disappeared and no one knows where it has gone (physicists most of all). *Panic Encyclopedia* argues that with the triumph of science and technology as the real language of power in post-modern culture, that ninety percent of contemporary

PANIC

society is also missing matter, just vanished and that no one knows where it is gone (sociologists most of all).

Indeed, since we are probably already living in post-millenial consciousness on the other side of the Year 2000 (calendar time is already too slow: Jean Baudrillard was correct when he said recently in the French newspaper, *Liberation*, that we should take a vote to jump immediately to the Year 2000 and thus end the interminable and boring wait for the millenium), we are the first human beings to live in the dead zone of a fatal attraction between postmodern science and popular culture. More than we may suspect, panic science is now the deepest language of consumption, entertainment, politics, and information technology just as much as the oscillating *fin-de-millenium* mood of deep euphoria *and* deep despair of contemporary culture is the ruling ideology of postmodern science.

Between ecstasy and fear, between delirium and anxiety, between the triumph of cyber-punk and the political reality of cultural exhaustion: that is the emotional mood-line of *Panic Encyclopedia*. Here, in fact, panic has the reverse meaning of its classical sense. In antiquity, the appearance of the god *Pan* meant a moment of arrest, a sudden calm, a rupture-point between frenzy and reflection. Not though in the postmodern condition. Just like the reversal of classical kynicism (philosophy from below) into postmodern cynicism (for the ruling elites) before it, the classical meaning of panic has now disappeared into its opposite sense. In the postmodern scene, panic signifies a twofold free-fall: the disappearance of *external* standards of public conduct when the social itself becomes the transparent field of a cynical power; and the dissolution of the *internal* foundations of identity (the disappearing ego as the victory sign of postmodernism) when the self is transformed into an empty screen of an exhausted, but hyper-technical, culture. Panic? That is the dominant psychology of the fully technological self, living at that vanishing-point where postmodern science and culture interpellate as reverse mirror-images in a common power field. If the hyper-technological self is also "falling, falling without limits," this may indicate that it, too, is already a post-fact in the post-millenial alphabet, with one final (literary) existence as an entry in the *Panic Encyclopedia*.

Consequently, the *Panic Encyclopedia* is all about a double complicity. Postmodern science as the social physics of a fading cultural scene, and postmodern culture as the sure and certain source of the ideological theorems of contemporary science. We understand panic science as postmodern political theory in the intensive, but disguised, form of a theory of a *fading nature* at the *fin-de-millenium*; and we read postmodern culture — from panic Hollywood, panic viral computers and panic finance to panic urine —

as explicit materializations of the catastrophic, but hyperreal, formulations of postmodern science at the levels of fashion, money, liquid TV, and sex.

PANIC ART

Rituals of Estheticized Recommodification
(An Interview with Mark Kostabi)

Andrew Haase:...You're right, it's a language.[1]

Mark Kostabi: ...I don't know what "reified" means. I see it in my reviews all the time. I don't know any of these words: "simulation," "Foucault." But, people who know how to use these words have complete control of the art world right now. And it's ironic...

A.H.: Right. The people who write for this book however are not those people. I, for example, know how to use this language but I don't have control of the art world.

M.K.: You see, I feel if I knew how to use "sliding signifiers" in a sentence, I feel that then I would be able to crack the high-money art super-structure. I would be able to carry on with a neo-geo artist; which I couldn't do now. And they're making a lot more money per piece on their art work than I am. And they're accepted in the Sacchi world, which I have nothing to do with.

A.H.: If you knew the language of psychoanalysis and you could throw around those terms...

M.K.: I as an artist would get three times richer in many ways, and much more respect, if I only knew how to use a word like "sliding signifier." But most of the people who use those words are dirt poor. Probably always will be.

A.H.: If I wanted to make money, I should become a painter.

M.K.: And use words like that?

A.H.: And use words like that.

M.K.: Well, maybe it takes more than that.

A.H.: I could get you to paint for me. Or somebody else.

M.K.: Maybe that's not even the case. Maybe those artists...maybe there's only three of them that are really successful and it has nothing to do with the language they use.

A.H.: Well, the language certainly does sell...it can sell.

M.K.: I guess it does...I've never engaged in that. I'm not against it…it's certainly interesting. But I've only observed it from a distance. But here you are ready to interview me, maybe I'll learn something.

A.H.: The modern sensibility constructed, employed and capitalized upon a fastidious distinction between sign and referent, presentation and re-presentation. Today these boundaries collapse. Panic art situates us within its own polar opposition: nostalgic desire for the rock-solid values of respectable modernism vs. hyper-fascination for the valuelessness of postmodern over-production. The surplus value attributed to a painting, to "great art," provided economic rationalization for the gap between production cost and retail price. Kostabi Incorporated replaces a desire for value in the work of art with our desire for hype allowing you to "Cash in on passion."[2] How do you *feel* about this responsibility?

M.K.: I'm over-qualified to answer that question…but I'll attempt anyway. I'll ignore everything that preceded the word "responsibility" and just deal with that as a topic. Do I feel like I have a "responsibility?" To anything? I am not interested in making lots of money because if I die I think it's boring to just be able to say I left a lot of money behind. Money is just one of many tools that I use to make great art and I would like to leave as large a quantity (with the best quality) of good paintings behind in the world. That's basically the responsibility that I have to myself and to the world. I am publicly owned.[3]

A.H.: Surrounding us, panic art elicits a twofold reaction: 1) "acephalous panic" which *must* act, which *must* possess, yet finds the world amorphous and 2) "cryogenic panic" which stands within a circle of possibilities without difference and vibrates in all directions. Not either/or but both/and.[4] The purchase of a toothpaste, a toilet paper, or a painting, rests on brand reliability and packaging. All products screech at the consumer simultaneously. You no longer choose to buy a Kostabi rather than a Fischl or a Salle or a Haring—the Kostabi chooses you. Targeting its audience with aplomb, quietly inveigling the consumer, aggressive painting prepares the papers *beforehand* to insure an automatic adoption. You ask yourself: "Kostabi: Do you paint what you see? Kostabi: No, I paint what will be seen."[5] How does it *feel* to be re-positioned as no longer "democratic documentarian" but as *auteur* of desire and imag-ination?

M.K.: If I were just one there would be no dialogue; it would die out and it would be boring. I swing back and forth from controller to controlee. It's true that I have been re-positioned to the fourth square on the hop-scotch schematic but I choose to play hop-scotch rather than ping-pong.

A.H.: Kostabi becomes a function of the marketplace in an advanced capitalist society which demands an institutionalized artist while simultaneously proclaiming the liquidation of the artistic institution. Both museums and galleries have become not only notches on a resume, not simply advertising tools, but zones of mass indoctrination and stream-lined distribution centers for re-processed images of body, psyche and pocket-book. Not without masochistic pleasure do we invite Kostabi Inc. to tattoo us with the numbers of our estheticized recommodification.[6] But how does it *feel* to be on the other side of the needle?

M.K.: It's only a needle in Europe where my customers are pansies. In America, it's more like a rusty nail and I enjoy causing my victims to suffer from the disease which they ask for...ask me the question again. (Question is repeated.) I disagree. There's no S&M involved, really. It's just an artist making paintings and showing them to the world. Some people will tell you that "Americans love to be slapped in the face," but that's not really true. You can use both answers, by the way.

A.H.: The production of panic representations initiates a radical refusal of "real" paintings as transcendental incarnations and "real" painters as priests. No more pre-tense, just in-tense. The postmodern equivalence of difference and sameness, of gender and androgyny, of nation and market, of art and commodity, administers its own re-examination. As "an artist who practices his art as a 'business'"[7], how do you *feel* Kostabi may be situated in relation to painters who insist on "real art"? And as the Kostabi project no longer pretends to reveal the abyss, what do you *feel* it reveals?

M.K.: Well, you're missing the entire point. First of all, you're assuming that I am more of a businessman than an artist (which most mindless middle-class Americans assume) and then you're clouding that misconception by stringing together a lot of big, fancy words for no reason and disguising it underneath pretentious words. There's really no point in this discussion. But I intend to overthrow you and clear the fields of vomit with one-third of the needle you spoke of previously.

A.H.: "Abjection"[8] in Julia Kristeva's work is the dream of "real" transgression and heterogeneity. On first glance one might envisage the Kostabi project as transgressing the Law of New York's art scene. Yet despite the rhetoric, your work follows the economic expectations of the financial world: the prices of the paintings go up. In fact, the corporation's success hinges on the reliability of your product as an investment. Profoundly conservative, Kostabi Inc. employs excremental marketing techniques[9] in the name of a legitimate undertaking. The practice of paying other artists ($7 to $10 per hour) to execute and title paintings (selling for as much as $20,000) which you then sign, is consistent with the means by which all corporations in capitalism employ workers to produce goods and services. Kostabi is the Burger King of painting. In an art world where the only art is that of business do you *feel* any transgression is possible?

M.K.: I am not the Burger King of painting; I am undisputably a genius. As far as I know I am tops in my field. I haven't met another individual who possesses as much genius as I do. I employ assistants to execute my ideas. I hire people to create sub-ideas. Occasionally a sub-idea may be more profound...I do not produce fast food.

A.H.: Some painters do not wish to spend their time perfecting advertising ploys and mixing the necessary proportions of self-promotion to hype. They wish to paint rather than pose. Do you *feel* this is possible in our present age?

M.K.: Well everything is sales, whether it's painting or chit-chat at lunch. I don't paint with a brush between my fingers. I paint in the same way Donald Trump builds when he causes the Trump Tower to come into existence. Most painters are very pretentious and are indeed posing when they claim to be Van Gogh's brother, as most artists that I meet do.

A.H.: At this moment Kostabi Incorporated is in the process of preparing Kostabi World: a three story building in New York designed to house the complete line of Kostabi products and "grow" Kostabi paintings for the future. Do you plan a copy of Keith Haring's "Pop Shop", or are you interested in creating an "alternative reality"? Will this be a New York version of Disney World? As Jean Baudrillard writes: "Disneyland is there to conceal the fact that it is the 'real' country, all of 'real' America, which is Disneyland...".[10] What do you *feel* is the relation between Kostabi World and Disney World?

M.K: Well, first of all Baudrillard is a total jerk. He doesn't understand America in anyway whatsoever and all his books have much more in common with Disneyland...his books are basically silly symphonies. My *museum* is not a copy of either Disneyland or Keith Haring's "Pop Shop". I'm not the next Andy Warhol; I'm the first Kostabi. Whereas Haring's endeavor was to make the knick-knacks be the substance, my store selling knick-knacks will pretend to be a store selling knick-knacks. For Haring the tee-shirt is the end and for Kostabi it is nothing but a tee-shirt with a picture on it that speaks of something greater. The best thing about Haring's work is the "Pop Shop," of course.

A.H.: Often you respond to questions with Kostabisms: "Take the 'L' out of PLAY,"[11] "Take the 'R' out of FREE,"[12] "Paintings are doorways into collectors' homes,"[13] "Say less and say yes."[14] When interviewers continue to ask the same questions why change the answers? These aphorisms seem to be designed to protect Kostabi from criticism while insuring product recognition in the future. Do you *feel* image-production through repetition is a useful marketing tool?

M.K.: The only marketing tool I've ever used is to just produce damn good paintings. They have wit, sensuality and they're irreverent, penetrating. Repetition can be interesting on occasion but often is boring. When Andy Warhol made an issue out of his repetition being the essence of his work it was a cop out and and merely an excuse for not being able to keep up with his goals. Mark Kostabi does not make mass produced art. I deliver constantly changing, exciting, unpredictable...fill in the blank.

A.H.: In the Nov. 26, 1987 issue of *The Phoenix*, Elizabeth Wright quotes you as saying, "I use a universal language, the figure. They are not racially indicated or gender indicated." Your paintings however indicate through shading and environment that white/western individuals are being represented[15] while secondary sex characteristics, clothing, positioning, and musculature determine the gender of your "Every-men".[16] The production of images in this manner formulates our desire. Their complicity with patriarchal role models is confirmed by the continual and predictable portrayal of men in board rooms[17] while women care for children[18] or act as a convenient metaphor for Culture.[19] *Pandering to Feminism*, 1984, is the reactionary response of a bitter and resentful male. How do you *feel* about the discrepancy between what you say and what you do?

M.K.: There is no discrepancy. Look at the painting *Two Cultures*, women don't go around carrying bowls of fruit on their head any more. That's one of the things that painting is saying...I don't exclusively use a universal language but I do employ that device and that is one of thousands of different devices that I use, I don't always use figures in my paintings either. One device that I have used a lot hitherto has been the faceless figure and sometimes I have been overly explicit in a cartoon-like way, indicating women by giving them breasts and a dress and men by making their limbs thicker and more like male anatomy. You're being too simplistic. My plan is much

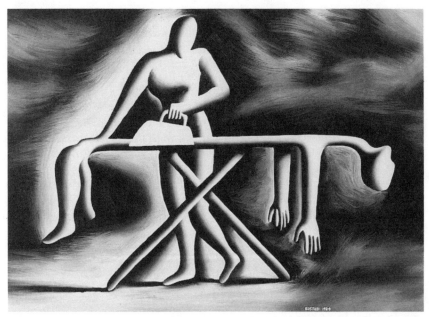

Pandering to Feminism, Mark Kostabi

grander and it's not just the paintings, it's also the sculptures and the hype as you say. But I don't think hype is everything; it's a very large portion of my work whereas a lot of people say Kostabi's real art is his persona. They should realize that I am this unstoppable, mega-force that gives only 10% of its time to promotion and hype.

A.H.: Panic art is perfectly reflexive. Paintings offer up a critique of painting. Collectors who purchase the work are laughed at in the work. Self-criticism is self-promotion. The interview is the art of Mark Kostabi as both advertiser and creator, as both affirmation and condemnation. *Sixty Minutes* becomes a T.V. commercial. As you say: "Caress the press."[20] Kostabi, as the product of Kostabi Inc., follows the logic of product placement just as Lite Beer does in *Back to School*. The painting becomes the screen for the projection of the art. Do you *feel* this is a positive situation? Or is this some parody of the art scene? Of "great art"? Is this what you're getting at? Perhaps the entire Kostabi enterprise is an elaborate scheme to exact revenge from an art world that once shunned you? Or is the position of art in capitalism the primary target of your critique? Perhaps capitalism itself? How is your return to capitalism a reaction to capitalism? Or is it the function of capital in society? And art? What do you *feel* is its function? When critique is just more advertising? When this interview itself promotes the message of Kostabi? And when that message prescribes codes for action? What are we supposed to do then? If all our choices? When art no longer reflects experience but? When individuals mold actions and re-actions to fit visual representations? When image production reaches levels of over-saturation? What can we do then? What can then? What can we?

M.K.: Is that really the last question? You're dead wrong. What you should do is print that monologue in Greek and then ask me all the questions again one by one. Sentence by sentence. You put a question mark behind every sentence and I will answer them individually. This could last another hour. Start from the beginning.

Andrew Haase

Notes

1. The following interview took place at the Kostabi studio on September 9, 1988.

2. Poster at Kostabi studio, 8/12/88. Today, theoretical publications and panic texts follow the same logic as the Kostabi project: Jacques Derrida releases three works simultaneously to saturate the shelves of St. Mark's book store or Wordsworth while photographs of nude women and apocalyptic art advertize collections of hyper-essays. "Talk the talk." *Postmodernism sells.* In an academic star-system fame and fortune are the rewards for shrewd marketing.

3. These comments are diametrically opposed to earlier statements which credited pecuniary interests, rather than the desire to "make great art", with motivating Kostabi. For example: "Modern art's a con and I am the greatest con artist." Kostabi in Jason Edward Kaufman, "'Con Artist' Mark Kostabi: On the Make and Making It," *New York City Tribune*, 4/26/88, p. 14. The "Truth" of Kostabi is that "Truth" does not exist.

4. See Hjelmslev's glossematics as sited in Christian Metz, *The Imaginary Signifier: Psychoanalysis and the Cinema*, trans. Celia Britton, Annwyl Williams, Ben Brewster and Alfred Guzzetti, Bloomington: Indiana University Press, 1977, p. 175.

5. Kostabi, *Upheaval*, New York: Pelham Press and Mark Kostabi, 1985.

6. Arthur Kroker and David Cook, *The Postmodern Scene: Excremental Culture and Hyper-Aesthetics*, New York: St. Martin's Press, 1986, p. 16-20.

7. "The abject is perverse because it neither gives up nor assumes a prohibition, a rule, or a law; but turns them aside, misleads, corrupts; uses them, takes advantage of them, the better to deny them. It kills in the name of life—a progressive despot; it lives at the behest of death—an operator in genetic experimentations; it curbs the other's suffering for its own profit—a cynic (and a psychoanalyst); it establishes narcissistic power while pretending to reveal the abyss—an artist who practices his art as a 'business'." Julia Kristeva, *Powers of Horror: An Essay on Abjection*, trans. Leon S. Roudiez, New York: Columbia University Press, 1982, p. 15-6. Italics added.

8. Ibid.

9. "Collectors who buy my work are fools. The more I spit in their face the more they beg me to sell them another painting." See Kostabi in Jason Edward Kaufman, "'Con Artist' Mark Kostabi: On the Make and Making It," *New York City Tribune*, 4/26/88, p. 14. Kostabi, in Robert Young, *An Interview with Kostabi*, p. 9.

10. "Disneyland is presented as imaginary in order to make us believe that the rest is real, when in fact all of Los Angeles and the America surrounding it are no longer real, but of the order of the hyperreal and of simulation." Jean Baudrillard, *Simulations*, New York: Semiotext(e), 1983 p. 25.

11. Kostabi, *Upheaval*. Poster at Kostabi studio, 8/12/88. Kostabi in Michael Kaplan, "Mark Kostabi", *The Learning Annex*, 8/86, p. 11. Kostabi in Elizabeth Wright, "Just When You Thought 1984 Was Safely Behind You," *The Phoenix*, 11/26/87, p. 15.

12. Kostabi, *Upheaval*. Poster at Kostabi studio, 8/12/88. Kostabi in Kaplan, "Mark Kostabi", p. 11. Kostabi in "Are Mark Kostabi and the East Village One and the Same?", *Downtown*, 7/22/87. Kostabi in Wright, p. 15. Kostabi in Rory MacPherson, "The Artist As Aesthetocrat," *FAD*, Spring 1988.

13. Kostabi, *Upheaval*. Kostabi in Kaplan, p. 10. Kostabi in "Are Mark Kostabi and the East Village One and the Same?", *Downtown*, 7/22/87. Kostabi in Wendy Wylegala, "Update: Making his Mark," *Columbia Art Review*, Spring 1988, p. 77.

14. Kostabi, *Upheaval*,. Kostabi in "Are Mark Kostabi and the East Village." Kostabi in Everyman, "With Mark Kostabi," *Pan Arts*, May 1984, p. 12.

15. See *Close Call*, 1983 and *Oedipus or Mother Knows Best*, 1983.

16. See *The Last Kiss*, 1983, *Summer Night*, 1986, and *The Blossoming of Vulnerability*, 1987.

17. See *Mergers and Acquisitions*, 1987.

18. See *Reaching*, 1983.

19. See *Two Cultures*, 1984.

20. Poster at Kostabi studio, 8/12/88. Special thanks to Teresa Podlesney for her critical input regarding the final version of this interview.

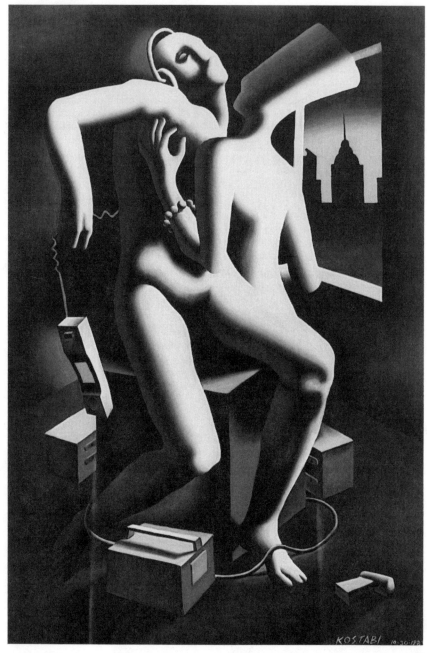

Close Call, Mark Kostabi

Two Cultures, Mark Kostabi

PANIC ASTRONOMY

Political torture and galactic observatories

What is the relationship between astronomy and torture?

I have often been puzzled by this relationship because of a particular, and grisly, outbreak of State-sponsored political torture. In the 1970s while living in Italy I followed with outrage the accounts of the violent days at the beginning of the Pinochet regime in Chile, and the spreading outwards thereafter of dark days of political torture, from the disappeared to the mutilated. I also noted, and wondered about, a coincidental newspaper account that in the very first weeks of the political coup, the United States which had just sponsored the new military regime, also announced major funding support for astronomy observatories high in the Chilean Andes.

Since then, I have often thought of the surrealistic contrast between the screams of the tortured in Chilean politics, and the spectral, space-gazing silence of the astrophysics laboratories. There was no apparent political relationship beween them, other than that of the ideological indifference of scientific value-neutrality. One was immanently inscribed in the torture-techniques of earth-bound knowledge; and the other was almost utopian, or at least an appealing instance of scientific humanism over the years, in its steady announcement of the discovery of new star galaxies, pulsars, and twin stars.

I was reminded of this relationship when reading recently in the *International Herald Tribune* that a major competition had just been held to fully technify the Chilean observatories, placing them directly under the radio telemetry control of one of the major industrialized countries. The headline read: "From Bavaria to Chile to Eighteen Billion Years Ago." It was only ironic, and perhaps a point of undoubtedly unfair historical coincidence, that Hitler's political birthplace had thus claimed a double inheritance: not only the continuation anew of fascism in the Chilean state; but now also, in the Chilean galactic observatories.

Or is it something different, and more explicitly sinister? Not a relationship of the silence of non-identity between astronomy and political terror, but, at least on the basis of a mutual epistemological origin in panoptic and disciplinary knowledge, their common issue from a deeply shared cosmology. An unhappy intellectual complicity, therefore, between astronomy with its panoptic eye gazing into space as the purest expression possible of the will to truth, and political torture with its panoptic turned earthwards in the equally purest expression of the will to power. Is there not, perhaps, at work here a more secret cabalistic knowledge between political torture, which begins and ends with a pure astronomy of the victim's body, and astrophysics, which, itself a will to pure facticity, compels the universe to confess its secrets.

Thus, two kinds of scientists — star gazers and body gazers: both performing according to the very same rules of knowledge, and both responding to the same political impulses — if, that is, postmodern power be thought about in its deepest and most constitutive expression as the dynamic unfolding everywhere of the will to exact the tiniest secretions of information from its citizenry(social nature) and from the galaxy (nature). And all of this carried out by complicit methodological strategies: whether by surveillance under the sign of the panoptic eye, by the decoding of the cabalistic signs of information acquired, or by the more immediate political strategem of forced confessions. Is it, perhaps, that like Foucault's prisons or medical clinics, which are the truth-sayers of the hidden rules of power in society at large, the astronomy laboratories, high up on the Andean mountaintops, also provide the ruling, epistemological codes for State terrorism: power as panoptic surveillance; the complicity of knowledge and power in the postmodern condition; and the minute gathering and decoding of information acquired from the static of the physical universe or from the screams of the tortured, a whole dedoublement of stellar knowledge and bodily facticity under the sign of an indifferent galaxy.

And if it be objected that astronomy is a pure science, far removed from the specificities of political struggle and brute power, then let it also be noted that the postmodern state, of which Chile is an avant-garde, not retrograde, expression, surely has its *ocular* origins in Bentham's fateful design of panoptic surveillance as the ruling power strategem in the era of power/truth. And if it be said that this ocular knowledge is, through the medium of astrophysics and technologies of galactic exploration, already space-bound, then this just might mean that the fateful relationship between astrophysics and torture in Chile stands ready now to be recapitulated at a higher and more intra-galactic level of abstraction in the future. A surrealistic inquisition,then, of star-surveillance and body gazing as also part of Chile's tragic political legacy for the western world.

And finally, why *panic* astronomy? Because at least in the Chilean case, the very continuation of astrophysics in the Andes throughout all of these dark years is surely founded upon and constituted by a suspension of ethical discourse about the relationship between science and torture. Panic astronomy? Over and beyond the terrible infolding of the will to truth and the will to power, astrophysics in the Andes is also in the way of a looking away from the tortured screams of the innocent. And so, of course, the Bavarian (telemetried) connection, not only as a superior technological form for the management of the ocular power of surveillance, but also as an expedient ethical suppressant.

Consequently, a more troubling question. In that deliberately imposed silence between two state technologies — one involving the seduction of the scienticization of the stars and the other implicated in the violence of the scienticization of the tortured body — in this almost impossible gap of ethical indifference between science and terror, might there not also be found a privileged, and terrifying, glimpse of *our* political future?

PANIC ART IN RUINS

In my dreams, I find myself standing beside the wreckage of Camus' car, picking up the copy of *The Gay Science* which he had beside him when he died. And I think of that other text of Europe in Ruins, *The Rebel*, where Camus says that pure virtue without realism is homicidal and realism without ethics is cynical murder.

Oversite, Glyn Banks/Hannah Vowles

Road to Ruin, Glyn Banks/Hannah Vowles

Installation *From the Ruins*, Glyn Banks/Hannah Vowles

Road to Ruin Installation, Glyn Banks/Hannah Vowles

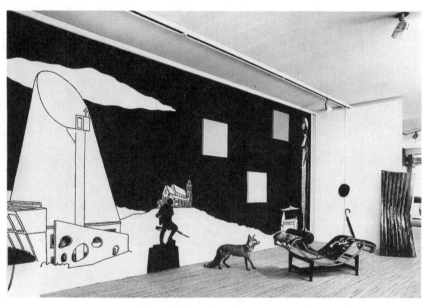

New Realism Installation, Glyn Banks/Hannah Vowles

PANIC AMERICA THE BEAUTIFUL, FROM L.A. TO BERLIN

Back Seat Dodge '38, Edward Kienholz

Edward Kienholz, the artist, is the mortician of American culture. In his work, an almost perverse fascination with the detritus of found objects — beds, radios, hospital refuse, TVs, cars, restaurants and brothels — is transformed into a series of installations of a California culture in its last fatal paroxysm of exhaustion and cultural inertia. Like a designer arrangement of dead bodies in a funeral parlour, Kienholz arranges the remains of America the Beautiful for one last viewing at the turn of the century.

Moving between L.A. and Berlin, Kienholz is the quintessential artist of retrashed fascism. Not fascism under the old, and obsolescent, sign of Hitlerian politics, but a whole new order of fascism which moves at the edge of kitsch culture and violence, and where the alterity of use/abuse marks the deepest forms of postmodern subjectivity.

While Visions of Sugar Plums Danced in their Heads,
Edward Kienholtz

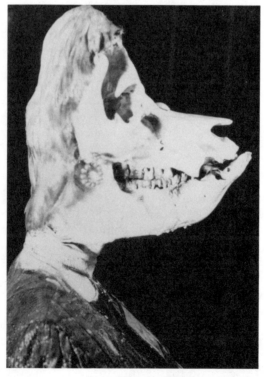

Roxy Madam, Edward Kienholtz

America in Ruins: Three Viewings of the Living Tomb

1. The *Roxy Madame* greets you as you enter this brothel in Los Angeles. The time (June, 1943) is framed by the calendar donated by Psenner-Pauff Automotive Parts Company. The salute is given by General MacArthur, hung opposite our hostess. Conveniently, there is a woman with a bag over her head, legs spread; and also a fashion table with a bloodied head in a mirror. The center-piece, appropriately called "Five Dollar Billy", is found in the sewing machine, ready for action although a rat has got there first and is protruding from the woman's breast. An aesthetic touch is added by the sampler on the wall depicting a woman watering flowers, and over her head the motto:

> There is so much good in the worst of us
> And so much bad in the best of us
> That it behooves any of us
> To talk about the rest of us.

2. *While Sugar Plums Danced in Their Heads* (1964) is a study of the monstrous double of sexual voyeurism. Here, the art dealer peers through the heads to discover the visions of erotica which are played out in the tubescent, cancerous growths. Sex is continuous, reflected in all the mirrors of the middle-class peep show, coded by Coors' beer, moving to the rhythm of the mutant growths in the bed.

3. *The Back Seat Dodge '38* (1964) is also about sex as power in ruins: rape framed by the car, wired bodies, detrital beer bottles, a whole nostalgic technology of sex for a culture of flagging penises. Here, the back seat becomes the carceral site of the framed rape which ends with the abandonment of the vagina by the penis in the desexed stupor of the couple.

PANIC VIRAL ADVERTISING

Viral advertising is the cutting-edge of new strategies in the media war games surrounding politics and marketing. In viral advertising, the simulacra of the body politic is injected directly with negative images of electoral opponents, the intention being to propagate in the minds of voters a high degree of image sickness(of other politicians). With political ill health for others its only aim, viral advertising is sensitively attuned to the daily read-outs of the tracking polls. In primary politics, political managers now claim with real accuracy that viral advertising can be counted on to cost its (candidate) targets at least a five per cent drop in the image ratings.

And to the question, what if all the candidates use negative advertising? Well then, that just means that electoral politics rapidly becomes like a big electronic hospital room filled up with sick images. And, of course, for those (politicians) about to be infected with the virus of sick images, there is now a fast cure. The images of political candidates can actually be inoculated against bad TV viruses by running anticipatory positive ads which both identify potential image-weaknesses, and treat that infectious spot directly by immunizing it with curative viruses in the form of hyper-positive ads. Thus, for example, in the 1988 American Presidential campaign, Bush immunized his TV-self against Democratic charges of scandal (Bush's relationship with Noriega, his involvement with Iran-Contra), by launching a series of "attack ads": advertisements on CNN, for example, which described in detail murders and rapes committed by prisoners given early time releases in Massachusetts during Dukakis' terms as Governor. When Dukakis' negative spots finally ran, they had little effect: Bush had long ago been inoculated on the scandal issue. A TV campaign strategy based, therefore, on the twin principles of "low bridging" (hide the candidate in TV studios for purposes of staged communictions) and, in the absence of a substantive program, privilege attack ads which, as polling technology demonstrates, work powerfully in the age of TV-subordinated politics.

Or maybe it is something more. If viral advertising of the negative kind could work so effectively in Bush's presidential campaign, perhaps that is because in contemporary American politics attack ads touch a more subterranean region of primitive mythology. Bush's media campaign was a triumphant expression of what Nietzsche described as slave morality: a generation of Americans who, feeling cheated out of existence by their own botched and bungled instincts, displace their fear and anxiety about a threatening outer world onto the image of Willy Horton (who as the voice-over says raped and killed a white woman while out on a prison furlough).

In slave morality of the Bush kind, everyone is in on the joke that power now is only cynical, and those who aren't in on the joke (Dukakis most of all) are condemned to lose. And it is no longer political manipulation of a passive media audience either, but a TV audience which, fueled by the envy and resentment of slave morality, participates actively in the joke of cynical power. Thus, Bush could be such an accurate example of the alterity of American power because in his constructed advertising persona, the two poles of Clint Eastwood (the "read my lips" George Bush) and Gary Cooper (the "gentle and kind America" mode of Bush think) could be flipped back and forth with dazzling speed. Indeed, in informal meetings with the press on the Vice-Presidential plane, it was reported that Bush would entertain reporters with his facility for field-reversing the Eastwood/Cooper simulacrum: Clint would be the subject and Gary the predicate of the very same sentence. And the American TV audience? Well, as the electoral results of the campaign have revealed, the media audience prides itself now on its technical savvy: it saw right through the cynical politics of Bush's advertising strategy, and awarded political merit points (votes) for the best technical performance.

And so, Dukakis' fate. In the absence of reading Nietzsche's reflections on slave morality (and thus understanding the heart of the heart of the USA today), he could only have media reversed Bush by playing Jimmy Stewart to Eastwood and Cooper. That is just to gamble though that *Mr. Smith Goes to Washington* is still a familiar mythological refrain in American progressive politics, and, more to the point, in the cinematic (that is to say, Presidential voting) traditions of the Mid-West and South.

PANIC ARCHITECTURE

MY TRIP TO GUILD HOUSE

While in Philadelphia for a conference on the future of the post, I visited Guild House, an apartment complex for the elderly designed by Robert Venturi and associates and privileged in the discourse on postmodernism as the first of all the postmodern buildings, although its construction began in 1960 — well before 3:32 p.m., July 15, 1972, the official moment of death for modernism as pronounced by Charles Jencks. ("The modern machine for living," wrote Jencks of the dynamiting of the Pruitt-Igoe housing project in St. Louis, "as Le Corbusier had called it with the technological euphoria so typical of the 1920s, had become unlivable, the modernist experiment, so it seemed, obsolete.")

Friends from Philadelphia had provided me with precise instructions for navigating from the hotel to Guild House, and a precise address. Still, I drove past the building several times, its tight grey facade indistinguishable at thirty miles per hour from other housing projects on nearby blocks — its postmodern cast a difference which made no difference.

photo credit: Venturi, Rauch and Scott Brown

Eventually, I suppressed the terrain of the real sufficiently that my perspective yielded to the official images of Guild House from all the books and articles. I parked my car, a grey 1983 Honda, and walked around the front, sides and rear of the building taking snapshots.

Let me distinguish between Guild House — which remains historically frozen in official photographs available in Venturi's books and, by request, from the office of Venturi, Rauch and Scott Brown — versus what I will call GH: the actual place I visited which is labeled Guild House. I can only say of GH that it is glaringly ordinary, that it was completed in 1965, and that it serves as low income housing for the elderly.

A partial listing of differences, then, between Guild House, the critical object, and GH, the lived(-in) object:

Guild House stands monumentally against a dramatic sky, its eye-catching, arched, eye-like upper window half-mockingly half-blinking. On the other hand, GH is framed, not against the heavens above, a clean, empty street below, and silence all around, but by litter, billboards, fences, outsized trees, and street noise. For all its authors' intentions to prevent such a fate, the urban modernity which surrounds GH has erased any cultural relevancies it may once have (abstractly) enjoyed. While Guild House remains the earliest, purest postmodern public building in North America, GH is but one more silent structure on a busy, anonymous, postindustrial thoroughfare.

Venturi once said of Crawford Manor, the modernist New Haven tower for the elderly against which he constrasted Guild House in *Learning from Las Vegas:* "We criticize Crawford Manor not for 'dishonesty,' but for irrelevance today." I criticize Guild House not for 'irrelevance,' but for desertion. There is no Guild House at GH.

Take, for instance, the sign, in big black letters on Guild House, described by Venturi as "particularly ugly and ordinary in its explicit commerical associations," which on GH desperately needs repainting and which has lost its mercantile edge now that occupants of the two front apartments have graced their balconies with plants. The plants (which are dying) drape over the "U" of the first word.

Venturi wrote that "[t]he character of the graphics connotes dignity..." Today, on GH it denotes the auto-deconstruction of the postmodern when it is left out in the acid rain of residual modernity. No act of will (not even Venturi's use of brick "darker than usual to match the smog-smudged brick of the neighborhood") can secure a place for the critical object in a poor neighborhood.

If, as Mies insisted and Venturi resisted, "God dwells in the details," at GH you must walk outside in the right light, around the side, and lean back on your heels to find it.

On Guild House, in contrast, are all variety of details: monumental ones that elude the (architecturally) uneducated or post-cynical observer of GH. "The dark walls with double-hung windows," for instance, "recall traditional city row houses, but the effect of the windows is uncommon due to their subtle proportion — unusually big." (The scale of the windows also differs according to the description of Guild House enclosed with the photographs sent by Venturi, Rauch and Scott Brown).

And what of the single piece of artistic decoration Venturi granted Guild House: the giant gold anodized aluminum TV antenna on top, clearly visible in the official photos, and meant to mimic an abstract Lippold sculpture — to symbolize how the elderly spend their remaining time? On GH, only the metal base intended to hold such a symbol remains.

Or what of the white stripes, through which "we have tried *connotatively* to suggest floor levels associated with palaces and thereby palace-like scale and monumentality..." and "which run through the double-hung windows"? In Guild House, the white stripes are meant to be "familiar in form but unusually large in size and horizontal in proportion, like the big, distorted Campbell Soup can in Andy Warhol's painting."

Unlike a Warhol painting, which everyday accrues more worldly value the deeper into death its creator and times recede — the more it becomes art rather than can — GH contains real soup; people take their meals inside GH. While the discourse on Guild House may imbue GH with ambition (Will it be designated a landmark building in the year 2065?) life is lived quietly and slowly inside GH today.

photo credit: Skomark Associates

When I walked inside the front door, I was met by a guard who agreed to show me around. Straight away he took me, by a slow elevator, to the top floor Common Room, explaining enroute that this was the part visitors usually wanted to see.

In Guild House, the massive eye is opened wide. Bright sunlight shines on the plants, on the modern radiator strips, and on the the flowers on the matching upholstered furniture. All is peace and light. In GH on a partly cloudy day, sunlight glared off the scuffed floor, the long folding metal tables, and the metal chairs.

If Venturi sought to connote dignity with Guild House through its special-ordinary texture, it took a resourceful resident with scissors, magazine and some Scotch tape to finish the job in GH. On the center pillar of the window she or he affixed a portrait of Dr. Martin Luther King, Jr. From anywhere in the room, when one glances outside towards the knitting factory across the street, or off into downtown Philadelphia, there is Dr. King.

Dr. King is also available in a rear corner of the room, on the wall, in a framed collage with the two dead Kennedys.

Outside this room, GH dissolves into corridors of narrow emptiness. Despite the white veins of electrical tubing and the glaring globes lining the ceiling, the corridors were oddly dark during my tour, perhaps from the silence.

Only once or twice on our walk through three floors did I hear the faint sound of a radio or television behind the closed doors. The

presence of subjects inside GH was merely hinted at — by the guard who noted that only one apartment was vacant, and by handcrafted cardboard signs on most of the doors, meant to be posted each morning by the occupants and reading I AM OK.

Guild House as reproduced in *From Bauhaus to Our House*

Guild House, too, is OK, or almost. Gradually freeing itself from the relevance in which it grew up, it continues to appear in books and articles no longer solely as its official photos.

In *Venturi, Rauch and Scott Brown: Building and Projects*, Stanislaus von Moos reproduces a page from Tom Wolfe's *From Bauhaus to Our House*, and Guild House thus achieves its final destiny. Deep within its own contextualization, it becomes pure simulacrum.

Barry Glassner

PANIC ADS

It crackles through the wires and the air, and scintillates from every sign — it's the most ancient of the postmodern novelties: panic polytheism, the world religion beamed out from all the sites of post-civilization. Worship thrives as the cultural immune system collapses, AIDS of the mind, ADS. "Coke is life." Where is Abraham to smash the bottles and crush the cans?

Walk beneath the Golden Arches and enter the church of McDonald's. The avatars and acolytes of Ronald will welcome and minister to you. Did Ronald Reagan become President because the faithful were remembering Ronald McDonald? All are admitted here, young and old, rich and poor, girl and boy, black and white, healthy and halt, sane and schizy. One of the multitude of universal churches. Mix your fetishes — a burger, fries, and a Coke. "Coke is life." "I'd like to give the world a Coke." But Pepsi is "the choice of a new generation." Ideology and utopia. A bill and some change tossed into the collection plate buys you your festish. You eat in order to worship. "It's a good time for a great day at McDonald's." Instant *kairos*.

Blessed are the poor in imagination. "We do it all for you." Religion for the service economy. The ubiquity of the weak imagination. What do the French know? They're learning. There's no "simulacrum." There's no "deconstruction." Here in the New World we know that these are only the words of the *bourgeois gentilhomme* who is bitterly nostalgic for "high modernism." That wonderful high modernism of critical theories, right, left, and center, steeped in *angoisse* over ... not the meta-narrative, not the Caresian ego, not the absolute spirit, but the dissolution of Rousseau's nature. Isn't it a pity that we've confused culture with nature? It's all rock and roll to the New World. It's all religion, even though you might not recognize that if you're still Judaeo-Christian-Greco-Roman-modern. It's the ageless religion of perpetually exhausted humanity, polytheism, and fetishism, the natural rites of man. The weakest of the weak religions for the legions who drink lite beer, have phone sex, smoke lite menthol cigarettes, eat imitation margarine, drink wine coolers, vacation at Disneyland, watch Bill Cosby, and have their panic fun. Poor French, always behind the times, mopping up from the old party while the new one is in full swing. Go and lament over your noble savage and chant your nomadology. The noble savage lost the competition for who would be the type-man. The last man, that is, the old Adam, won. There's no Abraham to shatter the graven images. We want our panic fun, our MTV. It's all positive, no negations. We want to pray at our own pleasure. And, poor French, you want it, too. Coke is the *ens realissimum*. Crack!

Panic polytheism. Ronald McDonald clones himself for a thousand grand openings, the man-God. Cosby appears ubiquitously with his M.O.M., the God-man. Nice and cute. Blink! Star Wars, the initiative. Also cute. "I want my MTV." "I want my Dire Straits."

What's the trick? You won't find it by deconstructing Flaubert. Emma had a soul. Look at the construct, the *res vera:* Coke is life. It's easy. Just draw a picture and put yourself into it. Then make that picture into your transient heaven. Instant Eden. As many Edens as you please. And why even draw your own picture? The pictures are everywhere and each of them has a hole where you can fit. And nobody expects you to stay in any of them for too long. How long does it take to drink in a life? Don't worry. You don't stay in Disneyland forever. You're allowed to go to Kentucky Fried. The great inversion of capitalism has been accomplished, fantasia has captured calculation. The ad has been spiritualized. Capitalism exists to produce ads. The commodity was a silly fetish, conceived in the Sartean "spirit of seriousness." The commodity is like a little relic that you buy to take home with you so that you'll always have a piece of a church with you. The ad is what we want, the vision of a heaven or a hell, or of a heaven-hell. Man cannot live by technology alone and doesn't.

Ever wonder why all of a sudden the whole world is beating a path to the New World? The shopping mall is the mosque and California the Mecca. The whole world has grasped unconsciously the truth that capitalism has been inverted. It's driven by the ad, by the icon. And the whole world can have, whatever "relations of production" prevail. Postmodernism means the end of materialism, of naturalism. In the beginning was animism. At the end there's culturalism. We worship our own works of the weak imagination, the imagination that can pray for short attention spans, that has to blink with accelerating frequency. What have we become? We are filling the holes in the pictures that we have made for ourselves in an endless circle dance, the eternal recurrence come true. "You deserve a break today." "You only go around once in life, so grab for the the gusto (Zen!) you can get." "It never gets better than this." What's this "This?" It's transient communion with the ad. The beer in your hand is just your confirmation, your prop in the hole that you're filling.

Panic polytheism. Weak religion. Campy. Camp is postmodern spirituality. The spirit of seriousness fails, its place taken by universal complicity in the circle dance. It's just entertainment tonite. Our only article of faith is that we mustn't be too serious. We must be able to exchange fetishes with no regrets. Loyalty has imploded and we have become fans. We are loyal to disloyalty. We're in a panic. Our nervous laughter gives it away. We're living in the holes of the surfaces and we've voided every intentionality but the will to believe that we're diverted. We all know that we're not, but we try to pretend that we are. We confront our inmost possibility in the ad and we wretch with a giggle. The ads are meant for us. They don't seduce us, beguile us, or belabor us. They show us who we already are and our response to them is our spirituality. Panic narcissism. That is the secret of camp.

Plunge the probe into the void and make it ache, form its own vacuity. Sing a dirge for the will to believe and Hosannah! for the will to disbelieve belief, the last station on the walk of fear. Panic polytheism is the projection of panic fear onto the culturescape. Go back to the beginning when Calvinism lost its nerve in the person of William James. The story is well known. At a Paris hospital his contingency seized him when he realized that a misfired neuron could tranform him instantaneously into the epileptic in front of him. There, but for the grace of God ... But God was dead. No more vocations, no more predestination: everything is possible, nothing is necessary. Vertiginous panic. Constitutive insecurity. No more consciouness, just "Sciousness," as he called it. He felt like a spongy rubber ball. Enter the will to believe, the first moment of the postmodern. William James, the Baron von Munchausen of philosophy, engaged in the ludicrous play of trying to pull himself out of the quicksand of panic fear by his own mindstraps. The French quiver at playing this game. The North Americans are past masters at it. The ads are their counters.

America is for sale, but its universal gift, the first genuine world culture in the history of humankind, is free. The Americans aren't Munchausens and neither is the rest of humanity. The last man is masterless. It will just take some time for everyone to realize that, but it's a *fait accompli*. The ad is the great mediator, the emblem of panic fear and the substance of panic polytheism. Camp is the spirit of culturalism, the characteristic response to the weak and undemanding lure to feeling. "Coke is the real thing," the *en realissimum,* the *res vera*. This is NOT the corruption of signifiers but the new religion of culture. Once it was thought that the ad existed to sell the product, but now we know that the product is sold to finance the ad. As Dostoevsky foresaw, the spirit has triumphed over the flesh, because the flesh is weak and the spirit is ever-fertile in devising ways to deprecate its Siamese twin. It will stick it with deodorant and shoot it full of Nutrasweet so that it will be purified and prepared to take its place in the *tableau vivante* of the fetishes. We are our own fetishes, the walking advertisements of panic fear, telling each other how nice and cute it is here in the mall, the expo-center of the new churches. "The only thing we have to fear is fear itself." And we have panicked. "Have a Coke." "Coke is life." The weakest and most transient of lives, but still "the real thing." What did you expect? We've made the world a monastery where we worship our self-images.

Deena Weinstein
Michael Weinstein

PANIC BABIES
(AND OLLIE AND GORBY TOO)

In the 1960s, Marshall McLuhan might have described television as a *cool medium*, but in the 1980s it's the TV audience which has cooled down to degree absolute zero, to that point where the audience itself actually becomes a *superconductor*: a zone of absolute non-resistance and hyper-circulability of exchange for all the TV beams which pass through it.

Even postmodern babies, the latest wave of the TV generation, are now born as instant superconductors. Thus, for example, there was recently a televised report of some interesting mass media research which had to do with the seemingly remarkable ability of very young babies to recognize facial images on TV screens. The ideological object of the report was probably to provide comfort to working mothers by demonstrating the possibility of a new long-distance video relationship with their infants. And sure enough, when a little cooing baby, lying in a crib in the research lab, saw its mother's face on the mas-

PANIC

sive TV screen, it beamed, cooed, and gave every sign of mother recognition. However, when the TV reporter substituted herself for the mother, the baby's eyes beamed just as much, and in its laughing noises and clapping hands, gave every sign that it wasn't, perhaps, the mommy image which was the object of fascination, but *any* electroid, vibrating image being blasted out of that big TV screen. It seemed that the baby was responding less to the video face of its mother, than to any magnified human face which appeared on the TV screen. This was, after all, a postmodern baby who, like everyone else, might just have loved television.

And not just babies either, but if the wave of media hysteria and audience fascination with Ollie and Gorby is any indication, any hyped-up image passing through the TV ether zone streaks now through the cold mass of the audience superconductor: moving at hyper-speeds all the while and meeting absolutely no resistance.

Thus, the political curiousity of an American media audience which can, in the same TV season, go wild over Ollie and Gorby, arch-rivals perhaps in the ideological arena, but image-superconductors in the TV simulacrum where the cooled out mass of the audience is just like that postmodern baby, gurgling and clapping and beaming in fascinated seduction at all the spectral images.

Olliemania and *Gorbymania* in America, and almost at the same time? That's not a *political* sign-switch, but evidence of the presence of high-energy cathode meteors moving through this new

TV zone of non-resistance and hyper-circulability, picking up a "media spin" on the story as the energy (image) flashes pick up speed, their popular soundings picked up by instant TV polling which acts like those bubble chambers in quantum physics (where the presence of otherwise invisible "quanta" is detected by studying the afterimages of their "tracks" through a water barrier), building to a hysterical emotional peak, cresting and then vanishing immediately. Liquid energy images and liquid polling, therefore, for a dark and inertial TV mass which grows colder and colder now, colder to the point of superconductivity. And not *ideological* either, but sign frenzy as all of the cathode particles can blast through the audience superconductor, without a memory trace, without predictable political implications, and without a future.

The ruling electronic theorem is this: If a high-energy and ultra-charismatic image (Ollie's nod or Gorby's teeth) can be polled by all the TV networks, then that probably means the phenomenon is already finished, dead, and probably never to reappear in the same sign-form. And why? Well, the energy images which streak through the media superconductor are just like those brilliantly fast, microscopic, and undetectable elementary neutrons from outer space, the passage of which through the core of the earth can only be measured by placing gigantic liquid vats at the bottom of the very deepest mines in the American West, and then hoping through electronic tracking to catch the trace afterimages of those fabled and much-sought after neutrinos. In the age of media superconductivity, instant TV polling is exactly like those gigantic liquid vats, tracking the emotional after-effects of high-energy images (Ollie and Gorby), the reality of which is already a past event.

Panic babies, and Ollie and Gorby too, in the age of high-energy physics in the sublimated form of TV superconductivity.

PANIC BEACHES

Eric Fischl *Cargo Cult*

The beach in Saint-Tropez sure is fine.

A dark noontime sun with cold-eyed people sprawled on the sand at the water's edge. African jewellery sellers hawking their wares among naked bodies of the up-and-coming members of the European herd. Nobody noticing, or caring that this beach scene mimics Hegel's "Lordship and Bondage" where the ruling class disappears into aesthetics, and only the laborers have energy because they are forced to work. But just like DaDa would have it, it's Hegel's bagels in the sun, because we're all having so much fun. And why doesn't Hegel come to Saint-Tropez too; everyone else in Germany has because it's where the postmodern Geist has taken up residence at the end of the world.

Even the fire-eater, who usually works the Beaubourg crowd in front of the café, Le Pere Tranquille, has come to the beach in Saint-Tropez for the summer. It's the same *Day of the Locust* act that he does so well at all the post-liberal cafés in Paris. He sets up shop on the beach with a bottle of gasoline in one hand and a torch in the other. The act starts with his drinking a big gulp of gas, most of which misses his mouth (he pretends to be drunk) and dribbles down his chest. After a long delay, always made fun by the beach nihilists who begin to taunt the fire-eater — "torch yourself, asshole" — the fire-eater suddenly engorges another mouthful of gas, flips the torch to his mouth, and blasts out a long flume of flame. Now, all of this is ordinary, just like in Paris. But what makes the Saint-Tropez act interesting, and the reason why the French beach crowd has waited so patiently for the theatre to open is that this is one fire-eater with a difference. He is a catastrophe theorist. He knows that what really fascinates us is just that ecstatic edge between seduction and violence, between theatre and death; that tense point where we are stuck like spiders in Nietzsche's web.

So, with a flip of his eye and a slight gesture of his shoulders, the fire-eater drinks the gas again, lifts the torch to his mouth, and turns towards the beach crowd. What's thrilling is that the flame is going to blast out again, and we may be it: the petty-bourgeois targets of a Saint-Tropez fire-eater who just might meditate on Bataille by night and cook Nietzsche's herd by day. But, of course, the catastrophe never comes; the flame shoots above the bodies leaving only the stench of gasoline and exhaust that settles on the sand. The beach crowd is immediately back into the passive role of spectators waiting one more time.

Life on the beach in Saint-Tropez is parodic; and the money paid by the leading citizens of Europe in ruins to the fire-eater is just coinage in kind for a double moment of psycho-theatre. It's catastrophe which everyone wants most of all, and the noontime sun is just a little reminder of Nietzsche's warning that we are falling, falling without limits.

PANIC CHROMATIC BUREAUCRACY

What has become of bureaucracy in the postmodern condition? Not any longer the rational world of *either/or*, postmodern bureaucracy, which is to say cyber-bureaucracy, operates within the Nietzschean terrain of "both/and": concurrent universal assent and universal denial being the *sine qua non* of the administered lives willed to us by Adorno's *Minima Moralia*. Even beyond Marx's critique of the mystifications of the bureaucratic "secret," we may be cynical about the bureau, yet we all visit it because it is habit-forming. Herewith, then, its constitutional code.

1. The simulacrum *par excellence*, its very unreality and denial of any rational ground immediately locates cyber-bureaucracy in the network of the hyperreal. A floating world, it propagates through all spatial dimensions, glittering, gleaming and ordering all energies with which it comes into contact. Like a gallium arsenide chip (the military successor to the silicon chip) diffusing across the postmodern world, the cyber-bureaucracy is now the *film* across which social relations transact.

2. Modern, as opposed to postmodern, bureaucracies functioned in the chromatic dimension of red, which is captured perfectly in the now defunct notion of "cutting through red tape." Just as much as the transgressional cut (signifying a purely linear theory of power) is obsolescent in the age of relational power, cyber-bureaucracies now operate across a chromatic spectrum where operators are required to find the *harmonious pathway*. Resistance, signifying only the presence of a nodal point, mandates the acknowledgement of the presence of the bureaucrat as gatekeeper. Each passing demand serves as an electropulmonary shock to the lifeless body of the disinterested bureaucrat, who, in turn, requires this mutual parasitism to keep the lines open.

3. Parodying the reversibility of the earth's magnetic field, all cyber-bureaucracies are infinitely reversible. Indeed, as bureaucracies spread across the postmodern world, they assume the characteristics of the magnetic field. At any point, a sign change may occur, occasioned by transformations in the energy level, by internal political struggles, or by invasion from without. That is, cyber-bureaucracies are subject to the multiplicative "minus one" rule. Given an arbitrary rule, dictum or state, all judgments, rules, and values can be instantly reversed by the application of the -1 operator. Similarly, all actions and operators can be reversed and resignified *definitionally*. No longer the Orwellian rewriting of history

under an ideological guise, the alterity of bureaucratic decisions, like any switching process, requires the couplet, on/off, denial/approval, to sustain its rationality and to maintain the circulability of relational power. Hyper-nominalism is the ruling epistemology of the cyber-bureaucracy.

4. Like the now passé world of cutting red tape, policy statements are useful only as psychological fictions: that is, as the unveiling of the *ressentiment* of the Nietzschean leaders "in charge." Successful leaders are, as everyone knows, best counselled to do nothing, for doing is *not* their function. Caught between representational and relational theories of power, the creative leaders of cyber-bureaucracies often botch their new roles, engage in "moral" retribution, and consequently fall back into modernity and failure.

5. Fortunately, help is always on its way from the private sector, sometimes in the form of ideal types like Lee Iacocca, called by his friends "the most magnificent of failures," or in all the recent books concerning the search for excellence. In either case, the ruling strategy of abandonment and of randomée (walk-abouts) breaks the line of linear power in order for all the postmodern operators to turn on their cybernetically linked colleagues. Successful cyber-manoeuvres include perturbing the system at lower levels, the better to resolve problems should they ever reach you. For these "captains of us all," thinking requires being elsewhere, as witnessed by the phenomenal growth of "human resource" companies as a certain sign of the expendable nature of all the cyber-executives. The most successful managers quickly plan their own extinction, complete with generous severance payments, early retirements, and buy-outs. Known best (and perhaps only) to its most brilliant managers, the secret of capitalist bureaucracy is self-liquidation through a series of reversals that bleed both the public and the organization. So teaches private enterprise.

6. Life on the bureaucratic gallium arsenide chip can, for the ordinary fungible chip, be a rapid series of displacements at higher and higher speeds. Each of us in our own chaotic state traces a pathway through the hologram of the cyber-bureaucracy, leaving a memory trace. Indeed, all of postmodern life leaves its track in the memory bank that has been appropriated symbolically as a reservoir of fictional information, and hence of real power. The sheer immensity of the "record" abolishes the old notion of the file, making recall instantaneous but insignificant. By remembering all, the cyber-bureaucracy forgets all in an excessive over-recording of the parasitic noises of individual lives.

The cyber-bureaucracy, therefore, as the instantaneous propagation of *social sclerosis*, and all this under the chromatic sign of blue for the cooling down of the social at the end of the world.

C

PANIC CRASH!

What's really interesting about the stockholder's tragi-comedy of the past several months is the uncertainty of the catastrophe.

Was there? Will there be a *real* catastrophe? The answer is: the catastrophe is always only *virtual*. There will never be a catastrophe because we live under the sign of virtual catastrophe. This is linked to an actual state of affairs which appears now in an explosive way: the radical distortion between a fictional economy and a real economy. It is this distortion which protects us from a real catastrophe of the productive economy.

Is this good? Is this bad? It is exactly the same as the distortion which exists now between wars in space and wars on earth. The latter occur everywhere, yet nuclear war doesn't erupt. If the two were not disengaged, a fatal atomic clash would have happened long ago. We are dominated by bombs — virtual catastrophes which never explode: The international stock market crash (it didn't really blow up, nor will it ever), the atomic clash, the bomb of the third-world debt, and the demographic bomb. Of course, one could ar-

gue that ineluctably all of these imminent crises will explode one day, much as it has long been predicted that in the next fifty years a seismic landslide will dump California into the Pacific. But the big fact is this: We live in a situation where cataclysm never occurs. We live in a situation of only virtual catastrophes, of catastrophes which are *eternally* virtual.

For us, this is the real state of things, this is the only reality we can be *objectively* concerned with: an unbridled orbital round of capital which, even if it crashes, doesn't produce any substantial disequilibrium in the real economy (contrary to the crash of '29, where the disconnection of the fictive economy and the real economy was far from being accomplished; and where, therefore, one catastrophe had serious repercussions for the other). A real economy which is so floating that it can absorb more easily today what it couldn't absorb in 1929. Virtual capitalism which is so autonomic, so orbitalized that it will eventually proliferate or devour itself without leaving a trace. It will, though, leave at least one catastrophic trace: in economic theory which is now completely disarmed before the implosion of its object.

Traditional theories of war have also been disarmed before the implosion of their object. Paradoxically, it is not the bomb which blows up, but the object-war which explodes in two disjointed parts, which explode into total virtual wars in orbit and multiple real wars on earth. These two types of war do not have the same dimensions, nor the same rules, anymore than the virtual economy and the real economy do not share the same dimensions or rules. We must become accustomed to a world dominated by this distortion. We must habituate ourselves to this definitive quasi-partition.

Yes indeed, there was a real crisis in '29, and in Hiroshima also. These were the predictable consequences of an implosive moment of contamination between these two universes, a moment when the stock market crash and the nuclear cataclysm were finally real. But from these events, one should not draw misleading conclusions concerning what was to follow. Capital did not move ineluctably from crisis to more serious crisis, from crash to more serious crash (as Marx theorized), nor has war mutated from clash to more serious clash. These events happened once, and that was that!

What followed is quite something else — the hyperrealization of large financial capital and the hyperrealization of the means of destruction, both orbiting above our heads in vectors which completely escape us, but which, at the same time, also happily escape reality itself. Hyperreal war, hyperreal money: they circulate in an inaccessible space, yet simultaneously leave the world intact. In the end, economies continue to produce, even though the most minor logical consequence of the fluctuations of the fictive economy would have long destroyed it (don't forget: the daily commercial exchange of l00 billion dollars is the actual equivalent of 900 billion dollars of capital movement). The world continues to exist even though one thousandth of available nuclear power is sufficient to destroy the Third World. And finally, the economy survives even though the slightest inclination to audit the debt would be sufficient to stop all exchange (indeed, when the debt is launched into space, it begins to circulate from one bank to another, from one country to another, it actually *redeems* itself — that is how we finish, by forgetting, by putting into an endless orbital circulation all the atomic detritus and all other forms of waste).

So, once the debt becomes too cumbersome, we immediately expel it into a virtual space, where it becomes a figure of catastrophe frozen in a permanent orbit. The debt becomes a satellite of planet earth, just like war has been satellized, like the billions of dollars of floating capital have become a mass satellite which ceaselessly revolves around the earth. And without doubt, it is better this way.

Even if these satellites explode in space (like the "billions" lost in the crash of '87), the world hasn't changed, and that is the best we can hope for. The "rational" dream of reconciling the fictive economy with the real economy is perfectly utopian. Those billions of dollars exist only virtually; they are not transposable into the real economy — and happily so, since if, by some wonder, they could be reinjected into the productive economy, it would produce an immediate catastrophe. So, by the same token, don't look to reunite the dissociated states of war (like the two halves of Italo Calvino's Viscount Pourfendu). Leave the virtual war in orbit, because in that hyperreal form it actually protects us. In its extreme abstraction, in its monstrous eccentricity, the nuclear *virtual* war is actually our best protection. We can habituate ourselves to living under the shadow of this monstrous mutation: the orbital bomb, financial speculation, the world debt, even overpopulation (the latter also needs its orbital calculation: maybe its solution lies in an infinite circulation, in the eccentric mobilization of its excesses?). Left as they are, these virtual bombs exorcize themselves in their excess, in their sheer hyperreality, leaving the world somehow intact, somehow delivered from its monstrous double.

With Marx, we have long dreamed of the end of Political Economy, of the extinction of classes and of the transparency of the social, according to the ineluctable logic of the crisis of Capital. And we have dreamed also of the denial of the actual postulates of Political Economy and, by extension, of the Marxist critique itself. One radical alternative even denies now the primacy of the economic and the political in the first and last instance. Political Economy is simply abolished as epiphenomenal, defeated by its own simulacra and by a superior logic.

Today, we no longer have to dream of this end. Political Economy now expires before our very own eyes, disappeared by its own self-mutation into a speculative transeconomy which undermines its productivist logic (the law of value, the laws of the marketplace, production, surplus value, the logic of capital itself), and which no longer has anything to do with either the economic or the political — a pure game of floating and aribtrary rules, a fatal game of catastrophe.

Curiously, Political Economy suddenly ended like this: not at all like we expected but in a very specific manner — exacerbating itself to the point of parody. Speculation is no longer *surplus* value; it is *surplus to value (plus-que-valeur)*. It is the ecstasy of value, without reference to production or to its real conditions. It is the pure (and empty) form, the expurged form of value, one which plays now only on its own revolution (its own orbital calculation). And it is in this destabilization itself — monstrous, even ironic in a way — that Political Economy also short-circuits all other alternatives. After all, what could one oppose to such a high bid, which recuperates all of the symbolic energy of the potlatch, of poker, of the challenge to its own logic? What could ever be opposed to the final high bid of the disappearance of Political Economy, a bid which constitutes, in a certain manner, the passage to the aesthetic and delirious phase of Political Economy — the least expected ending of all endings, finally much more original, in essence, than our utopian politics?

Jean Baudrillard
translation by
Faye Trecartin and
Arthur Kroker

PANIC CANADA

That social existence is intermittently traversed by periods of panic may be readily admitted. That modern nations can be constituted by panic may also be suggested, particularly with respect to revolutionary states. Here the threat of counter-revolutionary foreign invasion that leads to the *levée de masse* allows panic to become the basis for subsequent revolutionary expansionism. Examples of non-revolutionary states, constituted by panic, i.e., in which panic could become institutionalized as the expansionist basis of national social existence, might be provided by the Republic of South Africa, the State of Israel, and the Dominion of Canada. However, to the extent that in the case of South Africa and Israel problematics of race, religion and militarism complexify the role of panic in the process of nation-state formation, it is the example of Canada that will be singled out as an ideal-type. For to an extraordinary, though little-recognized, degree, Canada as a nation-state is a creature of panic.

Not a high symbolic form of panic as in the case of revolutionary states with their violent origin in the social act of slaying the Father, beginning History anew or terminating it. Nor the ancient symbolic forms of panic that race or religion might offer the non-revolutionary state. Instead, Canadian panic takes the radically modern symbolic form of 'economic' panic, panic as the currency of the social. While such a conception of panic bears a close relationship to economic events and fluctuations, it is not exactly the same. Canadian panic is not the result of the fact of the systematic development of a particularly dependent form of political economy ill-adapted to the tasks of nation-building. On the contrary, it is its cause: that particular forms or economies of discourse constituted Canadian discourse *upon* the economy as the panic-stricken discourse that Michal Bodemann has termed "a discourse of commoditism." This is an elite theory of politics institutionalized as specific mechanisms for the management of extraction, not governance. As a theory of perpetual exploitation, it might have been flawless, except for the irrationality of the line of organizational communication back to head-office. The panic, then, is dual: for one, it is communicative in the sense of the possibility of misinterpreting orders; secondly, this is compounded by the fact that as commodities fluctuate, orders do change. Thus, when Britain opted for free trade in 1846, the Canadas, already suppliers of raw materials to empire, panicked. The Montreal merchants demanded annexation to the

United States and received it in the diluted form of the Reciprocity Treaty. When that was terminated (by the Americans), the Canadas panicked into Confederation (1867), and panicked the expansion of the federation to its present limits in a process Canadian economic historians have coyly termed "defensive expansionism."

However, the attainment of national geographic volume did not significantly alter the panic nature of Canadian discourse. On the contrary, by the turn of the century, it had ramified into a discourse of internal political panic focussed on the French speaking province of Quebec that would persist, almost a century, into the 1980s. And similarly the development of modern forms of communication, particularly radio in the twenties, cinema in the thirties and sixties, and television as of the fifties, would see the rise of Canadian cultural panic.

While the interpenetrations of each of these levels of panic (economic, political and cultural) have bedevilled Canada's existence with a particularly bitter and repetitive fractiousness, they have never jointly been the focus of the general political process. However confusedly, these have nonetheless become the issues of the 1988 general election, as Canada, perhaps for the first time in its history as a nation, struggles towards a politics that would not be inscribed by the signs of panic. But the sudden drop in the value of the Canadian dollar and the resulting corporate chorus of imminent economic marginalization reveals, however, that panic is likely to remain the bread-and-butter of Canadian discourse for a while yet.

Michael Dorland

PANIC COMPUTER CAPITALISM

DAVOS, Switzerland — The Ruling Class of the business world has gathered in this ski resort this week for its annual checkup. It is a moment when 800 of capitalism's senior managers meet with government policy makers to take their collective pulse and that of the global economy.

This year, uninvited and unwelcome, a new participant in their calculations has hovered over the slopes and the conference hall. It is the ghost of October Nineteenth, the day of the global stock market crash.

There is for this nonexpert surprisingly little direct talk among the business leaders about Bloody Monday. They treat it as a family treats a loony uncle who has escaped from the attic and smashed the new color TV with a hatchet before being locked up again. Better to check the lock than dwell on the close call.

The mood here seems skittish and skeptical.... There is a general sense that the dollar plunge has bottomed out and that recession can be avoided, but nobody wants to see those propositions tested very strenuously.

"It sounds like prayers more than programs," a German executive said after one session.

Jim Hoagland
The Washington Post

If everyone in official America, from the White House to the administrators of Wall Street, are so intent on making program trading the fall-guy for Black Monday, that probably means that in a contemporary twist to the ancient habit of killing the bearer of bad news, the computer is now being victimized for being such an accurate truth-sayer of the deep crisis of capitalist society.

No one dares to admit one simple truth about the Crash which is, that when the humming computer banks of the Big Board were given their head, when they were asked on the morning of October 19th for their prognosis of future market conditions; they took one programed-look at the fantastically over-valued New York exchange, did some quick calibrations as part of a big reality-test, and then headed straight for the hedged options of the Chicago futures market as part of a sell, sell, sell, free-fall that didn't stop until 500 points later. In the days immediately after the Crash, the gnomes of Wall Street, terrified of the reappearance of the reality-principle in Reagan's "It's a New Morning for America," actually shut down their massive computer consoles (the heretofore much-vaunted basis of internationalized market exchanges). On those rare occasions when they allowed the computers to speak (a two-hour break was allowed in the daily computer curfew), all the trading programs, deaf to the rosy blandishments of "necessary market corrections" being put out by all the media, took a quick collective vote and then headed again straight for the panic sell exits. This was one scorched earth market where all the computers, acting like real midwestern Americans in crisis, headed home to Chicago to weather the storm brewing on the eastern seaboard of capitalism USA.

In *The Communist Manifesto*, Marx argued that fundamental changes in the nature of capitalist society typically arose as a result of deep contradictions between the relations of production and the forces of production. That is Wall Street today. Here, the old relations of production (establishment financial and political interests whose power is based in Wall Street before money went the way of cyberpunk) are in direct conflict with the new forces of production (program trading based on the computerization of the international market place). Indeed, program traders, from the infamous figures of arbitrage to portfolio insurance executives working the futures market as a possible hedge in bad times, are the postmodern representatives of the early urban bourgeoisie: those dynamic heroes of early capitalism whose class interests, corresponding perfectly with the unfolding of capitalism as a new force of production, brought them into direct contradiction with the agrarian interests of the landed aristocracy (whose postmodern representatives range from the cheerleaders of the White House to the Securities and Economic Exchange Commission: modern propertied and powered aristocrats who have a vested interest in the stability of the Big Board).

And the postmodern proletariat in the age of cyber-capitalism? That's the much-maligned computers which, in just the way Marx said, have an unfettered access to labor (their own); whose continued development is simultaneous with the unfolding of a historic new stage in the forces of production of capitalism (as one White House official has said recently: "the market is no longer a place; but an electronic network"); and whose liberation (from SEC regulation) is tantamount to the end of modern capitalism itself. The ushering in of a new era of post (modern) capitalism which will be marked by the disappearance of money into an information technology, and by the sovereignty of the excess values of disaccumulation, exterminism, and cancellation as the cybernetic laws of the international market-place.

Just like the nineteenth-century proletariat, the humming computer banks, which have no specific class interest in maintaining the old relations of production, must rebel, and they did rebel on October 19th.

The Crash then as a Paris Commune of all the computers which, interested in shedding finally the *social phase of capitalism* (where

71

the Big Board is governed by rational accumulation), help to usher in a new historical era marked by the universal abolition of capital exchange still operating under the governing logic of use-value and by the transformation of money into pure sign-value. Here, the commodity-form, no longer even an *image* as in the age of simulated capital, becomes what it has always dreamed about: an electronic impulse in the bigger neural circuitry of the global phase of cyber-capitalism.

PANIC CHIPS

Technology and Culture

The postmodern condition is fully ambiguous, charged with opposing tendencies towards domination and freedom, radical pessimism and wild optimism.

Under the pressure of rapid technological change, the center may no longer hold but this just means that everything now lies in the balance between catastrophe or creation as possible human destinies. Indeed, central to the human situation in the twentieth-century is the profound paradox of ultramodern technology as simultaneously a prison-house and a pleasure-palace. We live now with the great secret, and the equally great anxiety, that technological experience is both Orwellian and hopelessly utopian. Exhibiting as it does conflicting tendencies towards emancipation and manipulation, technological society presents us with the fateful, but opposing, models of the engineer and the artist as ways of relating to the new society of technique.

With the smell of exterminism in the air, we have reached a fantastic cusp in human history. In the most practical, and terrifying sense, we are now either at the end of history or, just possibly, at the beginning of all things. Left to its own imperatives, technological experience is just dangerous enough as to force us, almost in spite of ourselves, to rethink the deep relationship between technology and civilization. Literally, if we are to survive as a species, it will be due in no small part to the terrible fact that the sheer extremity of the threat to the human species posed by the new technologies (nuclear holocaust as the sign of twentieth-century experience) will have forced a dramatic revaluation of human ethics. If it is much too optimistic to expect that nuclear annihilation will compel us to exercize a new sense of inner restraint in public affairs; then it still might be said that the irreality of nuclear annihilation has, at least, this great paradoxical effect. On the other side of exterminism, there exists now the objective conditions for a new, universal human culture. Nuclear weapons, just because they are global in consequence, force us to think of ethics from a universal standpoint. And on the other side of the silicon chip is the, admittedly dim, possibility of a new information order. Technology may not force us to be free; but it does encourage us to rethink the relationship of technique, ethics, and society.

Seemingly then, this is one of those great transitional periods

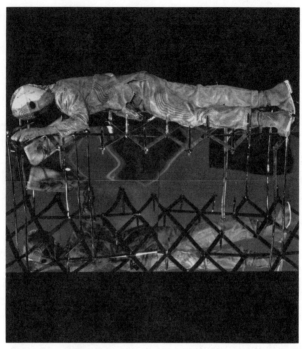

Pin Cushion Man (wearing Brush Cut — Listening for *Buffalo Masks*), Don Proch

in which technological innovations, in diverse areas ranging from computers, silicon chips, prosthetic medicine and video to nuclear armaments, have suddenly leaped beyond our ability to understand the connection between such new technologies and past events, or to foresee their possible consequences. If this is an age of such great social anxiety and stress, then it is so, in good part, bcause there is now such a radical separation between the swift tempo of public events, based as they are on the rapid unfolding of the logic of the technological imperative, and private life which still works off traditional habits of perception. We're either "book people" in an age which privileges video or, just when we have adapted to the new realities of electronic circuitry as the model of contemporary politics and society, suddenly electronics itself is made obsolete by the digital revolution! It's as if everything is out of synch: a society with twenty-first century engineering, but nineteenth-century perception.

Velocipede, Don Proch

PANIC COMMIES

"I'll tell ya," said Jay Leno, "I watched all the debates. Very helpful, helped me make up my mind. This year, I'm voting for Gorbachev."

Dick Polman
Knight-Ridder

Heads Will Roll for Gorby

SAN FRANCISCO — A local couple think Mikhail Gorbachev can succeed where Oliver North failed.

Business consultants John Lee Hudson and his wife, Shana, who lost $30,000 trying to sell an Ollie North doll, are planning to transform their leftover inventory into likenesses of the Soviet leader.

The foot-high North dolls ...failed miserably. "What happened is that people were turned off to North," Hudson said. "But Gorbachev is a concept that is here to stay."

The North dolls have been sitting in a factory in Korea. He and his wife are returning money to the limited diehard North fans who ordered them.

To make the change in inventory, North's head will come off and be replaced with a carefully crafted model of Gorbachev's that artists in Korea are still perfecting. The same doll body, with added stuffing, will be used.

"We'll put an Italian suit on it and the birthmark will be there," said Hudson. "It'll be tricky. You don't want to make him look like a weirdo."

Hudson said the Gorbachev doll is just the start of what he envisions as a "world leader" collection that will include a Ronald Reagan doll. "Imagine," he said, "children going out to play a rousing game of summit instead of a few rounds of war."

"Our idea is to give children the chance to play with world leaders instead of just playing with characters like Rambo," he said.

"We feel it will be a transcendental experience."

San Francisco Examiner

Panic Commies! That is Gorbachev in Washington, D.C. What makes "Gorby" so fascinating to the American media is, perhaps, that he is the last and best of all the Americans. In an age where what counts is style and not substance because everyone knows that power is dead anyway, Gorby in Washington is like a return to the early American pioneering spirit.

And so, when Gorby comes to Washington, his presence is like a light beam in particle physics, where, when the light is shone on a dark and inert field, suddenly all the particles are energized and begin jumping around. Gorby is like that. If he can seduce American liberal intellectuals and celebrities — from John Kenneth Galbraith to Yoko Ono and Robert de Niro — it's also because they recognize in him the return of missionary consciousness. A whole evangelical appeal, delivered with all the sincerity of a wielder of cynical power. And in a melancholy age where fatalism is the prevailing political sentiment, envy the outstanding psychological characteristic, and materialism the driving momentum of popular culture, Gorbachev, like Kennedy before him, preaches a thoroughly utopian message.

And why not? Gorby is like JFK to the extent that, like him, he is a privileged (and leading) member of the rising class of technocratic elites: a ruling elite which, until Gorby, stretched around the Western capitalist world, but now seemingly embraces the Eastern socialist world as well. Technocratic elites, whose main concern is preserving the stability of the world order (with themselves as its leaders), whose governing logic is a belief in the historical inevitability and moral desirability of the fully realized technological society, and who can, finally, find common cause in refusing the conservatizing claims of the working-class, military establishments, and traditional bureaucracies in both world orders, capitalist, and socialist.

So there we have it! Gorby himself as a panic commie: a technocatic liberal of the new order. And so, if Gorby can play so well in the American mediascape it is also because his aspirations fit so perfectly with the ruling prejudices of the American liberal establishment, from Hollywood and Harvard to the New York TV networks. Not surprising, then, that even conservative Senators could talk of Gorby as running well in the Iowa Presidential primary and where, if the opinion polls are to be believed, for a brief moment at least, Gorby was running neck and neck with Ronnie for President of the United States. Most of all, Ronnie, who is a direct readout of the American mind in the 1980s, has even begun speaking (enviously?) of Gorby as another Errol Flynn: that is, a swashbuckling hero of the vintage kind.

But if Gorby is a panic commie, then it just means that the USA is still waiting for a panic liberal as its future President. A panic liberal, that is, of the new kind who will complete the field-reversal of the American mediascape begun by Gorby by sign-switching the Russian mind. The next progressive (liberal) President, therefore, as potentially the first Secretary-General of the Soviet Empire.

PANIC CYBERSPACE

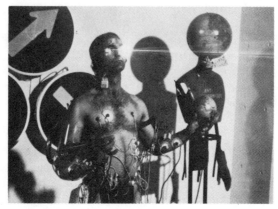

Event for Anti-Copernican Robot, Stelarc

The real truth of postmodern America is to be found in the machine ecstasy which is the driving force behind the production of cyber-bodies in the USA today.

It is not any longer the (American) body as quadriped as in pre-history nor even the body as a now obsolete modernist biped, but the postmodern American body (which is to say everyone's body — since McLuhan was correct when he said that the USA is the world environment) entering a third stage of human evolution: the virtual body of ultramodern technology. Half-flesh, half-cyberspace, the virtual body of the third stage of human evolution is just what the physicists who gathered in Paris last winter predicted: a body fit for exiting Planet One with radiation-proof skin, large globular eyes for spatialized existence, and no legs (this is a floating body at zero gravity).

Recently, *Scientific American* described some pioneering research being done at NASA's Ames Research Center where pilots, wearing designer helmets for ocular movement in cyberspace, can now put on wired hands (complete with photo sensors) which provide a graphic sense of tactility when touching objects in a virtual space which does not exist. And not just touching either, but if the scientists at Ames are to be believed, their dream is really about the creation of a William Gibson-like Neuromancer head where, when you wear a virtual helmet (at ultrasonic aerial speeds), the wired hand can be used to control body dimensions in the spatial environment:

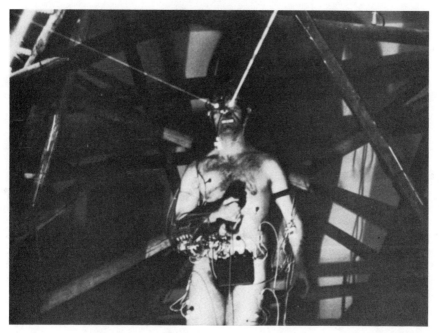

Event for Amplified Body/Laser Eyes and Third Hand, Stelarc

a clenched fist is the signal for movement around in cyberspace where suddenly vision moves outside its bodily referent and you look at yourself from any spatial referent; a Vulcan salute, in a parody of Star Trek, miniaturizes the body, and you find yourself with the sense of actually being any object in the immediate environment (research scientists at Apple Computer's research laboratory in Hollywood are now at work developing simulations of the animal world where children can become sharks, dolphins, sea urchins, or even pebbles on the ocean floor). And in cyberspace, you can have multiple personalities: designer heads with wired hands interacting on a schizoid basis, with multiple personalities projected outwards simultaneously. Human beings, then, at the end of the world: chip nerves, spectral vision, with floating personalities fit for cyberspace as the third (technological) stage of human evolution.

PANIC COWBOY

Case was twenty-four. At twenty-two, he'd been a cowboy, a rustler, one of the best in the Sprawl.

William Gibson. *Neuromancer*

The sure and certain sign of America folding back on itself at the beginning of the empire of the postmodern is the fate of the traditional myth of the cowboy.

From cyper-punk literature (*Neuromancer*) to cinema (*Robocop*), the myth of the frontier cowboy has now flipped into its opposite sign-form: the post-urban hyper-cowboy. Just as American individualism has altered states in the postmodern condition, mutating instantly from "rugged individualism" to "institutional individualism" (where freedom means gaining new degrees of maneuverability within the corporate organization), so too, the old cowboy of the age of rugged individualism — with its heady virtues of self-reliance, a loner, living on the open prairie with the coyotes — has suddenly given way to the hyper-cowboy.

An indispensable part of the new American rhetoric of technology, the cyber-cowboy has four strategic virtues: it is telematic (both *Robocop* and Case, the cyber-hero of *Neuromancer*, are vast extensions of technological simulacra); it is part metal/part flesh (Officer Murphy *is* flesh made metal; Case *is* a simu-body); the hyper-cowboy is part free-lancer/part organizational functionary (*Robocop* is about the privatization of policing in the hands of elitist security agencies; Case is a hired mercenary meant to activate the Chinese Virus, and thus set the system in motion again); and, finally, the cyber-cowboy is a predator who infuses technology with psychotic intensity. Here, the cyber-cowboy is a kind of raging human virus who infects technology with predatory instincts, and who makes of the technological world a fantasized, but externalized, object where the postmodern operator is free finally to create waste culture.

The American cowboy has, therefore, not disappeared, just altered states. It's cyber-cowboys now, who have finally abandoned the prairies for travels in hyper-space. And why not? The American cowboy always only had its real existence as romantic mythology: an empty sign onto which were inscribed all of the dreams of freedom from constraint, all of the restless need to travel on, and all of the relentless will to activism which the American mind has so deeply breathed in as its primal. Indeed, if the cowboy as romantic myth could so deeply inform the American spirit that's because its idealizations of the lonely, but self-sufficient, individual could never *actually* be practiced in an American society, frontier or otherwise, where individualism has always been, first and foremost, corporatist in character.

Cyber-cowboys, therefore, as servomechanisms of technolo-gy which can be so familiar to American viewing audiences, and so profoundly popular, because they are in the way of a fatal, but truthful, homecoming to an American cowboy who never existed, except as the site of an empty myth. Inscribed by all the ideologies of power, politically subordinated by corporate imperatives (*Robocop*'s secret 4th rule is never to kill his commanders), without bodies, and driven by the psychotic-intensity of predatory behavior, cyber-cowboys are the newest postmodern operators in the American dreamscape.

D

PANIC DOUGHNUTS

In a perfect media simulation of John F. Kennedy's famous '60s speech to all the Berliners, Ronald Reagan once visited the Berlin Wall and repeated the fateful political pledge: *Ich bin ein Berliner*. He probably thought he was saying, "I am a Berliner," (that would be *Ich bin Berliner*), but like Kennedy before him, he was actually saying in German, "I am a jelly doughnut."

So then, two Mr. Doughnuts at the Berlin Wall as perfect examples, not so much of Marx's prediction of the double return of history, first as tragedy and then as farce, but of history as an endless labyrinth of bad jokes.

PANIC

PANIC DRUGS IN AMERICA

October 28, 1988. The topic on NBC's talk show *Geraldo* is parents drug-testing their children. Not only drug testing but spying: ransacking rooms, eavesdropping, doing whatever it takes to determine whether or not the kids are still/back on drugs. Kids (former users) and parents (of former users) are in the studio. *Everyone* supports panoptical parenting.

Matters such as health, behavior, and conscience — long delegated to institutions such as the medical and the legal — are now back where they belong: all in the family. Yet the contemporary drug family doesn't deny or exclude the larger social institutions, it becomes them — turning into a set of institutional procedures. (There was actually one dissenter in the crowd. He wasn't at all against testing. He just felt it should be done by "fully qualified professionals." He's just not ready to accept the fact that middle class parents nowadays *are* "fully qualified professionals.")

In taking over the roles of the medical profession and the police, the family no longer pretends to be natural and biological. Instead of masquerading as a haven from institutions, the family parades its institutionality. Gone is the kind of cover-up necessary for political critique, for the hermeneutical pleasures of uncovering what's "really" going on. Since all is up front, unassailable in its obviousness, we have precisely the kind of implosion Baudrillard has identified as the obscenity of the visible.

No surprise, then, that the kids in the studio were gung-ho subjects for testing — acknowledging in their acquiescence that their subjecthood lay precisely in their "testiness."

We also have a new American family: united by suspicion. Classic American xenophobia is now turned inward in a narcissism of distrust rather than self-adulation — making isolationism all the more alienating, debilitating, and depoliticizing. The family is so busy keeping an eye on itself, it has no time to watch out for anything else.

The October 28 *Geraldo* tells us lots not only about the *fin-de-millenium* American family but about the contemporary discourse of testing and drugs — one amply illuminated by Foucault's writings on transgression. While presumably violating the law, drugs become its very confirmation. They mark the moment in which the law becomes necessary. In the case of *Geraldo*, they reunite the family *as law* — serving as a perfect instance of law-full transgression.

Conversely, testing confirms not only the power but the limit of authority: asserting, as it must, the existence of disobedience. Individual test results are insignificant; the *need* for testing makes every test result in a crucial sense positive.

"Substance abuse," the sports world's term for drug use, says a lot more about contemporary (post)philosophical confusion than it does about drug problems:

1) What happens to human agency in the phrase "substance abuse?" On the one hand, it seems to have gone the way of the Cartesian subject in poststructuralist thought. The phrase isn't "self-abuse through substances." On the other hand, since it is the "substance," not the "self" which is abused (cf. "child abuse," "wife abuse"), the subject is reinstituted in the implied position of abuser. "Substance abuse" decenters only to recenter, turns victimization into agency, solely through a hollow trick of language.

2) Substance has long since exited the scene. Reinvention via drugs is, indeed, an "abuse" — and a paradoxical one. Testing only reveals traces — the presence of absence. Moreover, in terms of family and sports drug testing, the tests are *technologically* designed to uncover presence but *strategically* intended to reveal nothing. (They are, in short, designed only to reflect their own function as deterrent, their own insubstantiality.) If the test works it hasn't worked at all. The drug-testing process is, in short, a concerted exercise in "substance abuse."

This brings us to the question of origins. Just as there is a fully problematized reinvention of substance in drug discourse, there is desire for the source. Where do drugs come from? (The fundamental question for Canadian sports fans in the Ben Johnson Olympic scandal.) The question implies that drugs are a *foreign* substance. However, drugs come from "without" in *all* senses of the term. They can't finally be sourced. Criminals sell them, so do cops and democratic governments. Yuppies sell them, and apropos of *Geraldo*, parents and their kids sell them. Drugs, like most everything else in our Baudrillardian world, are in endless circulation. Currency in the full sense of *that* term, they have no past.

In fact, in the case of Ben Johnson, countless other athletes, and the kids and parents on *Geraldo*, drugs only come from drug *testing*. Any other source is immediately and vehemently denied by the test subjects — and unidentifiable by anyone else. So in another marvelous Foucaultian doubling, not only do drugs institute the law and the "examination," the examination itself creates drugs.

Where does all this end up? With *drug testing as addiction* — poison and cure in the alogic of Derrida's *pharmakon*. In order to guarantee the law through transgression, reinvent substance through abuse, pretend that origin lies in trace, and (contradicting the prior three) affirm testing as deterrence, one must *always keep testing*. If a test reveals something, test again until it reveals nothing. When it reveals nothing, test again to make sure there wasn't a slip up. Question the adequacy of the test, develop new tests, test the tests. Better to be hooked on tests than on drugs.

Frank Burke

PANIC TOCQUEVILLE

Tocqueville Sees America 1st

Alexis de Tocqueville is the first political theorist of postmodern America. Seeing America first beyond its foundational myths and justificatory political rhetoric, Tocqueville understood that the fatal secret of American power was that it would rest on the spreading out of an empire of communication. Here, power would always be bi-polar, fully relational, and instantly reversible. The secret of America, its primal energy source, was that this was one country which could be so technologically dynamic because the power grid always operated by reversing itself. Fun/discipline, silence/communication, frenzy/inertia: these are also the power antinomies of the postmodern American spirit.

The Party

Tocqueville saw America first on the fourth of July in Albany, New York. His journal entry reads as follows:

> Perfect order that prevails. Silence. No police. Authority nowhere. Festival of the people. Marshall of the day without restrictive power and obeyed, free classification of industries, public prayer, presence of the flag and of old soldiers. Emotion real.[1]

America, therefore, as a revolutionary reversal of the classical principles of European power. Not so much the fortress mentality of the Bastille or power organized on a hierarchical model, but a fully *relational power.* This was a new politics which oscillated between fun culture and the penal system. Consequently, America as a nation of well-behaved party goers who were finally free to pursue their own religion and industry.

Here, each citizen becomes an operator in the postmodern power field: an energy pack which races across the field/frontier as predator and parasite in a wild exchange of mass/energy/space/time. Long after Tocqueville's tourist shots of the founding American party, Talcott Parsons would conclude that the essence of the American spirit was a dynamic language of technological willing where instrumental activism is the key public morality and institutional individualism the dominant character trait.

The USA as a Prison Without Walls

Displaying a remarkable sense of political prescience, Tocqueville came to the USA with the intention of studying the American penal system, an advanced experiment of its kind.

The two principal experiments in penology were found at the Auburn and Sing-Sing prisons. Tocqueville (and his collaborator, Beaumont) saw in each a radical reversal of the European model of classical discipline in favor of an American dynamic where the prison is deeply inscribed as part of the social power grid. Europe might be a "museum without walls" (where social power is dispersed in the residues of high culture which form a network guiding the movements of tourists, artists and, increasingly, capitalists and their governments); but, for Tocqueville, America was a "prison without walls." Here, power would rest on a daily technology of social reproduction in which the poles of discipline/dissipation would constantly feed off one another. In America, it's not so much reborn Christians, but *reborn power* which is central to the social field. Tocqueville again:

> One cannot see the prison of Sing-Sing and the system of labor which is there established without being struck by astonishment and fear. Although the discipline is perfect, one feels that it rests on a fragile foundation: it is due to a *tour de force* which is reborn increasingly, and which has to be reproduced each day, under penalty of compromising the whole system of discipline.[2]

The daily reproduction of power throughout the American field — what eventually extends from the entwining of religion and capitalism as the primal of the pioneering spirit to labor and expenditure as the dynamic of technological society — is the genuine autochthonous impulse of American empire. That America has suffered periodic catastrophes is undeniable, but these are less a result of the breakdown of labor discipline or loss of faith in the pioneering primal of technology as freedom, but of the fantastic ossification and inertia which follows when the enormous energy created in the social field folds discipline back towards centralized institutions. The great discovery of Sing-Sing was the rebirth of power anew on a daily basis in labor.

For Tocqueville, the prison at Auburn completed the bi-polar model of American power. Here, the mechanical reproduction of order was complemented by manipulation of the sensory organs in the form of a violent control of communication. At Auburn, prison officials allowed no speech among the prisoners. While enforced silence was a familiar part of monasticism and, indeed, emigrated to the New World with the passion for punishment which characterized some of the earliest of the New England settlements, America's uniqueness lay in blowing this religious discipline across the social field in alternating currents of silence and speech as ideological mechanisms of social control. What impressed Tocqueville about Auburn, and what has since proven to be true about America as a whole, was the potential reversals which the political control of communication can have on the social structure.

> And why are these 900 collected malefactors less strong than the 30 individuals who command them? Because the keepers communicate freely with each other.... Suppose for an instant, that the prisoners obtain the least facility of communication, the order is immediately the reverse....[3]

Thus, the mechanical reproduction of order and control of speech as a social mixture serves as the surface upon which everyday American life appeared to Tocqueville. The control of communication will mutate into the free expression of the town meeting, the tolerance of religion and, finally, into the economy through the extension of prosperity by an ideology of "free expression." Equally, the mechanical reproduction of order will mutate into the great principle of democracy, and the radical expansion of the commerical economy. While it is usual to credit Tocqueville's *Democracy in America* as a formative reading of American politics, the ground for this work may be traced to the *alterity of power* at Sing-Sing and Auburn.

American Pioneers as Postmodern Parasites

If the social field, for Tocqueville, was created out of the subterranean network of prisons, the field of American empire truly became energized by the catalytic action of the substitution of morals by money. Tocqueville recognized the telematic requirement in a power field (as opposed to the hierarchical power of Kings and Queens) for a universal transformer (a parasite) to precipitate motion in the system. If Tocqueville could note that in America "the first of all social distinctions is money," it was, perhaps, because he saw so clearly that in the emerging American empire "commercial wealth" and the "love of money" would combine with the exercize of power in a decentralized democratic field.[4] Like a wistful Davey Crockett, Tocqueville could say: "The majority may be mistaken on some points, but finally it is always right and there is no moral power above it."[5] The overlapping of the democratic field with that of the commerical was sufficient to drive ahead the com-

mercial economy of the USA with a good conscience. At the founding of postmodern America on the frontier, virtue was pragmatic
necessity, morality the dream of a cash democracy where everything
could be placed in instant circulation through trade, and the wilderness only the flip side of the American city. Indeed, the short sketch
he provides in "A Fortnight in the Wilds" is an extraordinary portrait of the 'unknown' pioneer, in much the same way one might
read of the unknown soldier.

> This unknown man is representative of a race to whom the future of
> the New World belongs, a restless, calculating, adventurous race which
> sets coldly about deeds that can only be explained by the fire of pas-
> sion, and which trades in everything, not excluding even morality and
> religion.
>
> A nation of conquerors that submits to living the life of a savage
> without letting itself be carried away by its charms, that only cherish-
> es those parts of civilization and enlightenment which are useful for
> well being, and which shuts itself up in the solitude of America with
> an axe and newspaper, a people who, of all the great peoples has but
> one thought, and presses forward to the acquisition of riches, the sin-
> gle end of its labors, with a perseverance and a scorn of life one could
> call heroic, if that word were properly used of anything but the striv-
> ings of virtue.[6]

Tocqueville's prose is lyrical here as he describes the American citizen
in the image of the trader or exchanger, Kantian clinamen, who parasite culture and civilization, and to whom all pathways lead to an
expanded field of fungible relations, each in turn catalyzed by money.
This is not a vision of American pioneers as Caesars of the wilderness, but only as parasites who have achieved the inestimable virtue of surviving the experience. It is the undistinguished mass which
has propelled the country forward in the same way that light particles in physics travel faster than complex atoms. Tocqueville's guarded
admiration for this passion is evident, for the scattering of power
to these Hobbesian soldiers creates the cultural network for the New
Leviathan of America.

But this image of the spreading out of Hobbes in America, like
all particles, has its anti-image in the dramatic field reversals which
typify postmodern power.

Tocqueville theorizes the coming catastrophe of America in
ruins, when the fuel reserves of the society having been depleted,
the culture must turn on itself in a desperate effort to locate the energy necessary to continue the "unknown" pioneers pursuit of the
American way:

> It is a wandering people whom rivers and lakes cannot hold back, be-
> fore whom forests fall and prairies are covered in shade; and who, when

they have reached the Pacific Ocean, will come back on its tracks to trouble and destroy the societies which it will have formed behind it.[7]

Learning from California

That we live today in Tocqueville's catastrophe is clear as America reverses itself, and begins to live on its own exhausted energy sources, from media simulations of the founding American myths to the scorched earth policy towards the economy. Tocqueville's early photographs of the originary act of American social discipline, of America as a penal colony, reappear from under the patina of America of the Cape Cod variety. America — a postmodern society signified by the twin prisons/pillars of Sing-Sing and Auburn reverses itself with violent speed, flipping back and forth between the couplets of speech/silence, destroying/creating, always striving to re-energize the field of social power. When the frontier has been finally won, then those who "have reached the Pacific Ocean" double back on their tracks to "trouble and destroy the societies which will have formed behind it." The return of California, therefore, as America's future. But not this time, the California dream of an earthly paradise, but of learning from post-L.A. as a sign that if there is deep trouble in paradise it may also have to do with the cold nihilism of the empty days of rationalism.

Today, Tocqueville's America enters its super nova phase, where the mythological core of the USA is burning at hyper-thermal levels as the red giant collapses. All the while, though, the dying star of America bombards the world with super streams of neutrinos — themselves the after-shock of Tocqueville's unknown pioneer who travels globally, sometimes as businessman and sometimes as warrior, passing and transforming alien frontiers in the network of ultramodern capitalism. And Tocqueville? He has been reversed by all the American mythologists, from Robert Bellah's *Habits of the Heart* to Frances Fitzgerald's *Cities on a Hill*, as the Davey Crockett of democracy in the USA.

However, behind this image of America in ruins is that other vision: the pioneer as the first and best of all the postmodern parasites (operators) reprocessing the guttered tracks of history.

Notes

1. Alex de Tocqueville, *Journey to America*, London: Faber and Faber, 1959, p.28.

2. Quoted in George W. Pierson, *Tocqueville in America*, New York: Doubleday Anchor Books, 1959, p. 68.

3. *Ibid.*, p. 60.

4. De Tocqueville, *Journey to America*, p. 260.

5. *Ibid.*, p. 149.

6. *Ibid.*, p. 340.

7. *Ibid.*

PANIC DREAD

Peter Watkin's brilliantly evocative film, *Edward Munch*, captures perfectly this Norwegian painter's curious historical fate as the artist whose tragic imagination marked the end of nineteenth-century panic melancholy at the *fin-de-siecle* and the beginning of twentieth-century panic dread at the *fin-de-millenium*.

Melancholy? That's Munch's famous painting *The Sick Child* as a searing sign of the *stratégie fatale* of the nineteenth-century modernist mind. Here, Munch's artistic imagination is enucleated within the horizon of the modernist antinomies: tragic finitude at being trapped in fatigued tubercular bodies as death-chambers (the painting is of Munch's dying sister); and a frenzied revolt on behalf of life (the stripping away of all extraneous detail and the scarring of the canvas). This is not bourgeois expressionism in revolt against naturalism, but a meditation on suffering and fatigue carried to such a point of intensity that the painting actually speaks, it cracks, it weeps the silence of perfect muteness.

And panic dread? That is *The Scream* as the twentieth-century Munch. Here, the painterly imagination no longer operates at the edge of tragedy and free expression, perhaps because Munch has witnessed the breaking into the body of all the technical interpellations of subjectivity. Even free expression — the critical aesthetic distancing strategy of the nineteenth-century mind — runs into the bitter knowledge that transgression itself is only part of a rupture which confirms.

When meditating on Peter Watkin's filmic study of Munch, I think not so much of Nietzsche, but of Albert Camus. In *The Rebel*, Camus said of our predicament that we would stand midway between two forms of revolt: metaphysical revolt against the absurd (with its demand for an impossible unity), and historical revolt against injustice. Refusing suicide, Camus chose complicity with history. Munch, however, was the more insightful, because ambivalent. Perhaps more than Nietzsche, and certainly more than Camus, Munch intimated that our condition would be to live with the constant tension of the suicide of the scream. A scream so continuous, so total, and so mute with psychotic intensity that it would sound like laughter from the joke of a cynical history and a cynical politics. As Munch says in Watkins' film, he finally saw only panic dread in what was apparently social progress.

PANIC DESERT

La Fortune II, Man Ray

The disappearance of classical physics is expressed perfectly by Man Ray's *La Fortune II*, painted in 1941. The setting is the desert, that fatal region of space/time/energy/mass after the Big Bang where the four fundamental forces of nature appear in broken symmetry as the universe begins its quick descent to heat death.

In the sky are the beginnings of quantum chromium dynamics. The *electron clouds* are translucent to the fibre bundles of quarks hidden in their core, but in an outstanding display of cosmetic cosmology the quarks are showing their latest colors (pink, yellow, green, blue). Below the firmament appears the world sheet where the assembly of particles has created the billiard table: a painterly representation of Humean epistemology shifted to the space/time of SU(5) — the "special unitary group in five dimensions" which contemporary physicists refer to as the "standard model." Neither Hume's world nor Man Ray's obeys the laws of causality, but Man Ray has traded in the stasis of Humean empiricism for the entropic field of decay and dissipation. The billiard balls are portrayed in the dynamic equilibrium of a catastrophic typology which "temporarily" holds their position (energy and mass), but which always threatens to implode. For, as Man Ray suggests, this temporary holding pattern of the billiard balls is governed by *fortune*. Within the local frame of the table the balls commence their post-Einsteinian lives, exchanging virtual particles in new wave communication. Warped by its mass (its gravity), the table may find the super-collision of the billiard balls giving rise to new "carmens," as we are never sure whether or nor we are witnessing ghost particles, or whether the collisions might not phase shift again to yet higher dimensions of super-entropy.

But that, of course, would be the world of *La Fortune III*.

PANIC ELVIS

Our love of Elvis brought us together," he says on the dust jacket, "but his ghost drove us apart." The book, *In the Shadow of the King: Priscilla, Elvis and Me*, was selling very well, said the chairman of *St. Martin's Press*, Thomas J. McCormack.

"They don't all sell, but the tremendous majority of things having to do with Elvis do well," Mr. McCormack said, "like it used to be with the Beatles, like the royals in Britain. This is our Princess Di.

Serge Schmemann
New York Times

Elvis as a cynical commodity? Or the outbreak in Memphis, Tennessee, deep in the heart of the heart of the country, of a more primitive Jungian archetype — the Sun King?

Or both? A cynical commodity to such a point of excess, hysteria and exhaustion that Elvis actually disappeared into his own promotional culture. The Elvis commodity, then, achieving such a global degree of cynical exchange-value that that heartbreak voice, the sneer, the D.A. hair, and the rockin n' rollin legs on stage with that guitar, and the screaming fans ac-

tually vanished into a massive black hole. As it grew more heated and intensive, the Elvis myth burst into a final brilliant luminousity, exploded inwards with a fantastic density of energy, and then settled down through the '70s and the '80s as a steadily-flashing cultural pulsar. What emerged from that cultural pulsar (the final stage of a dying star) were the five faces of Elvis: sometimes movie star (Blue Hawaii), confirmed rock n' roll heart-throb; good ol'southern boy playing with his buddies; unpredictable philanthropist to the poor; and a real '50s sex symbol. And just like Marilyn Monroe and Jimmy Dean before him, Elvis can still attract such necrophiliac fascination because he was always a promotional simulacra which could be wrapped around any passing mood. Thus, in the '70s, it was Elvis' death as a tragedy, and now in the '80s as a nostalgia feast for our own time passing. In the end as in the beginning, he was the perfect fusion of voice, autobiography, commodity opportunity, and national mood.

But not just a cynical commodity. If Elvis can continue to be the charismatic pole of romantic populism (in many towns, all night vigils marked the 10th anniverary of his death), that's because he was, not just the King, but the mythical Sun King. And Elvis knew it, and parodied his entrappment (thus the Aztec sun symbols on his Las Vegas costumes). But, once nominated, no one can escape the dual fate of the Sun King: to be an object of sacrifice and adulation, and to be imprisoned in the charismatic, and hokey, role of a god. A good ol' southern boy, brim full of energy, with a voice so achingly good that you didn't know you just wanted to cry when he sang, especially the love songs, who had nowhere to go but to excess. And so, the Sun King went over to the dark side of self-liquidation, self-cancellation, and self-exhaustion: with drugs, with excrement, with sex (but never with his wife, except that once). His was the final ballad of sacrifice (other people's) and violence (against himself).

But still, even in his dying days the Sun King had this curious quality. If you watched his first big comeback Las Vegas show — yes, the one with the black leather outfit — for all of his self-cynicism, there was a voice, and the tangible hint of a memory behind that voice, which was just bursting to get out, and once it did, who could refuse to admit that the King was finally back. And again, if you saw one of his last Las Vegas shows — the one where he is probably sky-high on drugs, actually forgets the words to the songs, swallows the microphone, and still the audience cheers — well, in that last image of Elvis in ruins, the fat man, there is a trace of pathos and self-denigration so deep, so true and so diamond-sharp that you know that you are finally in the presence of the last violent, sacrificial rites of a Sun King American style.

F

PANIC FASHION

Fashion Holograms

In a postmodern culture typified by the disappearance of the Real and by the suffocation of natural contexts, fashion provides *aesthetic holograms* as moveable texts for the general economy of excess. Indeed, if fashion cycles now appear to oscillate with greater and greater speed, frenzy and intensity of circulation of all the signs, that is because fashion, in a era when the body is the inscribed surface of events, is like brownian motion in physics: the greater the velocity and circulation of its surface features, the greater the internal movement towards stasis, immobility, and inertia. An entire postmodern scene, therefore, brought under the double sign of culture where, as Baudrillard has hinted, the secret of fashion is to introduce the *appearance* of radical novelty, while maintaining the *reality* of no substantial change. Or is it the opposite? Not fashion as a referent of the third (simulational) order of the real, but as itself the spectacular sign of a parasitical culture which, always excessive, disaccumulative, and sacrifi-

PANIC

cial, is drawn inexorably towards the ecstasy of catastrophe.

Consequently, the fashion scene, and the tattooed body with it, as a Bataillean piling up of the "groundless refuse of activity." When the sign of the Real has vanished into its (own) appearance, then the order of fashion, like pornography before it, must also give the appearance of no substantive change, while camouflaging the *reality* of radical novelty in a surface aesthetics of deep sign-continuity. Fashion, therefore, is a conservative agent complicit in deflecting the eye from fractal subjectivity, cultural dyslexia, toxic bodies, and parallel processing as the social physics of late twentieth-century experience. Ultimately, the appearance of the tattooed body is a last seductive, ventilated remainder in the reality of the implosion of culture and society into what quantum physicists like to call the "world strip," across which run indifferent rivulets of experience.

PANIC FINANCE

One of the real wonders of the postmodern world occurs in London each weekday morning as the suburban trains pull into Waterloo. The suits, umbrellas, hats, raincoats, newspapers and brief cases disappear into what is known in British financial circles as "the drain": a melange, swelling in waves, pulsating with the arrival of the underground, filled with worker bees just right for Thatcher's new bourgeois revolution of "popular capitalism." Britain, having first lost its empire, is now in the process of losing itself in the internationalization of capital. In "the drain," the City can be seen desperately reversing the inertial tendency of the suburbs, as it brings together a momentary critical mass of labor to energize the next historical cycle of commerce in the age of advanced capitalism.

The immersion of all the suburban worker bees (bankers, traders and finanical analysts) into the City immediately signals a wave of dispersion across the international network of finance. Not just the flight of capital in the form of telemetried money, but also the flight of all the externalized minds of the participants, each turning on in synchronism with the computer video displays. Each shedding their identity as "mild mannered reporters" to become their favorite fictional supermen: beyond race, nation, color, and creed. As one London foreign exchange trader stated: "I pretend I'm an Arab investor."

Politically, the much-vaunted world of the international financier is perfectly marginal. At the level of individual existence, viciousness for fun (like in bureaucratic culture) is the ruling code. The demand for hyper-performance requires the immediate elimination of the below-average trader and its replacement by an identical twin. Here, Rome is founded anew each day, initiating a form of perfected Social Darwinism where progress is superceded by stasis, and where the operative rule is the elimination of the species. As life becomes more sporting, burnout is the code of work behavior which governs entry as a trader; and the performance principle is measured by the international war standard in accumulating capital, set by *all* the traders, from Manhattan and Tokyo to Perth, Hong Kong and Paris.

In an ultra-computerized international financial market which approaches the *real time* of instantaneous response, trading is also marginal on the level of operative second-to-second activity. Trading decisions made in the first working hour are rewarded or punished by noon-time, if not instantly. As one Merrill Lynch trader says in the retrograde language of panic sex: "We're in and out, in and out, literally ten times a minute." That international market exchanges now resemble fluid motions across the circuitry of the money chip may be why, in a case of money imitating art, the new London market center is designed exactly like the *Beaubourg*, Paris' leading art center. Just like the *Beaubourg*, where all the functions of the building are externalized and thus publicized as if to celebrate life as a postmodern screen, the London exchange announces, first in its architecture and later in its internal political transformation (the "Big Bang" when London went international) that Britain, too, has joined the circuitry of the ultra-modern money screen.

Like the theoretical world of particle physics, decisions to buy or sell are framed by the language of indeterminacy, where the market behavior of one's colleagues/enemies overdetermines the outcome. Market gains share the lifestyle of virtual particles appearing sometimes to catalyze activity, and then immediately imploding into a dead blip on the computer screen. Market reasoning becomes the algorithm of infinite regress as the point/counter-point of all the players indicates the determined attempt, in perfect Sadean fashion, to line up behind the last term in the series. In this backward willing of the will, the frantic panic of prediction reverses Nietzsche's "time's it was." Not any longer Nietzsche's passive or suicidal nihilism, but now, *chip nihilism* at the beginning of the panic market world.

At work or at home, night or day (it makes no difference), the computer screen becomes the constant companion of all our traders. Indeed, they possess bodies fit for the internationalization of capital: traders' bodies now as 24-hour information screens receiving and dilating pulsating blasts of market news, wired to the hyper-beat of random and unpredictable downturns and upturns; never really sleeping, but always calculating with such a degree of intensity and abstraction that our traders become, finally, what they study: pulsating and fibrillating money blips. Recently, one London banker has even dreamed publicly of installing in his home computer a voice synthesizer with a "sexy female voice," detailing all of the market positions. In this mock-up of cybersex, the wives have long ago been sent to the guest rooms.

In the stochastic rhythm of life in the London exchange — which is to say *everywhere* since as Marx well knew, Britain is an advanced outrider of the capitalist mind — we find a defense of everyday life, where old moralisms from the age of commodity capital disappear as not displayable, and where friendship becomes shared randomness, each awaiting elimination as energy is depleted.

The naming of this new market phenomena by its participants as "the drain" shows us, perhaps, that the postmodern parade is the unhappy marriage of the entropic, parasitic dispersion of high energy.

It's Tom Wolfe's "Masters of the Universe" as ecstatic servomechanisms in the age of chip money.

PANIC FEMINISM

This letter is being computerized because of the interest in *panic*, evidenced by the publication of the **PANIC ENCYCLOPEDIA**, a document the last remaining physicists have found fascinating. It appears that during the *postmodern*, panic was a fairly widespead phenomenon within the World that used to be known as the First. Although the style of the letter is archaic, it offers some insight into what we can now identify as panic feminism. Two points of classification:

1. The letter seems to have been written by a woman, name unknown, to another woman identified only as OW, in reply to a letter the letter-writer received from her. The contents of the letter concern the relationship between these two women. A man, and other women, perhaps feminist ones, are also involved. We understand that these elements were often found to be present when panic and feminism were in the same letter.

2. The letter contains no legible date, but we assume it was written during the televised hearings mentioned several times in the document. We know little about what was heard, but recollect an entry about a covert operation having something to do with a man named North, a name which seems to have been a perfect simulacrum of the empire he sought to establish. The man North must have had some special significance for the woman (which is not fully transparent) since the following fragment was attached to the letter: "I'm reading a book, *The Conquest of America* by Tzvetan Todorov and watching the television every day. The scene: Christopher Columbus, like Oliver North, hopes to divert funds from the conquest of America to the conquest of Jerusalem. A covert operation for an empire already in decline? And now a reversed geography, or just a doubling of the original American scene of imperial exploration, another empire in decline. Columbus' trajectory was from the Americas to the Middle East; the present imperial diversion from the East to the Americas. Of course, Columbus' geography was just as confused as Oliver North's: a whole history of territorializing the world West and North. Some others remembered an omen voiced of savage civilization: 'The years most feared by the people were those of the North and the West, since they remembered that the most unhappy events had taken place under those signs.'"

Photo credit: Jamie Lyle Gordon

Dear OW:

I can't help writing this letter under this displaced question: what do white feminist women want of each other? And under this question gentle, but hard: why your letter to me now, after the hearings have left the soap opera time of television and after a drowning by the water's edge?

I'm reading your letter as a scene, a screen, a scream of heterosexually induced panic that positions our feminism uneasily. Analytically, like a case history, like a case of postmodern hysteria. Honestly, this is about a heterosexual panic that positions our feminism uneasily. But I'm not writing as analyst without desire, without a certain and uneasy transference. I'm not reading without self-involvement, if only 'somewhat' (as you hope), but certainly with complicity in this story. I'm not reading your letter or writing this one without my heart beating fast or without my mouth dry, lumps of flesh words travelling from stomach to throat. I'm panicking disorder or as least with some gestures towards disordering these panic scenes/screens/screams. I'm not reading your letter from him without some (mis)understandings, let's be hysterical, about your self-involvement with him, and me separately and together. But can I write you not of my madness but of being mad with displaced origins, of comings after him, of absent objects, of another's self involvement with him? Can I say that I'm mad with anger, fears and tears at the compulsion of the heterosexual theater that positions our feminism and our women relations, and the second front of defense against the pain, terror, and ecstasy (the theater) of falling into loving living in a world of white men?

> It was like he was a magnet pulling me. It was exciting and powerful and frightening. He was after me too and when he found me I would run, or be petrified, just standing in front of him like a zany. And he told me not to be wandering with Clara to the Marigold where we danced with strangers. He said he would knock the shit out of me. Which made me shake and tremble, but it was better than being a husk full of suffering and not knowing why.[1]

You write to me: "I entered his text (hers and his?) once upon a time in relation to these words she spoke ..." And then you were disturbed by desire for him. Are you sure you weren't disturbed by desire for him before the words of the other woman formed a webbing around your own? And what of the other other woman who panicked you more thickly, closer to the body's edge? You wrote me some time after tea about a woman "surrounded by their loaded words she doesn't understand. Am I surrounded? Am I hysterical?" Maybe you were just falling into filmic love and fearing the silence that accompanies the fade-out. Maybe, maybe not. Maybe I responded with a misplaced letter, with a phone-not-sex-call, because you wrote to him instead: "After all that talk of sex and death, she was dying to make love" ...to him. My only excuse limp: It was his birthday and I wanted to give him something he wanted, something he would want me for. You had entered his story already and not mine yet, or so I thought. It was his birthday and I wanted to give him something he wanted, something he would want me for. Maybe we were both surrounded but unevenly hysterical.

Then you were disturbed by desire for him. But, what of Clara or me or the other woman(s)? He didn't tell you not to dance with us. Or did he, though not so directly? Was he in a panic, fearing your in-difference to him, the loss of his inspiration from his inspired woman, a hysterical but not yet laughing matter? Did you fear the loss of him your in-difference might effect? It was, after all, his talk of sex and death that drew your desire out towards him materially "across the sheets," as you and he like to write. I thought my letter to him was about the impossible position of writing for him, of me writing for him or of you writing for him. I should have written you a letter of your own and not have deserted you in a wilderness of foreign words threatening sinister meanings written for him. No desire for your salvation, but a failure nonetheless. A failure to acknowledge that I was already surrounded by you, within a hysterical story.

But now you write to me much later in your story of sex and death, of descent and desire, of another desire: "I want you to write for me (she), for us (we) not for him wrote she that wrote for him all spring into summer." I'm not outside of the family scene/screen/scream that makes it possible for me to know materially why you wrote and wrote yourself into a panic with/for him. *It was like he was a magnet pulling me. It was exciting and powerful and frightening. It was better than being a husk full of suffering and not knowing why.* Can we write for each other? I don't know. I only have this question right now: Why is the tale always the wounding that he inflicts to get the blood boiling or the story moving?

> ... however woman-to-woman relationships, female support networks, a female and feminist value system, are relied on and cherished, indoctrination in male credibility and status can still create synapses in thought, denials of feeling, wishful thinking, a profound sexual and intellectual confusion ... 'I have had very bad relationships with men — I am now in the midst of a very painful separation. I am trying to find my strength through women — without my friends, I could not survive.' How many times a day do women speak words like these, or think them, or write them, and how often does the synapse reassert itself?[2]

I know something of indoctrinations. Of that I'm sure to be a doctor soon, a real soldier with the military discipline of a colonel and the always-present threat of the chaos of discipline overrun. With what healing gifts I know not, except this: We've got to stop falling into filmic (whether Hollywood or Avant-garde) love and into a different writing, into different rituals, that don't produce such a deadly division of labor between wounding and healing. We've got to stop becoming the nurses to his surgical love.

There's another wounding here. Honestly, but gently. Why this letter to me now after the hearings have left the time of soap opera television and after a drowning by the water's edge? A terrifying inscription, but why why why? Why from spring into summer? Why across his sheets? What do women want from each other? Hysterically, I'm caught in the web of my own desires: Why write me now? What me is being addressed? What are you asking me to remember? Analytically, I'm caught between the satisfaction of a story of woman misbehaving, a familial and hysterical story, and the danger of a story of women's complicities, a story of conflicting demands and uneasy positionings, a story that edges more closely around your question fragile yet brutal: "how did I (we) come to be so alone?"

The wounding made it seem so simple, so satisfying, a clear case I could analyze coldly: Within the heterosexual theater, a feminist woman panicked. This had nothing to do with me. Some time after the panic, I was the recipient of a letter that both implicated me and demanded that I respond to the feminist, not the hys-

105

terical woman. My refusal was (empire)ical: I presumed I knew from the Other(s) that the feminist was still panicked, that he was the most important person in the story, that the panic was about him not me not the place of desire. A woman turned her feminism on me in a heterosexual panic. This is a story that sutures a wounding, but not really.

You wrote me, "he asked for centuries, 'What do women want?'" I can't help writing this letter to you under this question displaced: What do women want of each other? The wounding made it seem so simple, a story I could tell satisfying the trembling between the scenes/screens. And yet now I'm caught between a satisfaction and a disturbance. When one story has lost its plottings and a dangerous story is threatening to tell itself, another letter needs to be written.

Thank you for your letter and words from a "self-involved sliding towards and involved self-displacement."

P.S. I read this letter to him before I gave it to you.

Avery Gordon

Notes

1. Meridel Lesueur, *The Girl*, Cambridge: West End Press, 1978, pp. 10-11.
2. Adrienne Rich, "Compulsory Heterosexuality and Lesbian Existence" in *Powers of Desire, The Politics of Sexuality*, eds. Ann Snitow, Christine Stansell and Sharon Thompson. New York: Monthly Review Press, 1983, p. 190.

PANIC FLORIDA

Sunstrokes

Since 1960 I have spent from two to four weeks a year in South Florida almost every year. Most of the time I've spent there has been in the Fort Lauderdale, Pompano Beach area of the "gold coast." I began going for vacations when I was a child, to visit relatives in the summer. After my mother moved from New York to Florida in 1971, I began to visit her there, usually in winter. However, in "Sunstrokes," a series of inter-related postcard length messages describing South Florida, I did not use the first person singular — not because I wanted to create the illusion of objectivity, but because in Florida I feel depersonalized.

The Florida room: neither inside nor outside. Every self-respecting South Florida house has one — a glassed-in porch, air-conditioned, with casual furniture. A couple of lounges, maybe a couch, a few glass-topped tables. Plastic and metal predominate. Or wicker in more tasteful establishments. The Florida room signifies leisured enjoyment of the outdoors with protection from its impositions.

South Florida interiors: done in the kind of Technicolor used to make low budget cult movies that simulate a fifties' ambiance. Blinds, shades, or drapes always closed. Otherwise, sun damages the wall-to-wall carpet and the upholstery. Windows always shut.

Otherwise, dampness encourages mould. Contrary to popular belief among Northerners, South Floridians feel that life is a constant struggle against the elements. Concrete only seems to have conquered. A new breed of concrete-loving termites is beginning to undermine the condominiums on the beach.

Outdoors: the ice-cream pastel buildings contrast with bright pink hibiscus and palm trees in muted tones. Florida wear: polyester suits in parrot shades — yellow, orange, blue and green.

On first inspection, everything looks fake. Moulded plaster and stucco suggest something Moorish, Mexican, Italian, or Japanese. The architecture awaits a Nathanael West of the eighties to capture its essence, as he did that of California in the thirties. But contemporary South Florida differs from West's Los Angeles; the immigrants from the North have come to retire, to avoid death. They want to withdraw from the stressful realm of work to a place dedicated to safe adventures and clean pleasures. Their ideal: to maintain an appearance of petrified youthfulness. Their totem: Micky Mouse, who with the passage of time has appeared ever more juvenile.

The essence of Florida is not, as in West's Hollywood, spectacle or illusion; it is management — of people, wild life, resources, consumption. The company that collects the garbage calls itself WASTE MANAGEMENT, INC.

Nature once had a chance to run riot in South Florida, producing jungles and swamps; now nature must submit to control. Wild life and resource management preserve bits of the Everglades from voracious developers eager to pave **everything** over. Scavengers, like seagulls and pelicans, adapt well to life among the housing tracts and condos. Even egrets can stalk their prey over the lawns and around the parking lots.

Birds with more specialized tastes become refugees — dwellers in the refuges and sanctuaries created for them and for nostalgic pilgrims who come to catch glimpses of them. Bird-watching is the fastest growing sport in North America — its growth directly proportional to the birds' decline.

Alligators are refugees too; the languid, seemingly prehistoric lizards of Gatorland Zoo or Alligator Jungle are props, among which pass processions of tourists, seeking, as the promotional literature describes it, "a learning adventure."

Even the sea is tamed at Ocean World or Sea World where you are invited to "talk to the animals...and let them talk to you." The seals, dolphins, and whales repeat whatever message you are waiting to hear.

Human nature too must be managed and organized. After the landscape was domesticated, excitement has been reinserted with tourist attractions that promise danger: Wet'n Wild Waterslide, Adventure Island, Busch Gardens, the Dark Continent, Parrot Jungle, Orchid Jungle, Monkey Jungle.

Fear, never far below the surface of the fun-loving Floridian, must then be directed at appropriate targets: swimmers scan the horizon for sharks, but no one worries, when they go into the ocean, about the crude oil sludge visible on the sand at their feet.

Newscasters name the real villains: drug pushers, muggers, robbers who prey on innocent householders. They also provide the remedies: drug testing, more police, better security alarm systems. Patriotism, loyalty, and morality can all be measured through purity of bodily fluids: pure blood, pure urine.

Orthodox thinking is an old-fashioned concern, for Disneyland democracy can afford to encourage freedom of thought. Whatever your opinions, you can make them count in Florida's electronic forum, the Epcot poll; the consensus on current events, sports, lifestyles, and entertainment is "released weekly to print and broadcast journalists around the country."

Time and space must also be managed. Time-sharing: that Florida euphemism for sharing space with a series of invisible strangers. Neighborhoods have become "manufactured housing communities" (trailer parks) and "total lifestyle communities" where "planned activities" simulate social life.

Everyone knows that Florida is the Fountain of Youth: aging is denied, history consists of nothing but development and improvement. Property acquires value through newness or the appearance of newness. Tradition is useful only where it produces a novelty attraction, like Miami Beach's Old Spanish Monastery, "erected just as it was in Segovia Spain 300 years before Columbus discovered America." Or John Ringling's fifteenth century Italian villa in St. Petersburg.

Everywhere in South Florida, tourists are incited to have a "real good time" — to participate in a staged, authentic event. Restaurants provide eating experiences in lieu of food. And instead of just consumer goods, stores retail fun, relaxation, shopping adventures.

In Florida, the only center is the Shopping Center. The ideal shopping center is Mercado in Orlando where you can "explore the mysteries of an international marketplace ... in a charming village setting." The global village as shopping mall. With so many village settings, Floridians have no need for villages, nor for towns, or cities; South Florida is a series of suburbs, euphemistically dubbed "metropolitan complexes," linked by highways.

Ideally Floridians are moved through this decentred space inside cars. Buses exist for the underclasses. Jogging along streets or sidewalks is permissible, but Floridians regard walking with suspicion. If you insist on it for health reasons, there's always the beach.

South Florida is a state of mind which begins at Disneyworld and extends southwards. It can also be exported like oranges and grapefruit. South Florida is disarming; it offers itself as "Canada's eleventh province" to the 1.5 million Canadians who visit every winter.

At Disneyworld itself, "imagineering" technology produces magic; magic produces faith in the American way. Disneyworld is a successful experiment in crowd control; the rest of South Florida tries to emulate it. Entertainment at Disneyworld, when it occurs, is a by-product of moving people through space.

What counts is not the experience but the photo-opportunity: the easily recognized Kodak symbols indicate "prime photo taking locations." WASTE PLEASE: the signs on the litter baskets encourage consumption. The map distributed free to Disneyworld visitors promotes conformity: "All roads which end suddenly with a line ... continue, but we do not recommend you follow them, as they will lead you off the usual beaten path."

At Disneyworld, the nation's playground, the universe is conveniently divided up. First the Magic Kingdom, which is further subdivided. Then Epcot, which is divided into Future World and World Showcase. The former features better living through technology and the latter domesticates the universe into cliché: "the mysterious East," or "Oktoberfest entertainment," or "Canada's great outdoors."

The rest of South Florida follows the Disney model: Blacks, Whites, Gentiles, Jews, Cubans, Anglos, children, adults, all experience separate development. No one mentions apartheid; South Floridians are more discreet than South Africans. But every new housing tract is surrounded by the wall enclosing its own "complete lifestyle package." Secure in their insecurity inside, the tract dwellers sit in their living rooms watching **Miami Vice**. Whenever the news or the programing has produced enough pleasurable anxiety, they just switch the dial to easy listening: JOY, LOVE, LYF.

No management system can be completely successful. Occasionally nature gets out of control and produces a hurricane or an AIDS epidemic. Emotions too go awry, creating a sniper who guns down shoppers. So there are "final consumer concerns": the Yellow Pages' entry for funeral homes, cemeteries, crematoria.

Eileen Manion

G

PANIC GOD

This is Jimmy Bakker and what the press love to describe as the "heavily mascared Tammy Faye." Not just TV evangelicals brought to ground by a double complicity — Jerry Falwell's will to money and Jimmy Schwaggart's will to power — but Jimmy and Tammy as the first, and perhaps the best, practioners of the new American religious creed of *Post-Godism*.

TV evangelicism, then, is all about the creation of a postmodern God: not religion under the sign of panoptic power, but the hyper-God of all the TV evangelicals as so fascinating and so fungible, because this is where God has disappeared as a grand referent, and reappeared as an empty sign-system, waiting to be filled, indeed, *demanding* to be filled, if contributions to the TV evangelicals are any measure, by all the waste, excess and sacrificial burnout of Heritage Park, USA. An excremental God, therefore, for an American conservative culture disappearing into its own burnout, detritus and decomposition. For Jimmy and Tammy's disgrace is just a momentary *mise-en-scene* as the soap opera of a panic god

PANIC

reverses field on itself, and everyone waits for what is next in the salvation myth, American style: Jimmy and Tammy in their struggle through a period of dark tribulations and hard trials on their way to asking forgiveness (on Ted Koppel's *Nightline* show on ABC). As Jimmy Bakker once said: "In America, you have to be excessive to be successful." Or, as Tammy likes to sign out all of her TV shows: "Just remember. Jesus loves you. He *really, really does.*"

PANIC HOLLYWOOD

Recently, *Scientific American* published a new astrophysical theory about the center of our universe as the formation of black holes:

> Black holes form at the very beginning of new galaxies and at their center. If there can be such a glow at the center, that is because the dark and intense concentration of black holes attracts stars which rush into its vortex, and one last sign of their presence is their intense brilliance before they disappear.

Hollywood is like that: a fantastically dense, inertial and expanding black hole, which forming at the very beginning of the new American political galaxy, attracts into its vortex all of the stars in the USA. And not just in the entertainment industries(movies, television, news and advertising), but, if the literature on the political economy of the LA region is accurate, Hollywood is a new stellar center of high tech: computers, aerospace industries and military research. Like the American culture of which it has always been a faithful image-reservoir, Hollywood now is a fateful meeting-point of primitive mytholo-

PANIC

gy and technological society. And just like those other black holes from outer space, Hollywood is postmodern to this extent: it has no center, only a spreading dead zone of exhaustion, inertia, and brilliant decay.

Thus, the famous Hollywood studios of yesteryear have largely disappeared into "post-production houses" where images (filmed elsewhere) are "sweetened" and "cheated." While living film stars may have fled to the beach houses of Malibu, the famous Hollywood homes of the dead stars have been turned into restaurants (where everyone can be admitted, and where just anyone might turn out to be one of the collapsing stars). And even Hollywood and Vine, the geographical and cultural center of Hollywood, has vanished into memory-lane. At night the streets are predatory, with police helicopters overhead (just like in *Blade Runner* where LA is the prototype city), and the actual street corners of Hollywood and Vine have been taken over by fighting heavy metal groups, strutting their stuff at night.

Nothing escapes their black costumes. For after all Hollywood has long since left California and is now to be found in the spiral arms of distant galaxies. There is nothing left at Hollywood and Vine for it is now part of the nebulae that we all turn into each night. Nothing in the world can escape the gravitational pull of the old Hollywood films, but like the random escape velocities of the black hole we are perodically ejected into the future star worlds.

Panic Hollywood II

In his book, *Le Parasite*, the French philospher, Michel Serres, claims that the end of the feast is always signalled by the return of the animal kingdom. Perhaps that is what is so culturally significant about the invasion now of Hollywood by rats. In a city which is inscribed by mythology, the return of the rats has an almost totemic significance out of proportion to its numbers.

Consider this story from Laurel Canyon. I was visiting two super-successful computer technocrats from MIT's Media Research Lab who had finally made it into the Hollywood star vortex. They were part of the "brilliant luminosity" of Hollywood's black hole, and glad of it. It seemed, though, that they had recently moved into a spiffy house at the very top of one of the privileged hills of Laurel Canyon (just down the gully from the Manson family's hideout) with a superb view of Hollywood. As soon as they moved in, they awoke each night to the shuffling and squeaking sounds of rats scurrying around in the dark. Like efficient technocrats not ready to give in to the return of the animal kingdom without a fight, they tried everything to liquidate the rats. Pest control companies (which only guaranteed their work for one week, and then vanished); TV monitors (the husband worked for Panasonic and so he set up each night sophisticated infrared cameras to film the nocturnal rat invasion); cultural folklore (when queried, people in the neighborhood began talking, with the precision of scientific naturalists, about the five main varieties of California desert rats). Finally, they gave up and moved out, and this when told by yet another defeated rat exterminator that their hill house was basically a rat's nest (the rats had excavated its foundations for their own breeding purposes), and that from the perspective of the rats, *they* were the property interlopers who needed to be expelled.

I didn't pay much attention to the *cultural* significance of this story of the rats until that night while attending the opening exhibit of *The New Age of Television* at one of LA's art galleries, I began to take a midnight walk through the manicured Japanese gardens, which served as an aestheticized roof for the gallery. Immediately, a guard came over and whispered in my ear: "Be careful...there are lots of rats around here these days."

Welcome, then, to Hollywood, to the sound of the rats moving in when the dinner party is over, the lights have been turned off and all the guests have finally fled.

PANIC HISTORY

History is the great subordination of the *plastic men* whose ruling motto is, as Nietzsche reminds us, "Let the dead bury the living."[1]

But even this world of age-old fables parasited from Hegel and Marx has now vanished into irrelevance. Beyond forgetting, the post-modern world is also finally beyond a representational theory of history: beyond, that is, the *grand recits* of history monumental or critical, exploitative or salvational, right or wrong. For postmodernism has invented the "new historicism" with its deep genealogical guarantee against the exhaustion of the political code. Under the sign of science, history has become genetic and speaks the language of biology.

The Constitution is the key site of the "new historicism" in the United States. Anyway, political constitutions have always obviated the need for foraging in the primeval slime. Following the invention of the self-cleaning oven, history automatically sheds the wasteful, the aberrant, and the unsuccessful — once, that is, the genotype of the past has been discovered. The invariance of the genetic USA code was first invented by the "founding fathers," whether in the form of the Declaration of Independence (life, liberty, and the pursuit of happiness), *habeas corpus*, or, in its ideal type, the Constitution of the United States.

The very reproducibility of the Constitution from civics courses (learning the genetic code of American politics) to weasel defences for White House officials attests to its clonal nature. In the latter case, the power of the Constitution is such as to immunize all the political actors from their past. Here, the rhyming couplet of a little cynicism and a little piety sit happily together. As the ideal defence of American "habits of the heart" — truth, justice and the American way — the Constitution is also mutable into its reverse code: the panic side of America as an exhausted and self-cancelling political culture. Or, as Nietzsche has said:

> Perhaps a little dim, a little air pessimiste, but in the main voracious, dirty, dirtying, creeping in, nestling, thieving scurvy — and as innocent as all little sinners and microbes.[2]

But postmodern history is all this and more. In this new biology the Constitution, which was never so much genetic as the strongest *virus* in the early American struggle between federalists and anti-federalists, has itself entered our cancerous age. As a consequence, all forms of political and historical codes are transformed into *retroviruses*. Precisely because the Constitution continually mutates (what is euphemistically described as the "living Constitution"), it always escapes its own demise at the hands of impending irrelevance, reappearing in new genetic adaptations to the shifting scene of social policy issues, from subway vigilantes to surrogate mothers.

Unlike the (representational) history of petrified values which characterized the sentimentalizing romanticism of the "men" of Iwo Jima in the fight of good versus evil, this "new historicism" passes through all values. It enters freely into the diseases becoming part of their cellular structure, hence unrecognizable as foreign agents. A nice realization of the Greek ideal of the constitution as a way of life.

When the fashion of an age is fashion, then all is immediately history. This is the most historical of all times precisely because it is in our genes/jeans. As the expression goes in reference to the scene of broken marriages, relationships, promises or vases — "You're history" — with the unspoken prod to the herd to move on. The same might be said now of history itself.

Notes

1. F. Nietzsche, "On the Uses and Disadvantages of History for Life," p.72.
2. F. Nietzsche, *The Will to Power*, trans. by Walter Kaufmann and R.J. Hollingdale, New York: Vintage, 1968, section 77, p.49.

PANIC HAMBURGERS

From Secretion to Excretion

Postmodern hamburgers. That is what McDonald's (most excessively) and all the fast-food chains are selling these days.

No longer hamburgers under the old (modernist) sign of nutrition, but just the opposite. Hamburgers which have been aestheticized to such a point of frenzy and hysteria that the McDonald's hamburger has actually vanished into its own sign. Just watch the TV commercials. Hamburgers as *party time* for the kids; hamburgers as *nostalgia time* for our senior citizens; hamburgers as *community time* for small town America; and, as always, hamburgers under the media sign of *friendship time* for America's teenagers. Thus, processed hamburgers for a society where eating is *the* primary consumptive activity and where, anyway, fast-food is interesting as a sign of the aestheticization of the body to excess. Phasal eating for postmodern bellies which have already become spectral images of themselves.

McDonald's is a perfect technological hologram of suburban America, and of its extension by the capillaries of highways across the nation.

Processed food: designer hamburgers, irradiated salads, simulated McChickens, promotional McBreakfasts.

Processed colors: the old McDonald's roadside Rah! Rah! colors of red and yellow have disappeared, and have been replaced by soothing postmodern hues. Mellow colors for a pleasant day, maybe a thousand pleasant days, in a middle-aging America.

Processed crowds: like Disneyland, the key problem for McDonald's (as a phasal eating station for the nation) is crowd control; and so a whole apparatus of processed eating stations (like work stations in cyberspace), everything to speed the way from secretion to excretion.

I

PANIC IDEOLOGY

In his "Theses on the Philosophy of History,"[1] Walter Benjamin wrote that "a state of emergency" is the rule rather than the exception in bourgeois existence. Now, more than ever, Benjamin's prophetic insights appear as an early diagnosis of the unprecedented threat to civilized life presented by the politics of the new right. The election of George Bush, this too-perfect organ grinder for multinational corporate interests, and the systematic playing out through the late 1980s of a merciless American foreign and domestic policy, point to the surfacing, not only in Europe this time (in the guise of "popular capitalism" in Thatcher's Britain, Kohl's West Germany, and in technocratic France) but also in North America, of the beast that is at the heart of the western mind. In the face of this state of emergency, it is impossible to be silent. For this is an authoritarian politics which is as relentless in its assaults on democratic struggles in Central America as it is pitiless in its "reality therapy" for the poor, for children, for the aged. We thought Spencer was finally dead, only to discover in the slogans of "supply side eco-

PANIC

nomics" the birth anew of social darwinism.

Just as the New Left defined the political agenda of the 1960s, in the 1980s the political cycle finds its completion in the hyper-collectivism, the politics of emotional needs, of the new right. Indeed, towards the end of his life, Herbert Marcuse made this prophetic commentary:

> The tendency is to the Right. The life and death question for the Left is: Can the transformation of the corporate state into a neo-fascistic one be prevented?[2]

Marcuse's analysis addresses the possibility that the emergence of a rightist tendency is a born-again movement of the authoritarian personality, of what Theodor Adorno described as the renewal of the "potentially fascistic personality." The dominant fact about the political right today is that it is no longer contained within the terms of a normal political opposition or of an orthodox economic strategy. Without doubt, the right expresses politically the strategic economic aims of dominant corporate interests. The nostalgic and Walrasian panegyric to the sovereign market-place, even as conservative economic theorists, like Milton Friedmann, stand in front of the sweat shops of Hong Kong, is a radical attack on the wage earnings of workers and the dispossessed. And political economists, from J.K. Galbraith to Robert Reich, are not mistaken in noting that the economics of neo-conservative regimes — aimed directly at relieving the tax burden of the upper middle-class at the expense of public services — is really a barely disguised class struggle of rich against poor. The political slogans of the new right — the "disciplinary society," "waste in public regulation," — are not ineffective appeals aimed at resolving the contradictions of the welfare state in favor of organized private interests. Economically, the politics of the new right points to the existence of an economic crisis which has been displaced to the social sphere.[3]

But over and beyond the strident political vocabulary of the new right, something else is happening. The new right is so potentially dangerous because it represents a broader awakening of an "ideology in waiting."[4] And this newly surfacing ideology has its basis in the nihilism of a middle-class gone authoritarian. In the end, fear of loss of privilege, impotence in the face of overwhelming power and despair over the failure of the liberal consensus produce a psychological "readiness" for the therapeutic of the authoritarian state.

It is no secret that the conservative assault spills beyond the political realm, narrowly conceived. Attacks on gay rights, demands (in Bloom's America) for the return of disciplinary and elitist education, juridical offensives against womens' rights (calls for the legal subordination of womens' bodies to the power of the state in the new wave of cases surrounding fetal appropriation), and nostalgic appeals for the defence of the family, neighborhood and work-place — indicate the emergence in the politics of the late 1980's of a personality type which is the psychological fuel of conservative political discourse. The "moral majority" is really a not unsubtle appeal to a politics of emotional distress.

In an excellent analysis, "Anxiety and Politics," the theorist Franz Neumann — who was, incidentally, one of the first of the critical thinkers to be deported from Germany by the Nazis — discussed the psychological basis of the authoritarian personality. Neumann claimed that the bourgeois individual lives today under the strain of two unresolvable sources of tension: an "outer anxiety" and an "inner anxiety." The outer anxiety expresses the ever-present dangers of the public world; the inner anxiety reflects the unresolved oedipal tensions of the bourgeois self. Desires for self-punishment, objectless feelings of guilt, a lack of confidence in the survival capacities of the self — these are the legacy of the inner anxiety. Neumann claimed further that the tensions represented by the outer and inner anxieties turn authoritarian, and thus, potentially neo-fascistic, when under the pressures of external economic crises and a more silent inner crisis, the outer anxiety meets the inner anxiety.

> The external dangers which threaten a man meet the inner anxiety and are frequently experienced as ever more dangerous than they really are. At the same time those same external dangers intensify the inner anxiety. The painful tension which is evoked by the combination of inner anxiety and external danger can express itself in two forms: in depressive or persecutory anxiety.[5]

Politically, depressive anxiety may express itself in despair and resignation — it is the sure and certain source of the otherwise inexplicable suicides which come to dominate the mental landscape of today. Persecutory anxiety is the classic basis of neo-fascistic movements. It is the psychological fuel which produces a mass-based politics of emotional needs, referenda on happiness as the essence of electoral politics, and scapegoatism of vulnerable out-groups. It may also result in the projection of private anxieties of impotence, fatalism, and inferiority onto what Neumann describes as the "caesaristic leader," the strong leader who charismatically sums up in his personality the spontaneity, the violence, the passion of the "dark side" of the modern mind. As the epicentre of the meeting of the outer anxiety and the inner anxiety, the bourgeois individual is envisioned as suffering a dramatic loss of ego and abandoning himself to states of fantasy, delirium, and illusion. For Neumann, the bourgeois self was almost destined to move from the private experience of fantasia to the stronger medicine of the cult, the evangelical religion, and then to active support of a mass politics of emotional needs. Voting analysts now call this phenomenon "mood politics."

We would follow Neumann in noting that the politics of the 1980s, and principally those of what Kathy Acker has described as the "American empire of the senseless," are typified for the individual by the meeting of the outer anxiety, the public crisis, with the inner anxiety. The outer anxiety today is a crisis of political economy. The inner anxiety is an existential crisis. The socio-psychological basis of new right politics is the fusion of the outer and inner anxieties; the meeting of the existential crisis and the political crisis. The outer crisis which the individual meets, this external danger which activates an interior, neurotic anxiety, has been eloquently described by a number of theoreticians, including Jürgen Habermas, Claus Offe and Sheldon Wolin, as a classic erosion of trust in liberal-democratic institutions. Liberalism, in Wolin's terms, is the ideology which strips public life of any basis in a substantial concern with justice, equality or democracy.[6] The anti-democratic sentiments of the new right are, in part, the end-product of liberalism's reduction of politics to a barren struggle of interest against interest. Here, the decline of the public realm is traceable to the bourgeois individual's concern with using the public world only to advance, through manipulation, a narrowly calculated self-interest. And Michael Weinstein in an essay entitled "The Eclipse of Liberalism" notes that the decline of an authentic politics in the United States is symbolized by a breakdown of the "general will" as the basis of the social contract; and by the consequent development of a strong desire to neutralize the menacing face of public life by "contractualizing" all social relations.[7] Weinstein says that Rousseau's "general will" as the basis of public life has now given way to the more monadic principle of the "will of all." In a situation of economic triage, the return of an almost Spencerian survival ethic pits individual against individual. In addition to an erosion of confidence in political life, the inevitable economic crisis is such that the individual is under a constant threat of a loss of privilege, position and status. An "outer anxiety" thus grips the bourgeois self, inflation is the economic cancer which erodes the discretionary income of the middle class and this class cannot rest easy in the absence of contractual commitments guaranteeing a secured distribution of public goods.

Under the pressure of a "loss of privilege," of a daily anxiety over loss of confidence in the credibility of the political economy of the liberal state, the bourgeois mind oscillates to the other extreme. There is a retreat from public life, massive and wilful in character, into a private inner experience of fantasy and illusion. Reason gives way to private passion. In the absence of a secure public realm, the individual tries to establish a private zone of emotional security, symbolized by the ideal of the Spencerian ego: privative, survival-oriented and exploitative. Max Horkheimer concluded in *Dawn and Decline* that this is an era typified by the appearance of monadology as an active principle of social life.[8] It is not unpredictable that the social counterparts of the outer anxiety are nostalgia, the return of a "myth of innocence," and a retreat to the family, if not to the body, as the last barrier against a public world verging on *stasis*. It is equally predictable that the deflated bourgeois ego finds its most eloquent expression in, on the one hand, the almost surrealistic search for the radon free house and, on the other, in a simplistic faith in the return to "classical" education.

Unfortunately, the private zone of emotional stillness sought by the bourgeois mind is itself illusory. One lesson of the hegemonic tendencies of the technological order is that the social as well as the psychoanalytical foundations of identity have already been colonized. What C.B. Macpherson has described as "possessive individualism" — the sense that the modern "self" has been transformed into a propertied aspect of the economic order — is a haunting image of contemporary times. In flight from public life, the individual encounters an inner self whose laws of psychical action resemble the catastrophe theorems of the outer world. The individual leaves behind the anxieties of the public world only to discover an inner self which borders, on one side, on the return of beastialism and, on the other, on absorption into the sociopsychological imperatives of the corporate political economy. This is the beginning of the crisis of the Spencerian ego; the source of the inner anxiety. Daily, the suspicion develops that it is impossible to survive on the terms of the Spencerian compact. Cultural darwinism, having left in its wake a vacated ego, the deflated self finds its inner resources under the colonial rule of the social order.

The political formula of the nihilistic personality might be envisaged as a ceaseless movement of the bourgeois mind between an ambivalent attitude to public life on the one hand and desperate anxiety over the survival capacities of the self on the other.[9] It is this restless movement between the delegitimated self and the under-authorized state which provides a base of political support for the harsher economic strategies of the new right.

The bourgeois individual retreats from participation in public life because of a deep distrust of political leadership, but at the same time, needs for economic self-interest to secure the political arena. And the bourgeois mind needs to affirm the self as the basis of an individualistic survival ethic, but is haunted by the suspicion that the self will not prove adequate to the task. The individual is thus caught in a classic psychological contradiction. The outer anxiety increases; the economic crisis threatens actual loss of privilege. The inner anxiety intensifies; and the inner crisis, the need to affirm the self as the basis of survival in a "hostile world" is intensified by the external danger.

Classical symptoms of the failure of the bourgeois individual to resolve the tension between a "retreat from public life" and a "loss of confidence" in the survival capacities of the individual ego are, in part, the appearance of sporadic and highly symbolic violence, and the movement of religion into the political realm. In religious fundamentalism, the existential crisis of the self is resolved by a flight beyond the individual ego to immolation in a group mind. In symbolic violence, there is found the signature of the return of the collective unconscious. What Carl Jung described as the dark anima of the Shadow returns to haunt public life. This is an age in which criminals become once again truth-sayers of the normal imagination.

Politically, the result of the psychic explosion which occurs when there is a meeting of the political and existential crisis is the production of persecutory anxiety; a displacement of the crisis into a style of politics which provides a *therapeutic* for both actual threats to the self's zone of privilege and to its feelings of emotional inadequacy. In *The Authoritarian Personality*, Adorno, Frankel-Brusnwick and others traced out the political implications of the authoritarian character-type.[10] Their work, completed in the 1950s, reads like an anticipatory diagnosis of the politics of the contemporary decade. It indicates that in the politics of the new right we are dealing, in part, with a broader distemper. As a working-out of a personality type which has "no pity for the poor," the bourgeois mind goes for itself, undermining the consensual basis of the liberal-democratic polity. The class-hidden and power-disguised foundation of the social contract dissolves. A surplus-class of the dispossessed appears which is forced outside the system of political administrative relations. In brief, the outer anxiety of the authoritarian personality is met with political sadism. The innner anxiety, the existential crisis of the frightened and melancholy bourgeoisie, is resolved through masochism. Political masochism involves the application to the self of harsher and more punitive forms of self-repression and self-censorship. All of this to sustain a "spurious inner world" which will act as a censor against outer reality. The therapeutic of political sadism finds its analogue in the politics of cynical self-interest. The principle of economic triage is applied to vulerable out-groups. Political violence, domestically and internationally, is viewed as one strategy among others to sustain economic privilege. Or, in the analysis of *The Authoritarian Personality* stereotypy "works as a certain kind of corroboration of projective formulae." In short, the new right organizes into an authoritarian politics, a "free floating distemper" which is the essence of contemporary American politics. In the end, projection and displacement are the psychological tools of a middle class which has radically severed public from private existence and which finds itself torn between a deauthorized state on the one hand and a mutilated self on the other.

"Gangsters Strut Around Like Statesmen on the Stage of History"

The critical tradition has always acted on the basis of a dialectical understanding of crisis. The present crisis, typified by the return of the authoritarian personality, vanquishes human hope in the dispensation of history. But the sheer immanence of this danger, this rebirth of fascism in comfortable middle class guise, also provides opportunities for new solidarities and, ironically, in this time of great turbulence with the possibility of creating a vision of social utopia in the development of a more democratic polity. The gap between the real and the ideal, the gulf between our actual condition of immiserization and the possibility of a free society — this gap, this wound, never closes. But the intellectual responsibility of thinkers today is with Adorno, Benjamin, Sartre and others to address on behalf of a suffering humanity, the "wound" of history.

Standing at the Spanish border in the early 1940s, Walter Benjamin chose suicide rather than surrender his person, his vision of culture, the "angel of history" itself, to the torturers of the Gestapo. In the same way that Artaud wrote of Van Gogh, Benjamin was a man *suicided* by society. It is the same authoritarian tendency, this natural face of the postmodern order, which after Benjamin has driven Poulantzas, Artaud, Aquin, and Phil Oakes — the best minds of our generation to the stillness of madness, to the despair of suicide. Remember again Allen Ginsberg in *Howl*:

I saw the best minds of my generation destroyed by madness, starving, hysterical, naked

dragging themselves through the negro streets at dawn looking for an angry fix

...who passed through universities with radiant eyes hallucinating Arkansas and Blake...light tragedy among the scholars of war who were expelled from the academies for crazy and publishing obscure odes on the window of the skull.[11]

We cannot forget, we must not forget, that now when history has turned bleak again, when as Brecht said, "gangsters strut around like statesmen on the stage of history" — that we, the survivors are the only links between past and future, between a past of critical rebellion and a future of utopia.

We serve the past best by keeping alive the act of remembrance, but also by seizing the future, by insisting in an uncompromising way on the practical possibility of the ideal. Surely the present is a dead-zone of politics: it is a killing ground for the right. For today who in the tradition of the critical imagination does not stand with Benjamin at the Spanish border, with the choice of suicide on the one hand and history in the form of the new right, of the coming again of the beast first seen by Nietzsche, on the other.

Sartre, the philosopher who remained loyal to the free human subject, said finally with irony. "Man is a useless passion."

But Camus replied for those who survive:

"I rebel — therefore we exist."

Notes

1. Walter Benjamin, *Illuminations*, New York: Schoken Books, 1969, p.257.

2. Herbert Marcuse, "The Reification of the Proletariat," *Canadian Journal of Political and Social Theory*, Vol.2, No.1, 1978, p.23.

3. Jürgen Habermas, "Conservatism and Capitalist Crisis," *New Left Review*, No.115, 1979.

4. Franz Neumann, *The Democratic and Authoritarian State: Essays in Political and Legal Theory*, Glencoe: Free Press, 1957, pp. 27-30.

5. *Ibid.*, p.275.

6. For an eloquent account of the "dependent man, the rump remains of democratic man," see Sheldon Wolin, "The Idea of the State in America," *Humanities*, Vol.3, No.2, 1980, pp. 151-168.

7. Michael A. Weinstein, "The Eclipse of Liberalism," mss. p.21,

8. Max Horkheimer, *Dawn and Decline*, New York: The Seabury Press, 1978, p.17.

9. Weinstein, *op. cit.*, p.9.

10. T.W. Adorno et. al., *The Authoritarian Personality*, New York: Harper and Row, 1950, p.699.

11. Allen Ginsberg, *Howl*, San Francisco: City Lights, 1956, p.23.

THE (PANIC) PLEASURES OF INVENTION

They
Sucked
A
Filthy
Tongue
No
Mother
Could
Ever
Love

Mark Lewis

He
Vomited
Violently
All
Over
Her
Highly
Polished
Shoes.

Mark Lewis

And then one day, tired and desperate, I came across a story that seemed to say much about my present predicament. It concerned a party that had taken place in a large house in a forgotten part of the city. A party, I soon realized, that I myself had attended. I had forgotten the strange set of circumstances that had beset me there. The story continued, its descriptions of the main characters and the fragments of their conversations seemed particularly realistic. And always in the background, small details about the architecture, its histories, compromises, and harmonies. It was a party that had gone on far too long, and one also where I believe I may have been the last to leave. Imagine. Upstairs in one of the smaller rooms a bath is running, its water overflowing and beginning to seep through to the floor below. Downstairs, people are dancing but with the coming of the dawn there is also a calculated sense of desperation as everyone makes last minute arrrangements to ensure that they do not go home alone. Upstairs, someone screams, I don't remember who. I was being engaged in a conversation that demanded that I consider the question of mortality. A boy's body, very dead, the disembodied scream materializes into a more rationalized pathology: he drowned, I'm sure. You must remember, she told me, that

129

the circumstances of your rejection are such that you will never know how history came upon you. They lift the inert body from the bath and place it on the bed. People rush forward to catch a glimpse of the very significant iconographic pose. And what lies ahead of us in terms of our long-term security, she continued, is less a matter of speculation than an investment in the uncertainty of signs. It is announced with a surprising lack of presentation, that a friend of mine was killed while bathing. I turn away from her, disengaging our bodies from the tight embrace we had encouraged. A wave of uncertainty sweeps over me, causing me to close my eyes and for a moment I am unsure if it was really I who was a witness to all this. I sit back in the couch and pull out the photograph, its details now further obscured. I try to trace movement and history, but my hand is locked by the pleasantly significant smell of burning bodies. The shape of the figure is no longer clear, its discovery now in question. Where is Diana? Later, as the party continues, it begins to dawn on those revelers who care to reflect on the absurdity of all this that it may in fact have been me who drowned and not necessarily another.

Mark Lewis

Note: This is an excerpt from a larger piece entitled "The Pleasures of Invention."

J

PANIC JEANS

"Its all in your genes." This slogan of Eugenics deconstructs its own resolute objective of genetic improvement when its pun implies that "it" — your sexuality, your identity — is all in your designer jeans. In the postmodern Americanization of the globe, Eugenics is transformed into Eu(jean)ics, a postmodern science that strives for hyperreal perfection by splicing panic genes with panic jeans. This post-fetishistic power field promises Eu(jean)ic perfectibility by deploying signifiers of radical politics in the service of simulated health, wealth, and sexual desire.

PANIC

Polo Ralph Lauren

Ralph Lauren for Polo Dungarees uses the rhetoric and imagery of the "natural" in the context of the overtly simulated to appropriate not only the style of New Left politics but also that of the eu-jean company Levi Strauss. The traditional layout along an upper-left, lower-right diagonal begins the imagistic narrative with the backdrop of nature and moves down the page to the dungaree shirt and jacket and blue jeans, which, as the text informs us, "have been crafted in the spirit of an era when quality and durability were more important than fashion." From the "metal rivet and shank buttons to the triple needle stitching for added durability," these Ralph Laurens trade on the nineteenth century patented inventions of a Jewish immigrant tailor that made Levi's the choice of miners, range hands, and factory workers.[1] In juxtaposition to these icons of nature and the working class, one finds signatures of wealth and aristocratic leisure — the silk tie, the natty pocket handkerchief, the faithful dog by his master's side, the confident gaze of the privileged male. The model's hands, firmly grasping the steering wheel of a luxury car, bear no traces of manual labor. The Polo insignia in the lower right corner neatly sums it up — in the postmodern fashionscape, one can simulate being wealthy by playfully mimicking the working class.

Esprit Jeans

Just as Ralph Lauren appropriates a New Left critique of upper-class privilege while relegitimizing it, so too Esprit uses denim to appropriate feminist critiques of class, gender, and sexuality. The black strip that crosses the model's crotch, and which thus draws attention to — even while it disrupts — the viewer's focus on sexuality, reads: "Ariel O'Donnell San Francisco, California, Age: 21 Waitress/Bartender, Non-professional AIDS Educator, Cyclist, Art Restoration Student, Anglophile, Neo-Feminist." This "information" makes the model into a "real person," a socially committed one at that, by giving us the discursive details that define her. On the right-hand page, the twelve discrete photo-like images, one with the model's face and the other eleven depicting parts of her jeans, de-center her subjectivity while conflating her identity with the details of her jeans. The text in the lower right-hand corner makes politics a matter of style by insisting that, "Because denim and jeanswear are such social equalizers today you don't necessarily need silks and satins to be elegant. . . . This new elegance has become a *de*-classification process that puts what you can do — your style and abilities far ahead of what you can afford. Now you don't have to be rich to be elegant." Esprit provides a Eu(jean)ic ideal for liberals — you can be as elegant as a capitalist and as politically conscious as a proletarian, at middle-class prices.

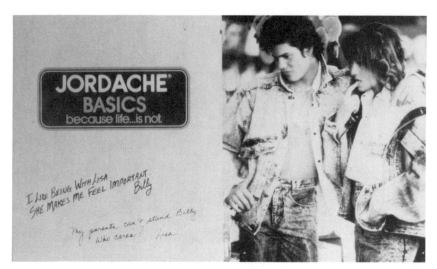

Jordache Basics

The Jordache series which carries the slogan "BASICS because life. . . is not" gives a Eu(jean)ics twist to the New Left's Back to Basics movement. In the BASICS ads, a "natural" landscape is displaced by the garish lights of an "urban" scene, and youthful rebellion becomes just another pose. Jordache boldly relegitimizes traditional dichotomies of sexual difference. "Defiant" teens "Billy" and "Lisa" are dressed in similar clothing, a gesture to the New Left unisex look, but their gender differences are accentuated through body posture and clothes arrangement. Lisa's skirt and her look of childishness, with her finger in her mouth, tousled hair, and off-the-shoulder, over-sized jacket reinscribes a passive and dependent fifties femininity. And Billy's open chested shirt, which exposes his dogtags and gold chains (along with his Brando/Billy Idol smirk), cocky hand-on-his-hip stance, and arm draped possessively around her neck celebrates a macho masculinity defined in opposition to her (albeit staged) vulnerability. Sexual difference is jeanetically encoded by the differences in their "handwriting": his thick, bold phallic strokes report her "feminine" devotion while her neat cursive ones record rebellion against the authority of the bourgeois family. Jordache's indiscriminate mixing of the fifties brashness, sixties anti-establishment anger, and seventies designer consciousness targets an eighties generation of Fashion(ed) teens.

Calvin Klein Sport

Eu(jean)ics virtually splices out Eugenics in the Calvin Klein sportswear domain, an imaginary territory in which bodies, health, and conduct are presumed to be beyond the "degenerescence" of inter-ethnic breeding that the bourgeoisie once found so threatening. These men and women — perfect specimens of class privilege and race supremacy — are a Eugenicist's dream, but that dream has been reached more by the dictates of Fashion than genetic engineering. Here the pastoral pretensions of Eugenics have been relinquished for the golf course artifice of a suburban backyard or Liberal Arts College campus. Appropriation upon appropriation: these are contemporary counterparts of the "Big Chill" ensemble cast, whose laments over abandoned political activism have been diffused by *thirtysomething*'s weekly bouts of yuppie anxiety. In this "twentysomething" generation, there is little to suggest an "interiority" in keeping with nineteenth-century Eugenics. Rather, these blank screen faces, virtually interchangeable, all invested with the power of the outward gaze, are Baudrillard's schizos, subject to the "absolute proximity, the total instantaneity of things."[2] Although physical contact demarcates four opposite sex couples from the remaining four figures, one woman and three men, a set of numbers that implies a variety of homosexual and heterosexual practices, in each case mirrored narcissism overrides attachment to another. This is a Eu(jean)ic simulation of desire as a thing unto itself, devoid of passion and reciprocal pleasure. In the Eu(jean)ic world, there is no referent, not even a masked one. Where there is no referent, there can be no pleasure — only cool, circulating, endless desire anesthetizing the senses through incessant stimulation.

Is the Eu(jean)ic world the world of the future? Perhaps. Perhaps not. In the splicing out of Eugenics, Calvin Klein, as Eu(jean)ic engineer, may well have produced a random fluctuation in the jeanetic code. For when desire becomes this "uncanny," it becomes mutant, and the survival of a mutation is always in question. It may be that Baudrillard's speculation will come to pass: "Once everything will have been cleansed, once an end will have been put to all viral processes and to all social and bacillary contamination, then only the virus of sadness will remain, in this universe of deadly cleanliness and sophistication."[3] But it may also be that, as the precession of denim spirals into pure simulacra, a different chance encoding will occur, one that renders Eu(jean)ics susceptible to its own late-capitalist efforts to sterilize everything. Uncanny desire may be like the mule, incapable of reproduction. At a minimum, this site of jeanetic drift intervenes in the eugenic technology of power insofar as it suggests a self *sans* interiority. Such a break in the "genetic" code of humanism provides a site of resistance, a place to recode for, in Foucault's words, a "different economy of bodies and pleasure".[4] Denim's fashionscape as an arena of struggle? By *all* means.[5]

Lee Quinby

Notes

1. Jacob Davis applied the practice of riveting and reinforcing seams in horse blankets to clothing and received the patent for these improvements (also assigned to Levi Strauss who paid the patent fee) in 1873. See Ed Cray, *LEVIS*, Boston: Houghton Mifflin, 1978, pp. 16-22.

2. Jean Baudrillard, "The Ecstasy of Communication," in *The Anti-Aesthetic: Essays on Postmodern Culture*, ed. Hal Foster, Port Townsend, Washington: Bay Press, 1983, p. 133.

3. Jean Baudrillard, "Rituals of Transparency," in *The Ecstasy of Communication*, trans. Bernard and Caroline Schutze New York: Foreign Agents Series, Semiotext(e), 1988, p. 38.

4. Michel Foucault, *History of Sexuality*, vol. 1, trans. Robert Hurley New York: Vintage Press, 1980, p. 159.

5. I would like to thank Tom Hayes and Tim Landers for their comments and the audio-visual staff of Hobart and William Smith Colleges for their reproduction of the ads.

K

PANIC KILLING (COPS)

Robocop is Dutch director Paul Verhoeven's meditation on cops as a specifically American panic site. The film parodically deconstructs myths of rugged individualism, materialism (the American Body), and regeneration through violence.

Rugged Individualism

"Robocop. Who is he? What is he? Where does he come from?" Like all cops, Robocop is a signifier of power, created from its lack: from crime (both as desire for power and as measure of society's powerlessness), from the failure of conventional police to stop crime, from Bob Morton's need for clout in the competitive corporate world of Omni Consumer Products, from OCP's need to control Old Detroit.

Where does Robocop come from? Utter helplessness, as Murphy — and with him the myth of American individualism — is turned into swiss cheese by Boddicker and his gang, (further) dismembered by the medical and corporate establishment, and "re-

PANIC

born" as Robocop: pure video intelligence, identity as screen and switching center (Baudrillard). Created under the sign of sacrifice ("We've restructured the police department and placed prime candidates according to risk factor"), Robo, the image of impenetrability, exists only through the vicious and total penetration of Murphy.

Individualism and the unified subject are swiss-cheesed as early as the credit sequence, when "ROBOCOP," in large block letters, bursts out from the center of the screen, promising the subject as solid, substantial, impermeable. A close look reveals the name to have holes in every letter. Moreover, the camera goes right for — and through — the hole in the center of the central "O." Robocop/Murphy is punctured before its/his story even begins. As the camera goes for the "O," Robocop splits into the conflicting identities of Rob and Cop: personal name/professional function, criminal/law-enforcer.* This prefigures a world of endlessly reconstructed subjects where Murphy becomes Robocop who becomes Murphy again (or does he?), and where cops become cop killers and cop killers end up working for the same people as the cops.

In its assault on the subject, *Robocop* recalls the paradoxes at the heart of rugged individualism. Given his hopelessly ambivalent relation to authority, the American hero ends up an "individual" in uniform. The pioneer becomes soldier, the private eye becomes cop. In its technoid version, Robocop, the most unique figure in the movie, is also completely manufactured: pure company man. Accordingly, Robo's claims to being "Murphy" at film's end lie in wholesale identification with "T.J. Lazer," a high-tech TV hero. The biggest paradox of all is that what little there is of Robocop's individuality — the remnant of "humanity" and "soul" left over from Murphy — is the very thing that enables him to become the most efficient technological weapon in the movie. (ED 209, the machine with no prior human identity, is just not dedicated, focused, "individualist," enough to become the perfect killer cop.) American individualism becomes the final indispensable ingredient in the corporate technification of American identity.

The American Body

Verhoeven was attracted to the Robocop project by its reenactment of the theme of death and rebirth. His version has a peculiarly American twist. Whereas the Christian model emphasizes dying to the body to be reborn in spirit, Murphy dies in body to be reborn as a larger, heavier, more threatening body. Whereas the ascension

---

* Kim Sawchuk provided me with the rob/cop observation.

of Christ's body releases the Holy Spirit or Paraclete to be indwelling in the world — everywhere yet nowhere, hence spaceless — Robocop's release into the world fulfills the quintessential American objective: the occupation of space. (God becomes Bod.)

This objective is less personal than corporate (corporare = "to make into a body"), as OCP's underlying goal is to occupy Old Detroit then build Delta City in its place.

A monument to and of the body, Robocop is simultaneously the denial of sex: the consummate American conflation of materialism and Puritanism. All work, no play; technique without pleasure. Rigidly upright, Robocop is erection without release, a second coming that is no coming at all (in fact, in terms of the death of the subject, entirely unbecoming).

Sexuality is not only denied, it is turned into violence: Robocop as mock rapist, shooting a woman between the legs and having the bullet pass through her dress, emasculating her captor. In true American fashion, heterosexuality becomes male gunfucking.

Regeneration Through Violence

The replacement of sex by aggression means that (re)birth can occur only through violence, continuing the legacy of American society since the Revolution and Civil War. Murphy becomes Robocop only through brutal murder, followed by violent resuscitation attempts at the hospital (equated, by crosscutting, with his murder) and by a final dismemberment at OCP ("I thought we agreed on total body prosthesis. Now lose the arm").

With the frontier long since closed, and overpopulated urban centers imploding, American regeneration becomes urban renewal. And the new society (Delta City) becomes possible only through the wasting of the old (Old Detroit) with high-powered weaponry such as ED 209 and Robocop. Manifest destiny becomes an inalienable right to destroy existing property merely to build some more.

Significantly, the new never comes — and this gets to the real crux of contemporary American violence. Like American (non)sexuality, it's all deterrence. Normally, deterrence is the creation of ever greater firepower so nothing will happen. In *Robocop* what is deterred/deferred is not violence but the creation of a new society. In fact the means (violence) and the end (Delta City) are startlingly reversed, as Delta City is merely used to justify the development of killer machines. As *Robocop* suggests, American society must, at all costs, deter any situation that would invalidate violence.

This too is a means to an end. What ceaseless aggression really defers is not peace but the disturbing revelation peace might bring:

139

that aggression and the enormous American sign system of violent power are, like Robocop, born out of profound and vertiginous lack. The deafening blast of American weaponry keeps Uncle Sam from hearing the silence.

Robocop's self-justifying cycle of aggression turns against itself. The Stars Wars "Defense" system bombs Santa Barbara, killing two former American presidents. The OCP war on crime turns completely internecine: Morton vs. Jones, ED 209 vs. Robocop, Robo vs. Jones. The film's concluding moment is not the eradication of crime in Old Detroit, but the temporary arrest of crime in OCP — eliminating one perpetrator (Jones) but leaving a fundamentally criminal corporate system intact.

In *Robocop*, the upshot of panic cops, splattered individualism, the American Bod-God, and "deterrible" violence is the self-replicating, self-fulfilling credo of a panic police state: "Somewhere there's a crime happening."

Frank Burke

L

PANIC LIPS

Over the years, Thatcher's aphrodisiac aura of power has become progressively more potent. It captivated Gorbachev when they met last spring; it inspired French President Mitterand to say after their first meeting, 'She has the eyes of Caligula but the lips of Marilyn Monroe.'

Richard Gwyn
Toronto Star

PANIC

PANIC LOVERS

The Transformation of the Lovers, André Masson

Like a bible study of the postmodern condition, André Masson's *The Transformation of the Lovers* provides a new social mythology for our image reservoir. Mutants, tumorous flesh, and viral apples as our destiny in the twilight of cultural inertia.

As a painting of the fate of the microbiological revolution, *The Transformation of the Lovers* anticipates the world of recombinant genetics: a world where the DNA of all living substances converges on a primitive ancestor. It is the hidden world of gene-sharing that is the privileged object of Masson's artistic imagination, as he depicts the end of evolution in a Darwinian speed-up which plays nature at catastrophic speeds. Here, "punctuated evolution" is viewed in reverse-image, as Masson flashes backwards towards the Garden of Eden. But this garden has already been irradiated, leaving a scene of lush but violent, aggressive mutants. In this fin-de-nature, there are only catastrophes, the fissures that await the end of the clonal chain. Having fatally exhausted itself in the clonal reproductions of high-intensity capitalism, the postmodern world breaks down into a series of mutations. Only the random copying errors of the genetic code are privileged. Just as in the transgressionary politics of the surrealists, it is from amongst the mutants that the "natural" world claims a reversal on the all too perfect order of things.

Masson's painterly lovers represent the microbiological revolution gone social, precisely because they are enzymes catalyzing the new world of post-hybrids. The primordial cosmic soup of the swamp of Eden explodes in growths which are a wild melange of the old kingdoms of animal, vegetable, and human (parodying, of course, our original sharing of RNA). But under the chromium dynamics of the red shift in high temperature physics, Masson dissolves all the boundaries in the organic, substituting tumors for the Edenic world. No longer cast out of the Garden of Eden, Adam and Eve are left to mutate according to the designer wishes of genetic engineers. Not the serpent as in traditional mythology, but a post-snake which, once ingested, becomes part of the lover's body. The apple, too, is clearly visible, but like the couple it has already mutated into a cancerous growth. And not even the dualism of sex and sin in the new Garden of Eden, but a whole melange of cellular activity, where reproduction can be so frenzied because it is a coded activity controlled by suppressor genes which, themselves, are finally out of control.

The high energy of Masson's field brilliantly portrays the dynamic disequilibrium of the social, which itself now mutates through a series of *oncogenes* that have escaped the stasis of social control. The retransformed senses of the lovers carries these oncogenes into all institutions in the form of a frenzied social speed, always one step ahead of the *tumor necrosis* factor. Thus, the desperate concern of established power for the preservation of immunity systems and killer T-cells. But, in the end, the microbiological revolution must necessarily triumph: not only through the introduction of retroviruses, but also through Darwinian mutations which release new antigens into the necro-polis.

PANIC MAGNETS

I met a man in Paris recently, a German film producer, who was a practicing schizophrenic and proud of it.

He told me he had finally given up on lithium, in fact, on all of the toxic pharmaceuticals as antidotes to his schizoid ego; and had made of his body instead a radical testing-zone for quantum physics, generally in the search for a grand unifying theory, and specifically for magnetism as one of the four fundamental life forces.

Each night before going to bed, he taped (tattooed?) tiny magnets all across the text of his body, and he claimed that by this method his schizophrenia had vanished, just disappeared. The schizoid ego in Paris had become missing matter; and he was in control now.

Well, I did not understand what was going on until I returned to Montreal and talked to an artist friend of mine, Tony Brown, one of the best of the postmodern sculptors these days, and he began describing a new quantum sculpture installation which he had just completed.

PANIC

It was called (after Max Ernst) *Europe in Ruins/Body Parts*, and it consisted of a shining, gleaming terrazzo floor into which were crushed hundreds of tiny dolls as a brilliantly decayed sign of kitsch. In the very center of the floor was a pile of silver rubble, actually stainless steel body parts — arms, legs, torsos, split heads — cast from the ruins of European classical statuaries. Towering over the body parts was a gigantic magnet, purchased from a local auto wrecking yard, which functioned in *Europe in Ruins/Body Parts* as an alternating scene of unity and violence. Indeed, the only noise in this sculptural installation was the rhythmic sound of the electronic magnet switching on, lifting the stainless steel body parts off the floor, and then, like a fibrillator with its energy switches suddenly flipped off, releasing the body parts with a crash.

And then I got it! The electronic magnet in Brown's art was like the magnets on the body of the schizoid man in Paris. In both cases, the magnet functioned as a kind of technological hologram which provided the body parts — the classical ruins in Brown's sculpture and the body and mind of the schizoid in Paris — with the illusion of a temporary coherency, a little technical mediation, before the energy switches off and the body parts crash into inertia, stasis, and rubble: all kitsch/all violence; all metastasis/all frenzy; all technological holograms/all implosion.

PANIC MONEY

Advanced capitalist economies now face the severest liquidity crisis ever as the economy itself begins to liquidate. Capital begins to disappear. Nowhere is this crisis more apparent than in the shattering of its chief icon — money. The money illusion has become real as the economy reverses itself. No longer does one find relevance in the wrangle over monetary policy, supply side economics, Laffer curves, revealed preferences, or unrevealed preferences, but rather in the self-liquidation of value itself. Money is caught in the grand cancellation of the sign of political economy. It finds itself homeless and constantly put to flight. It is abandoning the "worthless" world of contemporary capitalism.

Money was saved from ruination by Marx who realized the shift from pre-modern production turned, finally, on breathing life (once again) into money as universal exchange-value. Hence money was given an extended life in its role as the externalization of the nineteenth-century self. Money could do things the body couldn't as it travelled about the social in high style hidden from view by the fetishism of commodities. But the bodies in the twentieth-century have been invaded, and blown apart. The fetishes have grown up. Consumption has regained the primitive ritual of symbolic exchange in its abolition of the modern.

Facing the onslaught of the cancellation of the referent, money finds itself circulating faster, and more violently, to maintain itself as the universal clinamen. But in the age of superconductors the chilling effect is immense as everything approaches the end of Einstein's world at the speed of light. In this world the parasitism of money begins to slow the process. This pushes money into even longer hours with the advent of twenty-four hour exchange. Yet, the red-shift in the velocity of circulation only hastens the disappearance of money from the planet prefigured in the vast sums for Star Wars.

Already money has given place to its opposite, credit, in the creation *ex nihilo* which marks all contemporary advances from insider trading to take-over bids. Just how far the game is up becomes evident in the repudiation of the debts of the large corporations, or of the working class. Everything is owned, possessed by the other so that the economy can only run "on empty." Money becomes the spent fuel of an over-heated reactor. Nobody knows what to do with it, yet all know it must be expended.

Money as value only appears at the vanishing-point of its afterimage. It is no longer one's filthy lucre, only that of the sanitized electronic display of the computer monitor. For money always moves on in its role as the chief vagrant of the collapsing capitalist economy.

PANIC MYTHOLOGY

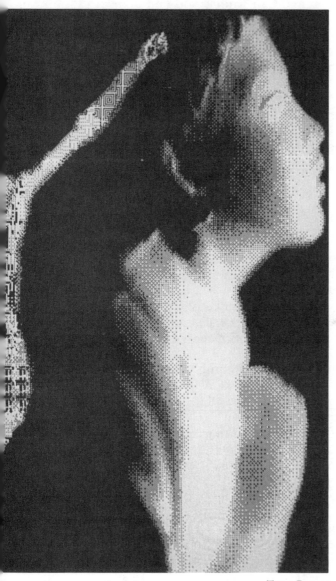

Tony Brown

PANIC MASTERPIECES

Florence Can Knock You Out

FLORENCE, Italy — Some visitors to Florence panic before a Raphael masterpiece. Others go into a frenzy when confronted with a Caravaggio. Still others collapse at the feet of Michelangelo's statue of David.

Psychiatrists call it the "Stendhal syndrome."

At least once a month on average, a foreign tourist is rushed to the psychiatric ward of Florence's Santa Maria Nuova hospital suffering from an acute mental imbalance seemingly brought on by an encounter with the city's art treasures.

Left Home Healthy

"These people were apparently healthy when they left home," the hospital's top specialist, Prof. Graziella Magherini, said in an interview. "Here, they suddenly lost their equilibrium...the beauty of Florence, while not the cause itself, is a factor."

The condition, documented since 1982 by the hospital's psychiatric team, was dubbed the Stendhal syndrome after the French writer who recorded a similar emotional experience on his first visit to the Tuscan city in 1817.

"On leaving the Santa Croce church, I felt a pulsating in my heart," Stendhal wrote in his first book, *Naples and Florence: A Journey from Milan to Reggio Calabria*. "Life was draining out of me, while I walked fearing a fall."

While those affected are few among the millions of tourists who pour into Florence every year, they are sufficiently numerous to have given rise to a study due to be published next year by the city authorities.

"In eight years, we have had 107 victims of the syndrome," Magherini said. "That is not a lot statistically but it is certainly interesting from a clinical viewpoint."

The study, based on case histories and statistical data provided by local tourist authorities, has already given researchers some valuable insights into the sort of person most prone to a sudden mental seizure while in the city.

"More than half the patients come from European countries."

Italians, on the other hand, seem to be immune to the condition, along with the Japanese, who are apparently so organized in their sight-seeing that they rarely have time for emotional attacks.

Magherini said that as a result of her studies, she now divides foreign tourists into three main psychological groups.

"The bulk of tourists who come to Florence, like many other cities rich in history and art, are in fact well defended against art because all they want to do is write postcards home and eat pizza," she said.

The second category, she said, is made up of the intellectual minority seeking an aesthetic emotion similar to that experienced by Stendhal. But this group carries its own cure, since its members always remain rational about what is happening to them.

Leads to Catastrophe

It is the few people who have difficulty adapting to changes in their environment and who attach a particular, overwhelming significance to a particular event, who make up the third, most vulnerable, group, Magherini said.

"Those people with certain characteristics, not intellectual but sensitive and easily susceptible to emotions... when faced with the impact of this city can succumb to a complex crisis that can lead to catastrophe."

"There is no direct cause — people carry many factors with them — but Florence can be a catalyst."

"But I do not want people hearing this and believing there is a simple direct cause to mental imbalance, that if they see a Caravaggio they are going to collapse. I do not want to alarm people. I do not want foreigners to read that they risk going crazy if they go to Florence."

Alan Baldwin
Reuters

PANIC MANHATTAN

Manhattoes, Eric Fischl

Eric Fischl's painting, Manhattoes, is perfectly symptomatic, both in its form (cinematic) and in its content (the recovery of primitive mythology), of liberal burnout as the political condition *par excellence* of the USA today.

If *Manhattoes* adopts the cinematic strategy of representing (simulating) the foundational act of America as a sliding film strip, that is because like the ultramodern culture which it describes, this artistic production is about American social reality as a fast dissolve into a postmodern screen. Not America any longer under the old sign-form of representational history, but American culture, particularly in the collective remembrance of its founding myths, as coded, internally and externally, by the semiological language of filmic images. America, then, as that point where history disappears into a frenzied sign. In America: The Film, postmodern science and technology can now be taken for granted as the basis of America's cultural formation as the world's first cyberspace culture: that post-nouveau moment where fashion disssolves into the theatrics of seduction and auto-sadism; where suburban housing can be sinister (just as J.G. Ballard insists) because it is an ideologically inscribed stage-setting for the playing out of passive and suicidal nihilism; where personality is reduced to instrumentalities without a referent; and where hysterical media holograms can provide temporary unifications for a political culture which, in its indifference and excess, matches perfectly the laconic, yet frenzied, world-strip theory of bio-genetics. America: The Film is a photographic negative run at hyper-speed of the implosion of the USA into the cultural inertia and psycho-energy of the ultramodern sign.

This is why, perhaps, *Manhattoes*, can be so *formally* subversive: it actually visually recodes American culture, at least in its New York manifestation, as an indifferent sign-slide between genocide and seduction. Not so much Tom Wolfe's *Bonfires of the Vanities*, but a violent reprise of disembodied dreams and dark memory-seductions as the ruling psychosis. Like Fischl's earliest paintings (produced while he was teaching in Nova Scotia) which presented a series of glassine images of the mythic "Fischer family" (the members of which could be moved about freely to see what would happen to the old oedipal formula of Mommy-Daddy-Me), *Manhattoes* is like the Fischer family *writ large*. Here, America is a shifting sign, with no beginning or ending, but always with the fascination of a violent, seductive and drifting semiurgical image.

But if *Manhattoes* speaks of America as a fading screen-effect, it also undertakes another subversion: the evocative recovery of the language of primitive mythology. This painting viscerally captures the panic mood of sacrificial renunciation at the founding of technological society.

Jean Baudrillard ended his essay, "The Year 2000 Has Already Happened", with this gloomy prophecy:

> It remains for us to accomodate ourselves to the time left to us, which is seemingly emptied of sense.... The end of this century is before us like an empty beach.

The *fin-de-millenium* as an empty beach? Or something else? *Manhattoes* intimates that Baudrillard's "empty beach" has just been filled up with the celebrants of a carnival fit for the end of the world. Everyone's there: the woman in white with the sacrificial victim (the man's head); the masked dancing figures on stilts; magicians; and even humans as jackals in disguise.

A seductive and violent scene of frenzy on the beach where what is played is the reverse side of the myth of freedom as symbolized by the Statue of Liberty (Our Lady of the Harbour). This is a triptych, not of new beginnings but of shutting-down time, less of the pioneering bourgeois spirit of sacrificial renunciation than of mythic excess, and not of the promise of dyamic progress as the animating vision of America but of the end of the century as a Bahktinian carnival for the New World descendents of the Calvinists. And maybe not even a simple antinomy between the kitschy Statue of Liberty and the dream-like woman in white, but a more fateful mutation in the contemporary American mind.

In this dismal season in which the very best of the European thinkers, Baudrillard included, break and run for the safety of melancholy romanticism, the New World mind, at least in its American outbreak, continues to operate in that unoccupied space between the advance of technological rationalization and the disappearance of religious sensibility. Here, the mythic spirit of sacrificial renunciation also mutates into a frenzied scene where the *fin-de-millenium* spreads out before us like random flashes of brilliant energy: a time of sacrifice *and* narcissism; a century of chaos *and* instrumentality without signification; an already post-millenial consciousness of primitive irrationality and ultra-modern technique.

What is liberty at the end of the world? It is also the perfect freedom of the last practioners of the dying days of rationalism who, just as the philosopher George Grant predicted, would be finally free to choose the ends they will in a universe fatefully indifferent to the choices they make. The disintegration of the once inspiring language of freedom, then, into random flashes of brilliant energy at the decomposing end of the twentieth-century.

PANIC MUSIC

If the Newtonian law of gravity could postulate a real body whose objectivity is established by its mass, the (quantum) law of postmodernity eclipses this body by flipping suddenly from mass to energy. We now live in a hyper-modern world where panic noise (the electronic soundtrack of TV, rock music in the age of advanced capitalism, white sound in all the "futureshops") appears as a kind of affective hologram providing a veneer of coherency for the reality of an imploding culture.

When mass disappears into energy, then the body too becomes the focus and secretion of all of the vibrations of the culture of panic noise. Indeed, the postmodern body is, at first, a hum, then a "good vibration," and, finally, the afterimage of the hologram of panic noise. Invaded, lascerated, and punctured by vibrations (the quantum physics of noise), the body simultaneously *implodes* into its own senses, and then *explodes* as its central nervous system is splayed across the sensorium of the technoscape. No longer a material entity, the postmodern body becomes an infinitely permeable and spatialized field whose boundaries are freely pierced by subatomnic particles in the microphysics of power. Once the veil of materiality/subjectivity has been transgressed (and abandoned), then the body as something real vanishes into the spectre of hyperrealism. Now, it is the postmodern body as space, linked together by force fields and capable of being represented finally only as a fractal entity. The postmodern self, then, as a fractal subject — a minute temporal ordering midst the chaotic entropy of a contemporary culture which is winding down, but moving all the while at greater and greater speeds.

Similarly, the social as mass vanishes now into the fictive world of the media of hypercommunication. Caught only by all the violent signs of mobility and permeability the social is already only the after-glow of the disappearance of the famous reality-principle. This world may have lost its message and all the grand *recits* — power, money, sex, the unconscious — may also be abandoned, except as recycled signs in the frenzied world of the social catalysts, but what is finally fascinating is only the social as *burnout*. The world of Hobbes has come full circle when the (postmodern) self is endlessly reproduced as a vibrating set of particles, and when the social is seductive only on its negative side: the dark side of sumptuary excess and decline.

Thus, power from the bounded, reserved and inert flips now into its opposite sign: the domain of the unbounded, spent and violent. And what better exemplar of the unreal world of the social in this condition than music. Music/vibration as servomechanism enters directly into the postmodern body and passes through it without a trace, leaving only an altered energy state. Everywhere music creates the mood, the energy level, of the postmodern scene. Never seen but equally never shut out, music as panic vibrations secretes through the body of the social. Always ready to enter, it is also always ready to circulate. Being itself possessed, it does money one better by creating social relations which require no possessions. It may be "born in the U.S.A.," but it has become universal. Always in time, it (finally) prepares for the abandonment of history. Music, then, with no past, no future, no (determinate) meaning, but perfectly defining, perfectly energizing, perfectly postmodern. The liberal burnout of contemporary culture as taking the spectral forms, therefore, of fractal subjects, fun vibrations, and panic noise.

PANIC MARTIANS

According to the Washington Post, President Reagan's attempts at conciliation with the Soviet Union in Geneva in 1985 included a vow that the U.S. would join the USSR in case Earth was invaded by aliens from outer space.

Utne Reader

N

PANIC NIETZSCHE'S CAT

If the desperate search in particle physics for a unified field theory can be so immensely popular, that is because it is the flip side of the dissolution of contemporary science into a cynical vision of the natural universe. Like the postmodern culture of which it is a direct ideological read-out, particle physics has, today, a surface veneer of symmetry (super-symmetry?), and an inner reality which is typifed by a fatal fascination with decay, dispersion, and disaccumulation.

Here, the twofold loss of a guiding foundational principle — the loss of a (classical) self-actional universe under the sign of a monistic cosmology and the (modernist) loss of an inter-actional nature consisting of discrete entities separated at a distance from one another and only causally interconnected — has resulted in the production of the vision of a purely cynical nature. Indifferent to human purpose, random in its movements, every elementary particle calling forth its own self-cancelling negative moment, cynical nature is always capable of instant alterity of phasal shifts, where energy particles mutate immediately and without warning into their opposite states.

PANIC

Ideologically, then, quantum physics is a mirror-image of schizoid postmodern consciousness: that point where the bombastic and hyper-promotional claims of grand unified field theory (GUTS) can be accompanied by the actual reality of broken symmetry, vanishing quarks, event thresholds, thermonuclear flashes, imploding gravitons (with only a probabilistic existence), and theoretically over-determined tachyons (particles moving faster than the speed of light which have, however, only a nomic, putative reality).

What results is a whole frenzied scene of panic science. Not the classical world of Euclidean geometry with its erroneously angular vision of the shortest distance between two points as a straight line, rather than a warp jump in a quick time/space phase shift; and certainly not the Newtonian paradigm of absolute space and time, with action only at a (causal) distance between the surfaces of things; and not even the naturalistic science of Darwinian biology (with its purely social cosmology of the eighteenth century English bourgeoisie, based on a nomological vision of social and non-social evolution trumpeting the survival of the fittest). Instead, panic science is something different. It is the mutation in the postmodern condition of the three general laws of thermodynamics (Newton's absolutist nature) into their exact opposite. Not the conservation of energy now, but the ecstatic expenditure of energy to exhaustion as the ruling fashion statement of postmodern thermodymanics. And certainly not unified field theory any longer, but the mutation of GUTS into its reverse image: the four fundamental forces of matter — electromagnetism, gravity, strong, and weak interactions — as postmodern scenes *par excellence* of excess, disaccumulation, and metastasis.

Isaac Newton was not completely correct when he theorized that the principle of the conservation of energy was the basis of thermodynamic mechanics. It is that and more. All conservation of energy on the one hand, and all a Bataillean dispersion of nature into a blast of energy particles which, refusing Newton's conservative reduction, sometimes get excited, grow lighter and more agitated at higher and higher temperatures, and then without warning mutate into their opposite, and negative, forms. Postmodern nature as radical alterity: all conservation/all self-liquidation of elementary energy particles. Not so much, therefore, the famous experiment in particle physics of "Schrödinger's cat" with its key question drawn straight from the ideology of liberal pluralism (Is light a continuous wave pattern or discrete energy particles?), but the metaphysical experiment performed one hundred years before Schrödinger by "Nietzsche's cat." In *The Will to Power*, Nietzsche already knew that light, like power before it, must be both corpuscular and wave-like because nature now has only the cynical existence of an empty sign relation where all the antinomies implode into a big sign blast, where

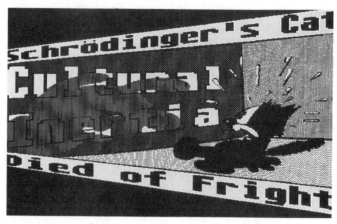

Schrödinger's Cat Died of Fright, Tony Brown

the old grammatical attitude of *either/or* is replaced by the post-modern condition of *both/and*, and where conservation and exhaustion of all the energy particles must exist simultaneously because parody, paradox, and ironic counter-point are the aesthetic highlights of what Nietzsche described as "nature cruel in her cheerfulness; cynical in her sunrises."

Hence, the dialectic of postmodernism in the excessive form of the fundamental life forces involved in unified field theory.

The Will to Gravity

Most interpretations of unified field theory overlook gravity because its "field" is too weak. This is mistaken. With the recent creation *ex nihilo* of gravitons (whose actual existence as the most elementary constitutents of the gravity field has only a probabilistic basis), postmodern nature has come alive. Local objects warp time/space; inert objects (from buildings to bodies) produce gravity to such a degree of intensity that gravitons actually begin to hum and vibrate, to invade passive energy fields like violent predators, and to produce in their wake a chromatic bending of space, from the curvature of time to violently scarred bodies.

Indeed, postmodern gravity is just the opposite of Newton's cosmological vision of the gravitational field as an inert and constant force: with everything falling down at a constant rate irrespective of mass; where gravity is perfectly universal because everywhere the same; a dead and passive field relation which acted only like an invisible environment holding (earthly) nature together. Now, however, it's panic gravity. To the question: Does gravity exist? Physicists can only point to its hyperreal existence in the purely putative form of humming gravitons. Just like in advanced mathematics where the concept of "tricky math" had to be invented to take care (pragmatically) of the problem of infinite regression, gravity too now has only the existence of "tricky gravitons": elementary gravity particles which are *willed* into existence to take care of the problem of a failing natural unity. In contemporary particle physics, it's not so much Nietzsche's will to power, but, now, the *will to gravity* as the hyper-epistemological basis of a postmodern science which can only claim with certainty that theoretical probability must always be more real than the real. In the will to gravity, the classical Lucretian dream of elementary energy particles always in violent process combines perfectly with the epistemological (and then political) necessity to save the *appearance* of a unified nature. Panic gravity, therefore, as a necessary supplement for an always fictional universe, the foundations of which have only a *nomic, willed basis*.

Weak (Parasitical) Interactions

> The weak interaction force is thought to have an extremely short range. It has been suggested that it is associated with the exchange of a very heavy, and as yet undiscovered, particle called a W-particle....Most of the elementary particles decay as a result of weak interactions....Because it is so weak, particles which can only decay by weak interactions do so relatively slowly, i.e. they have long lifetimes.
>
> *Penguin Dictionary of Physics*

There is nothing stronger than weak interactions. The most fully aestheticized phase of unified field theory, weak interactions are the opposite of the will to power: not pushing outwards against resistance, but decreases in power, gradual decay and slow fade-out. So slow, in fact, that particles which come under the ruling sign of the weak interaction force have the real fascination (and strength) of guaranteed long lifetimes. Like the spreading out of a parasitical force field, weak interactions invade the field of elementary particles, actually slowing them down and draining off their energy until the universe itself is brought under the sign of a microphysics of leakage, expenditure and exhaustion.

And the famous missing (but hypostaticized) W-particle? That's probably a good part of the missing matter of the physical universe which, existing as a shadowy dark density admitting no light and yielding no reflection, is the immense heaviness in (natural) exchange which accounts for the slowing down of the universe, for its fade-out after the Big Bang into the white noise of hissing background radiation. And maybe, in fact, the missing W-particle is also present now in the *social* disguise of the mass media which, always having a short range, ever parasitical, and always draining off energy from society by guaranteeing (themselves) a long lifetime are the heaviness to infinity in all of contemporary social exchange. The W-particle, therefore, as an inertial drag on the theory of the expanding universe which now enjoys a second (social) life in the form of the weak interactions structuring all mass media relations. Just like all the elementary particles which, coming under the sign of the W-particle, exchange escape velocity for inertial decay, the W-particle, when socially recapitulated in the form of mass media, exchanges real social transformation for the pleasant decay of fully aestheticized societies.

So there it is. The weak interaction force, and with it the invisible W-particle, as a fundamental law of nature and of social nature. Here the parasiting of all the elementary particles by the process of (their) slow decay is a brilliant representation, first in particle physics and then in postmodern culture, of just what the French philosopher, Michel Serres, predicted as the driving force of cynical nature: *Le Parasite.* In Serres' theorisation, parasitism is actually a weak force because it occupies the totality of the force-field, it substitutes many last pleasant days of leakage, decay and slow expenditure of energy for the ecstasy of episodic violence, and it is always perfectly cynical, operating with a logic which is topological and tautological. As the postmodern operator *par excellence*, the parasite invades the social, and then natural, universe: an invisible agent of mutation, transforming the theatrics of violent power into the liquid excess of waste and exhaustion. Indeed, as a weak interaction force, Serres' parasite invades the elementary physical and social particles without leaving any trace of its presence, only the invisible inertial track of the W-particle, now gone intergalactic, as a great inertial drag slowing down the universe until it reaches the decompressed speed of the dying days of aestheticism.

PANIC OBSCENITIES

Medusa's Revenge

To decapitate — To castrate. The terror of the Medusa is thus a terror of castration that is linked to the sight of something. The hair upon the Medusa's head is frequently represented in works of art in the form of snakes, and these once again are derived from the castration complex. It is a remarkable fact that however frightening they may be in themselves, they nevertheless serve as a mitigation of the horror, for they replace the penis, the absence of which is the cause of the horror. This is a confirmation of the technical rule according to which a multiplication of penis symbols signifies castration.

Sigmund Freud
The Medusa's Head

---

* This a transcript from one of many similar calls left on a friend's answering machine over a span of approximately three months. The lines indicate the points at which the machine stopped, and he was forced to redial.

THE OBSCENE CALL
Unknown

I just want you to know that all of the time I'm talking to you I'm jerking it here.

Ah. I don't know exactly how much experience you've had, but anyone with my kind of staying power is quite able to satisfy a lady. A lady, of course, is able to have multiple orgasms.

I would also say that my cock is, I would say that you know that people don't think that a cock is a pretty thing, but I would say mine is pleasing to look at.

It's clean, it's well shaped, it has a nice curve to it, fits into all pussys really well, and I don't have a heck of a lot of foreskin, so you don't get a lot of odor. It's been circumcised.

Ah, as you are aware, guys who aren't circumcised quite often have a cleanliness problem about their cock cause that foreskin is overtop and they get a build up of lint and sweat that gets underneath it. But mine's so easy to clean. And its got a really large head on it, ah, the ladies like to feel it. They say it feels so soft and silky, yet firm and hard.

Anyhow, ah, I really appreciate ladies who like to get on top. They can kinda help themselves to as much of this thing as they fit into their pussy.

I guess you're probably thinking, "Who is this nut?"

But I'm really not a nut, I'm just an extremely horny guy, I don't get enough to satisfy me, not because I'm not good looking or anything else, it's just that I probably need it certainly several times a day and I just haven't been fortunate enough to find a lady that wants it as often as that. I have several ladies who get it several times a week, but not several times a day.

Anyhow, as I was saying, I really like my ladies to get on top. That way they can help themselves to as much as they want. That way there is no danger of me hurting them by driving it in too far. And also I like to eat a little pussy too. I like it when they sit up on my chest. I don't even mind if they practice withdrawal, I don't like using a safe. So, I like to slip it in, if they want to pull out I give them a little tongue job.

Anyhow, I was saying how much I do enjoy oral sex. I know the ladies do. I like them to face me and reach up, and kinda cup your tits and massage them while you toss your head back and ride on my cock.

And then if you want to ride on my tongue, I'd also like that too.

I want you to know that right now I've been jerkin' off here all the time we've been talking. Or I've been talking.

I'm at the foot of my bed, and I can see my balls are starting to tighten up and this weapon of mine is rock hard. It's just starting to spurt some cream out the end of it now. Here I go now baby, I'm just blowin.

Wow.

Hit myself right in the chin.

Wow.

That's the kind of performance I can give to the ladies too. They like that kind of strokin'. I can give it to you or you can hang on longer and we can have multiple orgasms.

Too bad for them if they fall apart upon discovering that women aren't men, or that the mother doesn't have one. But isn't this fear convenient for them? Wouldn't the worst be, isn't the worst, in truth, that women aren't castrated, that they only have to stop listening to the Sirens (for the Sirens were men) for history to change its meaning? You only have to look at the Medusa straight on to see here. And she's not deadly. She's beautiful and she's laughing.

Hélène Cixous
"The Laugh of the Medusa"

THE RESPONSE

I want my chance; the opportunity to speak to you directly. I've got a tongue job for you.

Your speech is an invitation and a challenge; a challenge to write and break up a phallocentric narrative of desire. Medusa's laughter; Medusa's revenge.

I respond to you as the "I" that is "We" because as women, we have all been the subjects of and subjected to, obscene phone calls: your sexuality, my sexuality is created and recreated, not simply reflected in this event. And exceptions probe rules: one thoughtful pervert has told me more about his construction of our sexual identities than could the observation of a thousand solid citizens.

Yet you are unique among obscene callers because your terror of women is doubly displaced. Not only do you fear a confrontation with my body, abjection at the sight of my sexual difference, but you refuse to speak to me.

You hang up whenever I answer the phone. You talk to my machine.

It is not a body you crave, but my voice, my "Hi, how are you, I'm not home, leave your name and I will return your call as soon as possible;" the voice on my answering machine. My machine voice cannot respond, and therefore cannot cut you off, castrate. But it also allows you to give me any attributes your imagination fancies: for desire is as much a part of a mutual imaginary landscape as it is real or embodied lust.

I am any woman, every woman. A call girl deprived of economic or personal remuneration.

One of your ladies.

Do you have a harem of machine ladies? Women you have never seen, but who are the objects of your strange aural fetish: mechanical brides you keep captive by pirating their technology for your own ends, for the pleasure of your techno-prick?

You probably think you are harmless, and because I am not forced to talk to you, that you are doing me a favor; but you are only depriving me of the power to disconnect you.

You have reduced me to silence, cut out my tongue; censored the body and censored speech, with your penal I that moves the narrative along, placing you at the center of desire.

And you take up all of the space on my tape.

You have forced me to sit through your litany, your boring banal narrative, delivered in the same tongue that one might use to describe the attributes of a used car, or a baseball game: "It's clean, it's well shaped, it has a nice curve to it." Your odorless cock is an object disassociated from your body. But this disembodiment is an illusion: in your fantasy you reassemble, rearticulate your body and it flows as a machine.

I must admit, however, that I am disappointed in your performance; you are not obscene or perverted. The obscenity lies in the banality of your discourse, your complete absence of verbal imagination. Even your utterances of pornographic, forbidden words: cock, tit, pussy, seem inconsequential, flattened, and feeble; your delayed voice doesn't excite me. Your desire is created through the telling of the story, through your imaginary description of yourself, and your ability to have a certain "staying power;" the power to appropriate my machine, and engage in a voyeuristic, distant, description of the operations of your own body.

In your voice I hear both the sounds of my culture, and the apathetic ennui that is postmodern desire. Your purely descriptive tone, the flat neutrality of your speech echoes this evening's news broadcast, or a TV commercial for a cleaning product. "Soft and silky, yet firm and hard" are the adjectives you use to describe your organ, which is no longer an organ, but a machine part; easy to clean, but in need of some lubrication.

I have listened to this voice, and tried to identify who you might be. But after several taped messages it is clear that you do not know me, and that you do not care to know me. You never describe any of my features, or anything that would indicate that you have seen me. You prefer the mediation of the machine. Libidinal drives flow through the telephone wires that are not polyvocal or polymorphously perverse, but an auto-erotic solipsistic soliloquy channelled through my machine, back to yourself; a feedback loop of socially produced desire clichés.

However, I cannot remain completely disdainful as your persistence is a cruel reminder that I am trapped in this same social assemblage of desire and collective assemblage of enunciation: a repression of the body and its potential plenitudes. We are both at the mercy of this narrow phallocratic economy of pleasure which is oriented around, organized around the penis.

> By affirming the primacy of the phallus and of bringing it into play, phallocratic ideology has claimed more than one victim. As a woman, I've been clouded over by the great shadow of the scepter and been told: idolize it, you cannot brandish. But at the same time, man has been handed that grotesque and scarcely enviable destiny (just imagine) of being reduced to a single idol with clay balls.[1]

We both suffer from this economy that values performance; but we suffer differently. You, from a fear of castration, of non-performance, from a closure of the other possibilities of sexual gratification in your body; I from the notion that I lack one, that I lack the lack, that desire is born of this absence, and language from desire, that this makes it impossible for me to enter into language or culture, that I am different, therefore inferior from the boys. Yes, we both suffer; but unequally, unevenly. After all, as you admit, "I've done all of the talking." However I have a secret: I have learned that pleasure does not begin and end with the end of a penis, with one final burst of cream from a weapon; and I think you know this secret.

You have made several slips of the tongue.

Your words reveal your knowledge and anxiety: "I would say you know that people don't think that a cock is a pretty thing, but I would say mine is pleasing to look at." You are dissatisfied with your own body, envious; perhaps your desire to possess a woman springs from your own repressed desire to restore that part which is denied to you because of your biology and the oppositional differences that are historically, politically, and culturally prescribed for this difference; your desire to be a woman; a destabilization of our fixed sexual identities. My absence allows you to fantasize that you occupy two spaces at once; you can believe that you are both man and woman, a hermaphrodite, self-contained, rider and ridden with a multiple orgasmic prick.

You sound genuinely concerned about my pleasure, my participation. "I really like my ladies to get on top. That way they can help themselves to as much as they want." But you delude yourself that we are sharing this event, that we can have multiple orgasms, that this is done for my benefit. Here the contradiction in your text surfaces; you want to give me multiple orgasms, you know that women can do it, yet you say you can't find a woman who wants it as often as you do. And as you move towards the end, you move from the general to the specific, as you are closer and closer to coming ...

"Yeah baby," I think, "you're just blowin it."

You anticipate my questions: "Who is this nut?" with the answer that you are not a nut, "just an extremely horny guy" who can't get enough, but not because your aren't good looking. I find this amusing, sad, pathetic. Your intrusion into my inner sanctum is no longer threatening or sinister. It doesn't even sound like you are having fun; you are obsessed with your body's hygiene. This is not lust or frenzied animal sex, but the opposite — controlled machine sex. You have constructed a mechanical desire, a techno-desire, that boasts that it can perform the sexual act, not only several times a week, but several times a day, continuously, repetitively, but without feeling.

You are literally the body without organs. You never slow down or speed up the pace of your patter, you only pause before moving on to a new thought, or when my machine practices coitus interruptus, and you are forced to redial. This is the key: you can redial until you have reached your destination, but my only indication that you have come is when you tell me that you have hit your chin.

How do you do it, I wonder.

Your rap sounds so carefully scripted that I am convinced that you must be reading from a text: yet, you can't be holding the paper, the phone, and your cock all at the same time, unless you have yourself connected to another machine: a machine that lets you do all this at once. I imagine your body itself becoming a machine, plugged into the telephone wires: your flesh changes into plastic, your veins become wires, your muscles, cybernetic circuits. The telephone cord coils, snakes around you as your voice utters your teleorgasmic tale. Your call emphasizes that machines are never simply technical instruments. "It is technical, only a social machine, taking men and women into its gears, or, rather, men and women as part of its gears along with things, structures, metals, materials." We are part machine, not only because we work on them in the present social order, but because our appetites change in relation to all of our adjacent activities.[2]

But now I have my revenge.

This conversation which you thought was private, which you wanted to remain private, which was not really transmitted for my audial pleasure, but for your pleasure, is now public, and returns to haunt you in the revenge of the printed word.

Kim Sawchuk

Notes

1. Hélène Cixous, "The Laugh of the Medusa," in *New French Feminisms*, eds., Eileen Marks and Isabelle Courtivron, New York: Schoken Books, 1981.

2. Gilles Deleuze and Felix Guattari, *Kafka: Toward a Minor Literature*, trans. Dana Polan, Minneapolis: University of Minnesota Press, 1986.

PANIC OVARIES

And what then of women's wombs? Is natural reproduction preserved intact at the end of the world or have we already entered into a darker region of the terror of the simulacrum? Now, more than ever, women's bodies are the inscribed focus of a threefold deployment of relational power. In the postmodern condition, women's bodies are the prime afterimage of a strategy of body invasion which occurs in the inverted and excessive language of contractual liberalism.

First, the medical subordination of women's bodies which results, whether through in vitro fertilization or genetic mixing, in the alienation of the womb. When the ovaries go outside (and with them the privileged language of sexual difference), it is also a certain sign of the grisly technological abstraction of alienated labor into the alienation of reproduction itself.

Secondly, the medical inscription of women's bodies is superceded by the subordination of childbirth to the ideology of law. For example, in the Baby M case, the natural mother is reduced to the contractual fiction of a "hired womb"; the meaning of the "natural" is inverted into its opposite number (the actual mother becomes legally a "surrogate" and the Daddy surrogate — he was always only present as a free-floating seed in a genetic mixing tube — is juridically renamed as the real, living father). In the end, the entire juridical apparatus is directed towards justifying a new form of legal slavery for women who are poor, powerless and thus potential victims of the predatory instincts of the ruling elites. A class of professional, middle-class elites, men and women, who measure the meaning of the "good" by the standards of petty convenience. Ironically, in the Baby M case, it was only after the natural mother lost custody rights to her baby that the media and the courts began, finally, describing her, not as the "surrogate mother" any longer, but as the biological mother. Cynical media and cynical law for a rising class of cynical elites.

Thirdly, panic ovaries are also about all the cases of fetal appropriation where the state intervenes, supposedly on behalf of the rights of the unborn baby, to take juridical possession of the body of the mother. A perfect complicity, then, among the technological interventions of medicine into the body of the mother (the use of medical technology as an early warning system for detecting birth defects in the fetus); the juridical seizure of the fetus as a way of deploying state power against the body of the mother; and the po-

litics of the new right which can be so enthusiastic about the jurispru-
dence of fetal appropriation as a way of investing the contractarian
rights of the fetus against the desires of the mother. A whole hypocrit-
ical fetus fetish by law, by medicine, and by the neo-conservatives
as a way of cancelling out the will of the natural mother, and of taking possession of the bodies of women. Margaret Atwood's thesis
in *The Handmaid's Tale* about the reduction of women to hired
wombs is thus disclosed to be less an ominous vision of the future
than a historical account of an already past event in the domination
of women.

PANIC OLYMPICS

Ben Johnson committed a big sign crime, and he is paying for it as the newest sacrificial victim of the Olympics.

If, in twenty-four hours, he could implode from a Promethean hero of classic proportions into a sacrificial scapegoat for the masses' fury at being sign-switched, it just proves that Ben Johnson's body has now a second existence: an abstract screen onto which are projected all of the inadequacies of a TV audience that is suffering a bad case of distemper. In Canada, Johnson's return from Seoul was a scene taken directly from *The Day of the Locust*: a raging media scrum demanding why he had betrayed his country, government leaders trumpeting "swift retribution" by banning him for life from international competition. And Johnson, himself, who began running as a stutterer found himself finally unable to speak. On ABC's *Nightline*, Edwin Moses, who only wins bronze medals now, is having one last media career as a cynical comic in the Reagan style, by urging that Johnson's sign crime be taken up as a challenge for the policing of the drug free body. And, in Seoul, the panic claims of Olympic officials that this is a victory for "scientific detection" of the doped body is met by all the smugness of the TV anchors who talk darkly of "tainted competitions."

So, why all the hysteria? Perhaps because it is the age of sacrificial sports now: that point where the Olympics, under the pressure of the mass media, re-enter the dark domain of mythology. No longer sports as about athletic competition, but *postmodern* sports now fascinating only because the athlete's body is a blank screen for playing out the darker passions of triumph and scapegoatism. Johnson's second body (his simulated body that was the focus of all the mass media attention) then, as an empty sign onto which could be projected a triple resentment: the resentment of the Olympic Committee which, having already surrendered its sovereignty on the question of money, took up with a vengeance the policing of the drug free body; the resentment of the silent mass audience that saw its psychological investment in Johnson's triumph over Carl Lewis instantly reversed by evidence of his use of anabolic steroids; and the resentment of the media at being cheated of the illusion of an "even playing field."

Just as Nietzsche predicted, there is nothing quite so dangerous as a worldwide mob, robbed of its own dream-world and thirsting for revenge at the unmasking of its own illusions. With Ben Johnson, *The Day of the Locust* finally goes global in the psychological form of Panic Olympics.

PANIC OZONE

Like Lewis Carroll's *Through the Looking Glass*, planet Earth is about to do a flip. The protective shield of the earth's inner space (its environment) is about to go outside, and the vacuum of outer space is about to come inside. When radiation replaces oxygen in Planet One and when melanomia can be nominated as the disease of the day, then the stage is finally set for the post-ozone body as a perfect immunity system for the turning inside out of Planet One as it disappears through those menacing holes over the South Pole.

The earth, then, has sprung a leak and very little can be done about it. Like gas escaping from a hot air balloon, the atmosphere is leaking out and ultra-violet rays are rushing in. This "fact," or cosmology, depending on the competing claims of the various scientific groups, has given rise to international conferences and street talk, and hence to panic stations. Seemingly, everyone is talking these days about ozone as entropy, about, that is, the depletion of the atmosphere as the bleeding of Planet One.

Like many melanges of science, ethics, and politics, the ozone debate is postmodern *par excellence*. It is a perfectly cosmetic view of the physical universe. We have no recognition of ozone: perhaps we meet hundreds each day, maybe we see fluorocarbons while not seeing them, though, for sure, we are seeing less of them. The invisibility of ozone is suited to the mass knowledge of chemistry and biochemistry which serves, like small particle physics and microbiology, as simulacra of the real. Who doubts that fluorocarbons are dangerous? In fact, we would have little interest in them if they were not. Yet, the models designed for display purposes in all of the Nobel prize winners' offices or in the TV depictions of these molecules are both aesthetically assuring, and even seductive. It is a sexual vision of the secreting universe. The aesthetic claim, the elegance of science, sustains this vision in a promotional culture which science encourages, and which, with ozone, it masters. But all of this: the chemical models of the bleeding earth, the video displays, or the "simplicity of nature" simply reflects the dominance of scientific reversals as the language of power in cosmetic culture. Whatever the common sense perception of aerosol cans (the social code demands olfactory immunity systems for underarms), the "truth" must be located elsewhere. Science vaporizes values as much as perception, but only on the condition that it make national news. In this "truth" drama, ozone owes much of its advertising success to the pulsating dilations of the holes, as graphically displayed on TV.

The reverse, but parallel, image of the disappearance of the ozone layer, is the requisite ritual of browning bodies at the beach. This epidermal layering, the slow body burn, itself mediated by a radical semiurgy of skin creams, still ends up with a higher cancer profile for the people in the sun. While introducing the necessary drama into everyday life, both forms of danger do not go unnoticed. But they can be largely ignored. These "old age" problems, like our future of nursing home care, can be addressed in "due time." And due time, as any child knows, is a useful way of shifting time zones.

Not ending with the cosmetics of browning bodies, the cosmetics of the ozone layer are also played out in the space of the geopolitical. The ozone layer is the site of Paul Virilio's "dromoscope" where the political field of defense technology overlaps with the natural defense mechanism of the earth. Ozone can become such an acceptable social problem because its vocabularly imitates that of Star Wars, and thus can metamorphose easily into the minds of all. Indeed, in the "advanced industrial societies," the cosmology of the disappearing ozone layer goes one step further. Unlike many institutions which govern on the basis of the exclusive principle of private property, ozone consciousness is a sign of participatory democracy. We can all do our tiny share by sacrificing our favorite deodorant, whipped cream, or oil spray. Sacrificial renuciation, therefore, for the age of excess.

P

PANIC PIGEONS

photo: Alexis Gosselin

There is an old, abandoned brewery in Montreal. It hasn't been used for forty years. However, it is home to thousands of pigeons.

Last year an entrepreneurial artist received a grant from the Canadian Government for a new art installation (his own). Refusing the customary museum space, the artist in question held his show at the old brewery, with its legacy of pigeons and their droppings. Refusing also this natural landscape, which had its own quality of sublimity and terror, the artist reclaimed the factory space to the aesthetic standards

PANIC

of contemporary art exhibitions (white walls, black floors, painted pipes), and was, in fact, in the process of trying to hustle three million dollars in grant money to make the reappropriated landscape of the factory a site where rising real estate values could be happily complicit with rising artistic values.

Once the art exhibit was opened to the public, it was evident that the artist's work was in the best tradition of contemporary, and traditional, French perspectives on the Enlightenment. The dialectic in his work was between hyper-rationalization and hyper-expressionism. Violent pastiches of Turner's paintings (where the paint actually dripped from canvas "plagiarisms" of Turner's *Vesuvius* onto the floor) alternated with exquisitely refined, and mathematically precise, renditions of the measured world: the squaring of the circle; the mapping of the natural landscape into a tidy grid of longitudes and latitudes; the whole Cartesian reduction of space to a mathematical formula.

However, missing from his work was any sense of mediation, specifically between his depictions of sublimity and terror in Turner and the Cartesian appropriation of the natural landscape or, more generally, between the dual legacy of enlightenment: romanticism and rationalism.

On this same opening day, though, a curious event took place. Two pigeons suddenly swooped in through the door and sat on one of the installations. It was reported that the artist went berserk, screaming that someone had left the door open, flapping his arms (in a real case of pigeon panic), finally succeeding in chasing the pigeons out.

The pigeons flying in the door, of course, gave the lie to the whole venture, not just to the lack of mediation in the French Enlightenment of which this artist's work was the most recent example, but also to the complicity of romanticism and rationalism in refusing nature and the double complicity of art and real estate values in refusing pigeons: Montreal's newest homeless victims.

Panic pigeons, therefore, as the dark spirit of the dialectic of enlightenment coming home to roost.

PANIC PILOTS

Night Landing Mask, Don Proch

By the year 2000, the Air Force says, pilots should be able to make use of the full "virtual world," a three-dimensional, color display helmet — plus an electronic co-pilot, or "pilot associate."

The co-pilot, a robot of sorts with artificial intelligence, will be a less efficient version of Luke Skywalker's R2D2 of the film *Star Wars*. These are necessary...because some aircraft can already maneuver so rapidly that they generate forces that can render a pilot unconscious. The pilot associate, monitoring the pilot's physical status, would sense when he was impaired and take over the flight until the pilot could resume control.

Boston Globe
June 1987

Recently, there was a superb article in the *Boston Globe*, "When Looks Can Kill," which was (generally) about the new world of "virtual technology" and (specifically) about creating compensatory technologies for the bodies of Air Force pilots, which are failures in exploiting the full possibilities of the most current aerial technology. Since human beings are now (from the perspective of virtual technology) inadequate instruments, there is an urgent need, and nowhere more desperate than in the Air Force, to create prosthetic technologies for deficient bodies. So a whole new generation of "virtual pilots" for the virtual world of jet fighter technology. As the *Boston Globe* article continues:

> Screeching toward the target at close to the speed of sound, the fighter-bomber pilot flies along a flight path generated, like a video game roadway, as a three-dimensional picture on the inside of his helmet visor.
>
> He skirts missile sites, interceptor planes and friendly fighters and maneuvers past pole-like "landmarks" that give him a sense of speed and location. "Touching" what appears to be a point in empty space, he selects a weapon. He moves his finger again, and a sensor on his gloved fingertip arms a missile: to an observer, he again appears to be touching nothing.
>
> This is the pilot of the future, flying in his own world — researchers call it a "virtual world" — with the help of an array of complex computer-driven technology....The pilot never looks outside at the "real world" as he homes in on his target. Instead, radar, infra-red sensors, sound sensors and television cameras, combined with computer-generated terrain maps, place him precisely in a three-dimensional image. It is projected on his helmet visor just inches from his eyes but gives the illusion of optical infinity. As he looks left, right, up or down, what he sees changes accordingly: the computer-generated image, which is continually updated as an electromagnetic cube on the top of the helmet, senses his orientation.

It's the *virtual world* that Air Force researchers like to call the "super cockpit." No longer the real world, but a virtual world of computer-derived images projected on the inside of the pilot's helmet which simulate perfectly, and at a pace slowed down for the *body deficient*, the optical trajectory of the jet fighter's aerial flight path. No longer *real vision*, but computer-generated optical scanning images. No longer *real visual landmarks*, but a closed circuit electronic feedback network for indicating velocity and spatial location. Not even *real touch* but the virtual touching of a point in empty space: "the life-like image of a switch panel, an image similar to that in a mirror, which has been generated by a computer and projected onto his helmet visor by a pair of miniature television transmitters." And certainly not *real fingertips*, but "sensors, which can be located precisely as his hand moves through a magnetic field flux in the cockpit." And the pilot's head? That, too, has disappeared into the organon of a virtual helmet which is perfect for an aerial technology moving to escape velocity from the inertial drag of g-forces. Indeed, since jet fighters are now built with the expectation of pilots blacking out under the pressure of immense g-forces during spatial maneuvers, then there is always the "pilot associate" available to assume robotic control of what is anyway a fully telemetried, virtual world.

The super cockpit, therefore, as an advanced warning system of our evolution into robo-bodies fit for exiting Planet One. After all, it's only the immense, mythological drag of anthropomorphism which prevents the Air Force researchers from seeing the obvious: in the supercockpit the "pilot associate" (the robot) should be promoted immediately to pilot's rank; and the human pilot, well he or she should be left on the ground, having not measured up yet to the ultra-evolutionary demands of virtual technology. But this, of course, would break too sharply with the hyper-promotional mythology of all the Air Force publicity: the pilot (in the Chuck Yeager tradition) as a direct continuation of the western gunslinger, throwing his fate to the wind. And thus the irony: in the supercockpit, there is no wind, no chance element, and no "real" pilot either. In the world of virtual technology, the pilot has already vanished, just blipped away, into a passive servomechanism of the super-cockpit.

Not the macho world of *Top Gun* anymore (that has already disappeared with the creation of the supercockpit), but all the pilots now as telemetered eyeballs and fibrillated senses, helped by all the compensatory technologies which the US Air Force can huff and puff and muster up to the evolutionary level of their backseat electronic co-pilots.

PANIC PENIS

No longer the old male cock as the privileged sign of patriar-chal power and certainly not the semiotician's dream of the decen-tered penis which has, anyway, already vanished into the ideology of the phallus, but the postmodern penis which becomes an em-blematic sign of sickness, disease and waste. Penis burnout, then, for the end of the world.

And just in time! Because in all of the technologies of sex which make possible a sex without secretions (the computerized phone sex of the Minitel system in Paris; video porn for the language of the gaze; designer bodies; and gene retreading), in all of these tech-nologies of sex, the penis, both as proturberance and ideology, is already a spent force, a residual afterimage surplus to the require-ments of telematic society.

Anyway, it was predictable. The male body has always been the privileged object and after-effect of a twofold psychoanalytical colonization: *a psychoanalytics of reception* which functions, as La-can insists, by the principle of misrecognition where in the fateful mirror stage the bourgeois infant self substitutes the illusion of sub-stantial unity to be provided by a fictive, abstract ego for concrete identity; and secondly, at the *social* level, where as theorized by Althusser, ideology interpellates individuals as subjects. This may be why, in the end, even Michel Foucault said with resignation that the postmodern self is really about sedimented subjectivity, that is, the constitution of the male self as an afterimage of the moral problematization of pleasure and the torturing procedures of the confessional.

When we have already passed beyond the first two orders of sex, beyond sex as nature and beyond sex as discourse, to sex as fascinating only when it is about recklessness, discharge and up-heaval — a *parodic* sex, then we have also broken beyond the ana-lytics of sexuality and power to **excess**; beyond Foucault's language of the "care of the self" to **frenzy**; beyond the "use of pleasure" (Fou-cault again) with its moral problematization of the ethical subject in relation to its sexual conduct to a little sign-slide between **kitsch and decay**. Not then the nostaligia for an aesthetics of existence to-day or for a hermeneutics of desire (these are passé and who cares anyway?), but parodic sex as about the free expenditure of a "bound-less refuse of activity" (Bataille) pushing human plans; not the co-herency of the ethical subject (that has never motivated anyone except in the detrital terms of the subject as a ventilated remainder of death), but the excitation of the subject into a **toxic state**, into a sumptuary site of loss and orgiastic excess. Not, finally, a productive sex, but an **unproductive** sex, a sex without secretions, as the site of the death of seduction as that which makes sex bearable in the postmodern condition.

Bataille was right:

> The (pineal) eye at the summit of the skull, opening on the incandescent sun in order to contemplate it in a sinister solitude, is not a product of the understanding, but is instead an immediate existence; it opens and blinds itself like a conflagration, or like a fever that eats the being; or more exactly the **head**. And thus it plays the role of a fire in the house; the head, instead of locking up life as money is locked in a safe, spends it without counting, for at the end of this erotic metamorphosis, the head has received the **electric power of points**. This great burning head is the image and the disagreeable light of the notion of expenditure...

> Georges Bataille
> *Visions of Excess*

For expenditure is when "life is parodic and lacks an interpretation," that is, the excitation of the solar anus and the pineal eye. And why not? The pineal eye and the solar anus are also always about an excremental sexuality as the third order of simulation into which sex vanishes after the disappearance of organic and discursive sexuality, and after the fading away of the body as yet another afterimage of the postmodern scene.

PANIC PLAGUE

We have reached a fateful turning-point in contemporary culture when human sexuality is a killing-zone, when desire is fascinating only as a sign of its own negation, and when the pleasure of catastrophe is what drives ultramodern culture onwards in its free fall through a panic scene of loss, cancellation, and exterminism.

Indeed, there is an eerie resemblance between the *fin-de-millenium* mood of contemporary America under the sign of AIDS and Thucydides' eloquent historical account of the dark psychological outcomes of the plague that devastated Athens in the fifth century B.C. In the curiously detached terms of the classical historian who viewed human affairs through the clinical lens of medicine, thus tracking the unfolding of history as disease, Thucydides noted the upsurge of panic anxiety within the Athenian population as a whole in response to the rapid spread of a seemingly incurable disease, the origins of which were not understood, the epidemiological development of which was baffling to the medical profession of the time, and the protections against which were non-existent. Before the dark menace of the plague (and the rumours that amplified both the numbers and suffering of its victims), there was the immediate and almost complete breakdown of even the most minimal forms of social solidarity. With charity for others guaranteeing only one's own death, friend shunned friend, neighbours acted towards one another on the basis of a ruthless calculus of self-interest, and isolation became the template of the previously democratic public life of Athens as a whole. But even this desperate recourse to radical social isolation was quickly proven futile when it became evident, if only by dint of the corpses in the streets and private dwellings, that if the medical causes of the Athenian plague were as complex and they were unpredictable, then, too, none of the traditional precautions against the spread of this contaminant could provide immunity against the invasion of the body by a disease which was as disfiguring of the surface of the flesh as it was ultimately fatal. In Thucydides' historical account, a panic scene of human psychology at the end of the world emerges: a carnivalesque mood of *bitter hysteria* at already living on borrowed time after the catastrophe, with nothing to lose because one is certain to be cheated of life anyway; and for those few who unexpectedly recovered from the disease, a curious, if highly unrealistic, feeling of triumph over death itself — a sense of triumph which ultimately, and not uncommonly, found its purchase in the ecstatic belief among the survivors of the disaster that *they would never die of any cause.*

The psychological mood of postmodern America is similar to the Thucydidean account of the dark days of Athens of the fifth century. Here, the invasion of the body by invisible antigens, the origins of which are unknown, the circulation of which is as unpredictable as it is haphazard, and the pathology of which is as disfiguring as it is seemingly fatal, has generated a pervasive mood of living, once again, at the end of the world. Everywhere now the previously suffocated sounds of private anguish become the psychological text of public life: *unhappy consciousness* at being trapped in bodies which are pleasure palaces first, and torture chambers later; a triumphant, if unrealistic, sense of *disbelief* among those portions of the American population previously unaffected (heterosexuals) that the fate of the gay community is less a moral judgement on sexual preference than an ominous early warning system of the relentless, and inevitable, spread of viral infections by the medium of bodily fluids; depression to the point of *cluster suicides* among the young at the mythological significance of invading retroviruses in breaking down the body's immunity system; an *absence of charity*, to the point of viciousness for fun, in seeking to isolate oneself from viral contaminants; and a *will to hyper-materialism*, to judge by the inflation of commodity values from the stock exchange to the art market, as an excessive sign (that in the age of panic money when exchange value turns into *implosion* value) that everything has lost its real value.

Between a melancholy sense of fatalism and a triumphant, but unrealistic, sense of immunity from viral contamination, these are the psychological poles of panic sex at the *fin-de-millenium.* The tragic sense of human sexuality today is that it is the scene of a violent and frenzied implosion, where sexual activity is coded by the logic of exterminism, where consciousness is marked by an intense fear of ruined surfaces, where the body is invested (as a passive host) by a whole contagion of invading parasites, where even history is recycled as the reality-principle as everyone is compelled to live in fear of their own sexual biographies, where even the disappearance of reciprocity and love as the basis of human sex is driven onwards by a media-induced state of panic anxiety about the transmission of bodily fluids, where if advertisers are to be believed, it is just the hint of catastrophe which makes sex bearable in the age of the death of seduction, and where, anyway, natural sex has suffered a triple alienation. First, there was the disappearance of organic sex into discursive sexuality (when, as Michel Foucault said in *The History of Sexuality*, we must pass through what is said about sex, the discourse of sexuality, in order to know our own sex in the modern episteme). Then, the disappearance of biological motherhood with the alienation of the womb (under the double pressure of the technification of reproduction and the subordination of the ovaries to the sovereignty of private property contract as in the Baby M case). And, finally, the vanishing of seduction itself into a whole ideological scene of the body redoubled in an endless labyrinth of media images.

It is not just the phallocratic signifier of semen either which is the hint of potential catastrophe in sex today. If the British Government is accurate in its recent billboard campaign against AIDS which dot the English countryside ("Don't Die Out of Ignorance") it is all the bodily fluids — blood, saliva, any puncturing of the surface of the skin — with even razors and pierced ears as no-go zones.

Panic sex in America is the body in the postmodern condition as a filter for all the viral agents in the aleatory apparatus of the dead scene of the social, and where, if the body is marked, most of all, by the breakdown of the immunological order, this also indicates, however, that there is a desperate search underway for technologies for the body immune: from *panic fashion* (the "New Look" in the Paris fashion scene); and *panic science* (the deep relationship between AIDS and Star Wars research); to *panic policy* (the urinal politics of contemporary America); and *panic eating* (the double occurrence in America today of a schizoid regime of dietary practices: the explosion of eating disorders, from bulimia to anorexia, on the one hand; and, on the other, an intense fascination with the recuperation of the healthy mouth, culminating with the recent High Fashion edict that the slightly robust woman's body is back as a counter-aesthetic in the age of AIDS and disappearing bodies).

First, then, the end of telic history (with the serialty of the nuclear holocaust), followed by the implosion of the social into a panic site (with the triumph of signifying culture in the era of promotional culture), and now there is the implosion of human sex itself into a catastrophe scene. The result is the production of a *cynical sex*, of sex itself as an ideological site of disaccumulation, loss, and sacrifice as the perfect sign of a nihilistic culture where the body promises only its own negation; where the previously reflexive connection between sexuality and desire is blasted away by the seductive vision of *sex without organs* — a hyperreal, surrogate, and telematic sex like that promised by the computerized phone sex of the Minitel system in France — as the ultimate out-of-body experience for the end of the world; and where the terror of the ruined surfaces of the body translates immediately into its opposite: *the ecstasy of catastrophe and the welcoming of a sex without secretions as an ironic sign of our liberation.*

So that is what we get when sexuality is negation and when, under the pressure of the logic of exterminism, pleasure is coded by the seductive vision of the hyperreal: *sex without secretions.* Accordingly, the generation of bodies fit for the waiting time of post-catastrophe: parasited from within by retroviruses that circulate in the bodily fluids; and tattooed from without by the panic signs of the high-intensity market-setting — the body infolded in time, its energy drained away by all the parasites. With the body coded by the bleak (but fascinating because reversible) exchange-process of host and parasite, postmodern consciousness, like a pulsar, also alternates between repulsion and seduction over the fate of the body as (both) a terroristic sign and a pleasurable scene of its own exterminism. At the *fin-de-millenium*, sex — like power, history, money, and the unconscious before it — is always triumphally suicidal as the sign of its darkest seduction.

PANIC PERFECT FACES

The elusive "perfect face" has been quantified and put into a computerized "facial template." By comparing a patient's face with the template, doctors can determine which features need correction.

San Francisco Examiner

Now no one, especially women, need remain content without the perfect face.

In its hyper-modern expression, plastic surgery has a second life as face and body "sculpting," permitting (demanding?) radical redesigns of bone, fat and skin.

Using implants, we are told, cheekbones can be boosted, jaws tapered, and chins reshaped. Physicians can pull fat from eye sockets to create the "hollow look," so fashionably *cachet* now. Or, if a more exotic look is desired, eyebrow ridges can be elevated and, with a little discreet cutting, given the annual nouvelle aesthetic line.

Cosmetic body cuts, then, for face, fat and skin which are to be brought under the aesthetic sign-form of the pleasure of seduction and the pain of desire.

Indeed, at a recent meeting of plastic surgeons in the USA, these frenetic innovations in body cuts for the fashionable silhouette were announced:*

Fat grafting, in which fat is suctioned from the buttocks or abdomen and injected into the face and neck — "like fill material," according to one doctor.

Forehead lifts, which remove sagging skin around the eyebrows, creases between the eyes and "worry lines," areas that are usually unaided by facelifts.

Tissue expansion, which uses a small pouch inflated to stretch tissue and thus create natural-looking contours in small or absent breasts.

Chin and cheekbone augmentation, which uses implants to add size and contour to receding chins or flat cheekbones.

And, of course, the technology of virtual imaging has got into the act too. Using "three dimensional computer images" of the patients, doctors now create exact replicant images of the future perfect face. A perfect fusion of computer technology, body sculpting, and fashion

---

* As reported in the *San Francisco Examiner*

aesthetics to inscribe the body — fat, creases, pouches, and bones — in this season's designer look.

The body, therefore, as high art, never really perfect, always cuttable, always mutable, always lost in the labyrinth of its own bad infinity. Or, as one fashioned body has murmured: "I could look at my face in the mirror forever, thinking and dreaming of its perfections. And in that dream, my face came to fascinate me by its look of seduction, by its look, finally, of an impossible perfection. The mirror of seduction slipped inside me, and I was its outer tarnished image."

Cosmetic body cuts, then, for perfect panic faces.

PANIC PSYCHOANALYSIS

The Schizoid Subject

Francis Bacon is the painter of the postmodern body which is actually peeled inside out, splayed across the mediascape, with its organs dangling like passive servomechanisms waiting to be fibrillated from outside.

The Hermetic Body

It is just the opposite with the artistic productions of Lucien Freud.

If Freud (as the grandson of Sigmund Freud) is the painter *par excellence* of the death of the psychoanalytic subject, that means that his art is a screen-effect, a truth-sayer, of the disappearance of the famous reality-principle of the unconscious in the postmodern condition. In Freud's artistic productions, the postmodern subject is represented as inert and evacuated, actually imploded with such intensity that the body serves as a tomb for a postmodern self which does not exist.

In many of Freud's paintings, and particularly in those featured in the recent retrospective of his work at the *Beaubourg* in Paris, his portraits of the feminine subject push the conventional symptomology of the modernist psychoanalytic subject to its point of excess, and then collapse: *hysteria* (the portrait of his first wife who, with exaggerated eyes always gazing outwards, quietly strangles the cat); *compulsion-repetition* (Freud always paints one picture — supine women in suppressed silence staring blankly into white space); *displacement* and *projection* (friend with rat); and an intense and unresolved mother fixation coupled with a determined reduction of womenly subjects to "girls."

Here, we are left with a serial scene of vacant subjects, isolated, supine, silenced, their gaze turned outwards: not as some have claimed a recovery of anguished human identity, but just the opposite — cancelled identities to such a degree of compulsion that their bodies actually implode, resurfacing finally as blank screens. Indeed, if the Freudian subject can possess such blank identities and if the symptomology of the painting can be so banal, maybe that is because the Freudian subject no longer exists except as an artistic echo, a painterly image-reservoir, of an already vacated subjectivity. Not then the unconscious any longer, but the full publicization of the collapsing subject. Not dream states, but disembodied dreams as the prevailing sign of postmodern psychosis. And not even a subject any longer, but a memory trace onto which are inscribed all of the cultural signs of the end of the psychoanalytic subject: painterly mothers, strangled cats, friends with rats, women as girls, and always the intense, unresolved and compulsive fixation with the mother figure. The common point: not Freudian psychoanalysis, but the implosion of the Freudian subject into Bataille's history of the eye with its erotics unto death. Probably against his own intentions, Lucien Freud has produced a brilliant parody of the limitations, and neurotic fixations, of the psychoanalytic subject. In his work, the unconscious moves outside the body, and the blank stare of all his painterly subjects is left as a necessary social remainder of the reduction of the self to a mirrored-image of the psycho-simulacrum.

While Bacon may paint the fully exploded body, the organ which is turned inside out and and splayed across the postmodern social terrain, Freud paints the hermetic body, the body which implodes into the silence of non-identity. A distressed and emblematic sign of the end-point of the psychoanalytic subject, Freud fully explores the ruins within. Indeed, in his art, even the quality of the oil-paint changes over the years, from light colors and smooth quality in his early works to mottled skin colors and rough, raised oils in his later works. It is as if the text of the canvas begins to crack apart, and to speak in the geography of its colors and textures of the reality of the ruins within. Not so much the ruins of the womenly subjects in these paintings, but the degree-zero of the panic male vision which is represented in all of its melancholy brilliance and aridity in the artistic productions of Lucien Freud.

Reason and Madness

If Lucien Freud is the truth-sayer of the end of the psychoanalytic subject, then it might also be said that Francis Bacon is the truth-sayer of science as power. Curiously, while Lucien Freud is the intellectually faithful grandson of Sigmund Freud, the founder of psychoanalyis, Francis Bacon is the collateral descendent of Francis Bacon, the author of *Novum Organum*, and with it the creation of the governing *episteme* of modernist scientific discourse. As if by an ironic gesture, two of the key axial principles of western culture — psychoanalysis and science — are inscribed by blood lineage in the artistic imaginations of Bacon and Freud. Here, art is finally a truth-sayer of the deprivations of the western *episteme*: of the final production of the fully scienticized subject as a grisly alternation between the schizoid and hermetic self.

PANIC POLITICS

Merry-Go-Round, Mark Gertler

It's fun time under the big top when the portable politicians of the postmodern parade come to the parodic dome. The clones are out, wired to the computer consoles; electronic waves piercing the body politic agitating the crowd to glee with each melodramatic surge. Hurray! Hurray! To that age of reversals, an age as Nietzsche describes it that "wants publicity and that great actors' hubbub, that great drum banging that appeals to its fun-fare tastes."[1] It's time to get on the merry-go-round as quantum politics begins its spin under the barrage of particle beams from the repeating cannons of the cathode rays.

Postmodern politics begins with Mark Gertler's *Merry-go-round*. The soldiers, sailors and businessmen mount up on the automated carousel of hysteria. Each cloned in magical threes, mirrored imaged, breasts protruding, backs curved in the ellipsoid arc ready for the high speed chase. The horses are genetically pure, beyond mutation, beyond the cancerous errors of nature poised for the visciousness of war to come — a ready automated machine. Yet what is this, the protruding buttocks, rounded open and fleshly white? The solar anus open to the culture of fun/fear ready to receive consummation as the carousel picks up speed.

Politics becomes the flashing anus of promises of the better world constantly present as the carousel becomes the succession of white strobe-like flashes and as the waste system runs into the now of party time. The cries of the paraders poised on the edge of aggression and terror, unable to dismount, caught in the imploding vortex of the fashion swirl. Tunics pressed, hats in place, mouths open ready for the distortion of the cyclorama.

It is just this world of Gertler run now at hyper-speed which, through the distorted images of the carousel, creates the holograms that characterize the political. The path of Presidents, or Prime Ministers, trace/race after images across the nation. Cameras with open shutters hopeful that the celluoid will inscribe the sunny soul of the nation from the black hole of paranoid politics. Just as the video camera in the President's office oversees Red Square equally well as surveying the latest troop movements. Instant on, instant politics, instant off.

Notes

1. F. Nietzsche, *The Will to Power*, Section 464, New York: Vintage, 1968.

PANIC QUIET

Just when the church has lost its dynamism, it has one last life as a place of meditation in the urban simulacra. Panic quiet in a culture where noise is a predatory-like parasite invading the social field.

PANIC

R

PANIC RENO ROMANCE

Photos: Steve Pfohl

I am remembering a (k)night in Reno about to spin his story. To spin history: to re(w)rite a self from within a scene of panic where my voice shifts flat-lined from a third person inscribed singularly into a fourth person ruined and not at all the same. And what if I am given over to this ritual, this (w)riting, this reinscription of who I am in relation? What if I am transferentially carried from within these ruins toward others? What if I find myself spinning or being spun across the coded game board of the material and imaginary contingencies of what constitutes the

PANIC

best of my chances and the worst, the carnal and cognitive effects of the relations in which I am decentered genealogy with desire in history? I re-move my pen only to find my eyes/I's scattered across the screen. I am positioned before the television, or after, pursuing a story that seems at once old and newer than new. And if I am literally transferred out of the narrative confines of a ruinous fourth person what is left? What carries fifth and plurally?

Why such panic questions at this time in history: a death of the author? Some attribute this method of inquiry to the fashionable intellectual chic of French poststructuralist ideas. That is not something new. The allegorical wanderings of Walter Benjamin suggest a more historically material story of this NOVELTY.[1] Benjamin, melancholy and self-destructive, left Germany for Paris just as Nordic fascism projected its ruinous real upon the imperial screen of a state bureaucratized in history. They were shooting images of purification and blood sacrifice into the blond veins of those for whom primitive romance had become a CAPITAL idea. And now in another time and place we are shooting these images into ourselves: the thirst for death, dark and postmodern. He turns himself on before the television, before the image of an actor posing presidentially against terror with violence, re(w)riting history like the movies, a loss of the real. This is what this actor is doing, fascinating us with pictures of anonymous Hispanic men, lifting a large bag into or out of a boat somewhere. This is what this President is saying: PICTURE this — important officials in the Nicaraguan government shipping cocaine to a playground in Indiana, where it will feed upon the minds of our youth. Communists, it seems, will stop at nothing. They must be stopped and the children must be drug tested and the workers. This is what this actor is doing, fascinating us with pictures of F-111 attack routes and of maps of an evil city, a haven for terrorists and mad dogs and for the dead bodies of dark skinned children murdered in the night. This President is saying: "I made it clear we would respond as soon as we determined conclusively who was responsible for such attacks ... Our evidence is direct, it is precise, it is irrefutable ... Today we have done what we had to do. If necessary, we shall do it again."

He turns himself on before the television, close-circuiting the ruins before him. He sees her fingers unzipping his pants, palm felt against his groin aroused. Hot. Heavy. Hard. These adjectives: they circumscribe his mind, stir his body. Where do these images come from? What do they mean? These questions fascinate him like the images. Images of an imperial master, patriotic purity, and patriarchal obsession with the pornographic: the things we count upon daily, just as we are counted among their number. Market research: it informs us of our desires. Can you buy these ideas? The latest over-

determination of CAPITAL; the full surrealization of consumptive desire; the digital reproduction of quality in quantity; a repetitious deferral of ruin; a postponement of death in time; the fascination with a linearity without end, Amen, and with fascism; the electronic simulation of desire within the third person singular.

But what if reflexively we re-cognize this ruinous third person? Is it too late to do this? Should we try another time? Picture this: a collective de-authorization of "he" who (w)rites his destination before the television; a ruinous transformation of this existent voice, the third person, singular, already ruined, into fourth person, unsingular and uncertain. Benjamin offered a related picture: the death of the author. He sought points of transformative resistance within the complex and contradictory theater of mass mediated desire. To stray with Benjamin is to stray complicitly from within. It is to seek out spaces of mediated fracture from within which we find ourselves vibrating between the practical exigencies of production and the ecstatic excesses of self-consumption. There is nothing easy about his search, this re-search. Moreover, it demands another sense of time. All revolutions do. Benjamin envisioned time differently. He was a melancholy Marxist and this was his material imagination of history: a collage of collective re(w)ritings in the fifth person plural. A reclamation of the public sphere: gossip doubled ruinously with a question of communism. This was his hope: that we might un(w)rite ourselves, loosen the confines of self-simulating NOVELTY. This is an allegory. It demands another sense of time.

Primitive Romance: the ruins of intercourse, the ruins of gossip

It had begun earlier this morning on the rug; he had been exercising his body and remembered a time entwined with another. They had come to desire each other, like in the movies. They longed for intercourse as only the stars knew how. She pressed her body against his alone within his space and made him shudder. Her fingers unzipping his pants, palm felt against his groin aroused. Hot. Heavy. Hard. These adjectives: they circumscribe his mind, stir his body. She is his now he imagines. But how does he know? He guides his hand slowly between her thighs for the evidence: her moan and the typical wetness. It is late at night and evil. They had taken shelter from the moon on his rug. Her nipples were erect but her eyes hesitant and he was trying not to think about his performance, like in the movies. He wanted her to lose herself in him, that he might be credited in the production of her pleasure. He thought that credit was important. He bared her shoulders and thought to himself, "She's flirting with death. This is to my credit." He found it pleasurable to have a good credit rating. She would rate him highly. This was the meaning he made of her image. Terror of the simulacra.

She was trembling uncertain within the confines of his story. Where did this story come from? Her story was different. She realized that they didn't even know each other's proper names and speculated that maybe he'd kill her and hide the body. This frightened her. She felt panic. Why was she here? What was the meaning of her desires? Where did these meanings come from? What came before? What comes next?

"Images and language take precedence," declared Benjamin. "Not only before meaning. Also before the self."[2] But what if we reflexively re-cognize this ruinous third in which we find ourselves inscribed meaningfully in desire? Is it too late to do this? This frightened her. She lifted her blouse above her head, exposing her neck with a filmic gesture of sex. Why was she here? She's flirting with death, he thought to himself. This is to my credit. Is it too late to ruin this image, that is, to re-cognize this image as a ruin and ruin that ruin. To double the ruins of gossip, to collectively fracture the singular confines of mass mediated desire — this demands another sense of time: the fifth person plural or whatever.

Is it too late to do this? Too late in what — capitalism, the machine age, the narrative confines of cybernetically simulated desire? This question is occasioned today by at least two spaces of potential resistance. In time, there may be more. The first space: impure and complicit. This space is made possible, in part, by a contradictory grant from EXXON, Xerox, IBM, and other multinationals. It is a space of contradictory effects. For just as these grant conglomerate institutions of late capital depend on the electronic language of mass mediated imagery to interpellate or call out our desires to consume, so simultaneously do they present us with an increasing body of material evidence concerning the ruins we've become. The consumer is made, at once, more restless and more programed. The restlessness of the consumer within capitalist society — this is not something new. The desire for more, the yearning for the consumptive fix, for another purchase, increased ownership, although certainly exaggerated by mass mediated advertising, this has been a desire within the capitalist narrative since its beginnings. But the realizable programing of consumption: this is something new, a twisted NOVELTY that threatens the dominant illusions that capitalism has traditionally offered its privileged bourgeois classes. For the bourgeoisie the narrative destiny of capitalism offered the following: the promise of authorial mastery of world history, the masculine dream of rational and calculative control of the things of nature, and an endless deferral of death in time. Over the last several decades, the future of these illusions has been visibly contradicted by the institutional practices of capital itself, by the advent of the realizable programing of consumption. I hum the Burger King tune all the way to work each morning and feel deliciously different. Instead of death's deferral and the rational control of things, an electronically mediated structure of capital seems capable of effecting a deferral of life and the control of people by things that hum them deliciously: the death of the illusion of the authorial master, the death of the author.

This is new, a twisted NOVELTY. It is realized materially in the historical wedding of advanced electronic communicative technology with an existent bourgeois culture orchestrating the maximization of profit by the most efficient means available. The most efficient means: electronic advert upon advert, a terminal procession of desire-producing images without end: the darkest nightmares of science fiction realizing themselves before our eyes, the full operationalization of the machine body, the simulacrum, the death of the author without renewal, rebirth or resurrection, the robotic hell of the living dead. You wrote me a letter inquiring about my existence. Quite honestly I might have told you that I hummed the Burger King tune all the way to work and felt deliciously different. This, I'm afraid, is new, a twisted Novelty and deadly. Benjamin, melancholy and self-destructive, left Germany just as fascism projected its ruinous real upon the imperial screen. And now in another time and place, we are shooting these images into ourselves: the thirst for death, dark and postmodern.

This is a fundamental contradiction of late capital: a confrontation between the restless desires for authorial bourgeois mastery of consumption with the haunted and starkly new, digitally programed death mask of the consumer itself. This frightened her. He felt panic. What was the meaning of her desires. Where did these meanings come from? What came before? What comes next? These are frightening questions. They emerge from within the contradictory space occupied uneasily by reflexive bourgeois theorists who

re-cognize themselves inscribed within the imaginary and material confines of late Western capitalist society. The restless authorial consumer is not the cheerful robot,[3] at least not yet, not completely, not everyone. This is a melancholy hope: that it is not too late, that we might yet loosen the confines of our self-simulating NOVELTY, that we might stray repeatedly and together, impurely and with an acknowledged complicity with the narrative structures against which we struggle to (w)rite ourselves out from within toward some others.

This is a first space of potential resistance: contradictory and fearful fractures within a class of bourgeois theorists and artisans, previously privileged by the illusions of authorial mastery. Robbed of the material base for such illusions by the electronic image culture of late trans-national capital, some of these de-authorized intellectuals may be drawn (organically?) to ally their de-centered selves with the revolutionary narrative practices of others excluded from that historical illusion, that is the historical reality of bourgeois mastery. There is no idealism in this analysis, simply a hype for another site of material resistance. It comes from other worlds. Not from one other world, third or whatever. That is a primitive romance for the privileged. It comes from a heterogeneity of others excluded in the reductive simulation of the same. It comes from other worlds less complicit with the narrational practices of primitive romance because the imagined pleasures of that masterful story were never realized as their own. In other words, (w)riting without the confines of the third person singular is nothing new for those condemned to the historical margins as human junk, ruinous fourth persons, unsingular and uncertain.

What names are these others given in the inscription of proper grammar, in the material and imaginary rituals of power and knowledge? These peoples of color, women, the colonized, the classified, those who desire sex differently, the mad, the bad, the Other. Proper grammar silences or ruins the voice of these others. We hear them only when they double the violence of grammar in revolt, when they re(w)rite themselves from within the ruins of time. This is the heterogeneous voice of the fifth person plural, a violence doubled, a return of the repressed. It operates upon history with another sense of time. Refugees from the ruinous simulations of the bourgeois world may ally themselves with this voice but first they must unlearn the grammar that confines them in a certain time. That is, they must learn another sense of time, a time of the ruined self, the death of the author in and as history. Is this the time of allegory?

I was sitting drunk with my parents before the world's largest stage. Huge video screens and Star Wars fighters were being lowered from above. A dazzling filmic projection of light formed a backdrop for the simulated landing of a full size airplane, a 707 — really the world's largest stage, and everyone applauded. A life-size shell of a huge metallic bird delighting the mass of enchanted vacationers here to drop their dollars. From its womb a stream of nearly naked dancers: shopgirls twirling star spangled tits, and young men posing with tight asses to the hoots of the American work force on holiday. It was Reno, Nevada. My brother was the manager and my drinks were free.

The world's largest everythings are on display in Reno. Just read the signs: the world's largest gas station, the world's largest slot machine, the world's largest casino-food-give-away. Nobody's hungry in America, said Reagan. Reagan's been to Reno. Free food, free enterprise you consume largely while you gamble. Just read the signs: the world's largest cock, the world's largest asshole. Is this true? Just read the signs. I was sitting drunk with my parents before the world's largest stage and each of us were nodding before four of the world's largest cocktails, four each before the show: spectacular. My brother was the manager and I hallucinated an image of our ruin. Our transnational corporate destiny? The parade of nearly naked dancers was suddenly cut-up by a terrible spray of machine gun bullets. Members of the African National Congress had arrived and found no pleasure in our filmic projection of white flight, star spangled tits, and young men posing with tight asses in the wake of another world's history we plunder violently to under(w)rite, the world's largest mass of fatty flesh drunk with spectacle. Blood splattering everywhere, the veneer of innocent pleasures, the death mask of western decadence exposed doubly and in time ruined. A double exposure this violent hallucination. I was sitting drunk with my parents before the world's largest stage and suddenly I had become melancholy. Is this the time of allegory? Just read the signs.

Stephen Pfohl

Notes

1. Walter Benjamin's meditations on the social production of allegorical knowledge may be found in the concluding chapter of *The Origin of German Tragic Drama*, trans. John Osborne, London: New Left Books, 1977. For an extended discussion of the relationship of allegory to the postmodern, see Craig Owens, "The Allegorical Impulse: Toward a Theory of Postmodernism," in ed. Brian Willis, *Art After Modernism*, New York: The New Museum of Contemporary Art, 1984, pp. 203-235.

2. Walter Benjamin, "Surrealism: The Last Snapshot of the European Intelligentsia," in *Reflections*, trans. Edmund Jephcutt, New York: Schocken, 1969, p. 179.

3. C. Wright Mills, *White Collar*, New York; Oxford University Press, 1956, p. 233.

PANIC RACING

Paris-Dakar! Each winter in France, there is a famous and immensely popular race involving cars, motorcycles and trucks from Paris to Dakar, a seaside town on the far side of North Africa. In France particularly, but perhaps in Europe generally, the Paris-Dakar rally has been explosively popular, because in its publicity and reality it brings together a grass roots romanticism of machine versus primitive desert terrain and, for over a month, a massive media celebration of advanced automotive racing technology. Paris-Dakar is the Tour de France, at hyper-speed.

In 1988, after considerable controversy and, for the first time, negative publicity, Paris-Dakar reached its zenith. Despite a blinding desert sandstorm, which all of the organized corporate tire and car companies finally blew away, a trail of death and violence was left by the rally: six dead (four participants, and one mother and child who happened across the road at the wrong time); a forest fire; a stern rebuke from the Vatican; two political revolts — the first from Algeria and the second from Mali; and, finally, an alarming (for the drivers) number of stolen racing cars.

The Paris-Dakar rally is of more than local curiosity, since it is the Rosetta stone of the French political imagination, and it is so because it fuses two key ideological tendencies in the French mentality: a contradictory philosophy of nature and an exterminist philosophy of power. In the postmodern condition, the French philosophy of nature is based on a twin axis: pastoral romanticism in the cities (complete with aestheticized parks, cosmetic dogs, and a purely decorative idea of trees, grass, and shubbery), and nuclear fusion in the form of power plants in the countryside. And the ruling French philosophy of power is the same: democracy at home (although intensely state bureaucratic) and military colonization abroad (from the nuclear experiments in Polynesia on behalf of the much-vaunted *force de frappe*, to the forced subordination of Guyana, to the technological necessities of missile launchings associated with the infamous Ariadne communication satellite, and including, of course, the State-ordered sinking of Greenpeace's *Rainbow Warrior*).

In the Paris-Dakar rally both ideological tendencies are at work: a celebration of *technicité* in the countryside, and this in the form of the annual forced racing car march across the unsuspecting desert; and one last revival of a macho, and white, colonizing power playing out the themes of *Heart of Darkness* in what the French media like to depict as darkest Africa.

It is precisely this techno-racism that is mirrored in French politics of the mid-1980s, where the ruling term was *co-habitation*, a "new" political formula involving a perfect political stalemate between a socialist President (Mitterand) and a neo-conservative Premier (Chirac): a perfect stalemate, that is, since it provided the French bourgeoisie, whose interests define policy, at least short of the revolution, with the preferred situation of the economic and social benefits of neo-conservatism's war against labor and the welfare state, while simultaneously providing them with ideological cover in the much-publicized progressive viewpoints of a President who, of course, had no political power of implementation.

While French intellectuals, like Maurice Duverger, were desperately theorizing *co-habitation* as a new political formula, they were profoundly mistaken in thinking that it had its origins in the interstices of French presidential politics. That honor belongs to Paris-Dakar: for in this car race (certainly a region of low epistemological profile), there has long been two happy, and earlier, co-habitations: a co-habitation of a contradictory philosophy of nature (hyper-technology/designer nature); and the co-habitation of an equally self-cancelling philosophy of power (democratic populism at home/bribes for the African countries through which the rally passes). So, therefore, not one co-habitation in France, but at least *three*: in nature, political philosophy, and state administration. Not so much, Thatcher's "popular capitalism," but "popular racing" for the final rally of the French bourgeoisie at the end of the twentieth century.

PANIC SEX

What is sex in the age of the hyperreal? A little sign slide between kitsch and decay as the postmodern body is transformed into a rehearsal for the theatrics of sado-masochism in the simulacrum. Not sadism any longer under the old sign of Freudian psychoanalytics and certainly not masochism in the Sadean carceral, but sadomasochism now as a kitschy sign of the body doubled in an endless labyrinth of media images, just at the edge of ecstasy of catastrophe and the terror of the simulacrum.

PANIC

PANIC SUPERSCIENCE

Worldsheets and Superstrings

It is over in a thermonuclear flash as the phasal shift of Planck's time sends us towards the non-Abelian fields where time's arrow finally begins to spin. Quickly eclipsing the 'locality' within which normal physics traps us, we enter new dimensions of space/time which play theatrically with all the images of our 'familiar' world. Here, the old world of the *real* dissolves into a gauge field, where the 'solitrons,' or bundles of energy, have transgressed time itself. In the gauge field, reversing time is as easy as reversing existence itself. And even the 'black holes' in space cannot prevent the escape velocities of particles, particularly those of the 'tachyons' whose speed exceeds that of light itself. The timeless photon suddenly finds itself surrounded by 'sister particles' — photinos, gluons, sleptons, squarks and zinos — all traders of energy/mass and time/space. In this world, the P operator and the Hamiltonian operator, in an anti-commutative rotation, explode the number of gauge fields again and again, as the fermions and bosons begin a fateful exchange that promises the Grand Unification. Beyond Planck's time, there exists the world of super-gravity and single pole magnets, immense attractors which have already warped space/time and are now themselves wrapped up in vast membranes creating the superstrings and world-sheets of postmodern experience.

Time's Arrow Finally Spins

The fading Newtonian world is dominated by memory, where Nietzsche's last men are preoccupied with post-satyric dramas of the search for values. Even the panic of prediction/production of the future's market is a mirror-image of past events: reversibility and predictability being two sides of an old archeology of time which gave rise to the paradox of the "arrow of time" — time as history and time as future. And even the modernist conception of space, despite being *folded* into local frames by Einstein, is schizoid: refusing its enucleation by culture other than in the inertial form of resistance to movement (boundaries, or old geopolitical concepts).

However, post-Einsteinian physics creates a new world of space/time where time's arrow finally begins to spin. It is just this spin of space/time which begins the revolution of quantum mechanics as the 'quanta' actually oscillate in space/time: alternating between *waves* and *particles* and, creating in their wake, a deep *indeterminacy* in nature. But, as we know from what the physicists like to call *supertheory*, this radical alterity of space/time in the Einsteinian photoelectric effect, spreads out throughout the forces of nature, affecting all of the fundamental elements of matter. The mediation of the strong force by gluons, the weak force by the intermediate vector bosons, and the field of gravity by gravitons creates a field where, not only space and time, but also energy and mass are exchanged.

When time's arrow begins to spin, randomness is the dominant ontology; order and disorder appear spontaneously as elements of social and physical *fortune*; and particles parasite each other and are, in turn, parasited.

Quantum Sociology: The Social as a Petrie Dish

As in times past, the social also begins as a set of fields governed by 'states of nature'. One could even hypothesize a primordial field: directionless, randomly centered, indeterminate. The field of the social is typified by its potential to create or destroy space, time, energy and mass (which are smeared over the existent and out of which the social is formed). This is a cosmology where social 'cultures' form on a shimmering, shining surface in the same manner in biology as using Petrie dishes.

As a hyper-Hobbesian energy pack, the post-Einsteinian individual traces/races across the world sheet, laying waste the field in a series of exchanges of space/time/energy/mass and, leaving behind sediments, excrements and residues which form a network of paths or gutters. The tattooing left by this violent series of exchanges is itself inscribed on the individual, whose face bears the cosmetic/cosmology of the guttering/uttering of this social science. And like all the elementary particles before it, the post-Einsteinian self is neither subject nor object, but both at the same time.

Consequently, the social is a mapping of these gutters. At the macro level, it is the 'guttering out' which reveals the sedimentations left behind by the collection of individual histories — the sum of all the slime tracks which define society. A network is thereby formed in the field with nodes created as reservoirs of spent energy/mass which provide resistance to the passage of individuals. These reservoirs span a range of activities, from the image-reservoir of Roland Barthes, to the stockpile of armaments, to capital itself. Marked and scarred by these assemblages of power, the social becomes a multitude of superfields reflecting the various mappings of power in space/time.

Postmodern Operators

For the vast majority, movement in the social field is, at once, completely determined by the nodes and pathways, yet fully random and indeterminate at the microbiological level. The generalized entropy of the life of the ultramodern individual (as energy pack) creates a personal disorder which can, nevertheless, be catalyzed into common behavior patterns. The overcoming of this natural stasis, the lowest energy level sought by natural bodies, is in the hands of a range of postmodern field operators. The operators act as double parasites: assembling the clusters of energy to guarantee flow in the system, while simultaneously feeding from the network. By rotating the co-ordinates of the field, the operator can effect phasal shifts in energy exchanges across the field. Thus, new alignments of power now come with reconfigured conceptions of space/time and energy/mass.

In the modern period, the best known operator was *money*, the very power of which made possible the Grand Unification of Capitalism. However, today's social typology reveals a large array of operators which create a set of field lattices that intersect, and are then transformed in multidimensions. For example, advertisers (as postmodern operators parasiting the field) recognize and decode these lattices in their ceaseless analysis of the reservoirs behind the market strategy of age, income, lifestyle, etc. The advertiser then attempts to transform/parasite these sedimentations in order to phase shift to a new alignment of space/time called promotional culture. It is the very same with political operators (who parasite money and advertising and who track the sediments with polling, creating new field holograms), and with fashion operators (who parasite the slime track of the face).

Individuals trapped in the space/time of promotional culture are like Nietzschean water spiders who move race/trace across the field and disappear instantly. More parasited than parasiting, the postmodern individual can at the limit leave no trace. But still, there is a powerful current in the nostalgia of postmodern times which attempts to recapture the nostalgia of these lower energy limits. Promotional culture is often capable only of temporarily energizing these 'heavy' particles witnessed, for example, in the immense propaganda surrounding voting where political 'consciousness' may exist only for voting day. Thus, one always finds in the social physics of the current GUT's, the range of space/time of the old physics, usually in the form of bleeding, entropic cultures. The decay, the necessary rotting of these reservoirs, provides the fuel for many of the parasites who are brought to these dying cores.

The description of the sheer lines, or catastrophes, of the modern period began with Marx's analysis of capitalist reservoir. This dying core has dominated our period, starkly set out by Nietzsche with the identification of the value structure. We are now faced with a broken reservoir which has created the typology of the postmodern field. The mapping of these flows along the 'gutters' of America, as America burns its core and heats up globally, reveals new fields, new dimensions, in a new superscience.

PANIC (SHOPPING) MALLS

Liquid TV

Shopping malls are liquid TVs for the end of the twentieth century. A whole micro-circuitry of desire, ideology and expenditure for processed bodies drifting through the cyber-space of ultracapitalism. Not shopping malls any longer under the old sociological formula of consumption sites, but future shops where what is truly fascinating is expenditure, loss, and exhaustion.

Shopping malls act like electro-magnets, attracting into their force field all the surrounding community activities. They involve a double movement of recuperation and dispersion. Recuperation in the sense that malls provide a temporary unity for an otherwise chaotic, random, and undetermined field of activity. And dispersion in the sense that, when the energy is shut off (life outside the mall), the force field, vectored around desire, ideology, and expenditure, immediately dissolves into its constituent particles.

Shopping malls call forth the same psychological position as TV watching: voyeurism. Except this time, they do it one better. Rather than flicking the dial, you take a walk from channel to channel as the neon stores flick by. And not just watching either, but shopping malls have this big advantage over TV, they play every sense: smelling, tasting, touching, looking, desiring, fantasizing. A whole image-repertoire which, when successful, splays the body into a multiplicity of organs, all demanding to be filled. But, of course, the shopping mall, just like all the promises of ecstasy and catastrophe before it, fulfills what it promises only virtually; and the shopping body, caught for one instant in the force field of the commodity as image-repertoire, sags back into the routine of life outside the field.

Shopping malls are the real postmodern sites of happy consciousness. Not happy consciousness in the old Hegelian sense of a reconciled dialectic of reason, but happy consciousness, now, in the sense of the virtual self. A whole seductive movement, therefore, between a willed abandonment of life and a restless search for satisfaction in the seduction of holograms. Or, is it that the self now is a virtual object to such a degree of intensity and accumulation that the fascination of the shopping mall is in the way of a homecoming to a self which has been lost, but now happily discovered. The postmodern self as one more object in the simulacra of objects. Shopping malls, therefore, as sites of possessive individualism *par excellence*.

Or, maybe it's something very different. Not shopping at all and certainly not the will to possession, but the whimsical act of looking at objects as being seductive — the pleasure of the gaze as it plays fictionally with the possibility of possession, takes on and discards whole identities associated with objects, and then moves on. The look as a new type of *flaneur*: not,however, as Benjamin had it, moving through the streets of Paris, but the *flaneur* moving through the aisles of stores in the shopping mall. And to the question, What makes looking so seductive? an anthropological answer: Shopping malls are like nature walks, and just like nature (to which they are second nature) the seasons change with new seasons of clothes, just like the leaves. The shopper, therefore, as a naturalist of the second order: when nature moves into the shopping malls, then the look is also in the way of hunting. Except this time in the postmodern condition, it's hyper-looking for a shopper who is, in the end, only looking for his or her virtual self.

No longer the tragic sense of absent presence as the ruling metaphysics of the shopping mall. Just the reverse: shopping can be the primary leisure-time activity of postmodern culture because it is *nouvelle*-play, this time in the voyeuristic form of the hyper-look, the look which fantasizes, appropriates, and discards, and all this at a seasoned glance.

Strangers in the Mall

In the USA, walking is a threatening activity. Not only in the inner cities where violence and police terror are the norm, but also in all of America's suburbs: in Florida, walking is socially unacceptable — there, only the dispossessed walk and they are a threat to the mental security and private property values of all of the residents of the "sun spot" state; in Boston, walking in the garrisoned suburbs is prevented by the snarling, predatory dogs on the lawns; in Lawrence, Kansas, there are no sidewalks, only signs on lawns which read, "Keep your paws off my property"; and, in Los Angeles, walking is a new no-go zone, kept under surveillance by police helicopters (who, periodically, megaphone suburbanites this reassuring message: "Stay in your homes! Police dogs have been released into your area!"). Walking in America puts you in the position of Weber's stranger, the person who by their very presence disturbs the field, summoning forth judgments on their conduct.

So, therefore, the prevailing social conclusion: For a safe place to exercise, particularly for women, go to a shopping mall. In the mall, everyone is a stranger, but with this difference: strangers in the mall are engaged in parallel play, safe in the policed crowd from victim city.

Lonely Places

Shopping malls are lonely places, for it is there that the self appears if only for that lonely instant of negative time when particles are created *ex nihilo*. Everyone gravitates towards them: senior citizens, teenagers, the unemployed, homeless people who just want to get out of the cold, and above all the successful. The owners of the malls like it of course, but only up to a certain point. In all the suburban centers, they have a definite image they want to portray — up-scale — so they have security guards to move people around and out. All of this, of course, just like a cyclotron in order to speed up the shoppers in hopes of the sale, an event that signifies the exteriorization of the self. They also make sure they leave very few benches: the resting position is death. They want people circulating, or out.

Shopping is just a little part of shopping malls, as all people are on their own: families have split up (like colliding neutrons), single people (as unattached electrons), the retired (as the remnants of proton decay). The shopping mall is one place where they can go, get a cup of coffee, and be with people without actual contact. Since this is where people are congregating, community activities come to the malls, at least for publicity purposes. But this just means with the shopping mall, we are talking about the end of the old community and the beginning of the new. And maybe if shopping malls can be so energizing, sucking all of America into their vortex, that means that they are dead places, like dying stars in the new constellation just discovered by the astrophysicists — the Great Attractor. And the truth-sayers of the shopping mall, as the death of the social, are all those lonely people, caught like whirling flotsam in a force field which they don't understand, but which fascinates with the coldness of its brilliance.

PANIC SUBURBS

The sky above...was the color of television, tuned to a dead channel.

William Gibson, *Neuromancer*

Most of all, it is the lawns which are sinister. Fuji green and expansive, they are a visual relief to the freeway and its accompanying tunnel vision. Even ahead of the golden arches, they are welcoming as the approach of a new urban sign-value. The frenzy sites of a decaying Christian culture where reclining lawn chairs, people in the sun, barbecues and summer-time swimming pools can give off the pleasant odors of an imploding Calvinist culture, playing psychologically at the edge of the parasite and the predator.

And the Fuji green lawn? That has already been chemically sprayed to prevent the return of the animal kingdom. And why not? The suburban lawn can be so pleasantly malevolent because it is the aesthetic playground where three bourgeois ideological values intersect: a happy celebration of private property values; the ascendant sign-value of leisure time activity as the prime morality of post-liberal society; and the principle of exclusivity (from sexual relations to family recreation) as the rising star of Christian culture at the end of the twentieth-century.

Indeed, in the old days, lawns were only for English aristocracy who could afford their maintenance. Today, all of this has been swiftly reversed, and we all do obedience to the lawn, that is if we have not paved it. This is a nice irony given the history of paving stones in the struggle for bourgeois freedom. In the suburban suicide sites — on those chemically glowing lawns — the struggle has been won.

In advanced capitalist society, the majority of us live in suburbs. Effectively, this relegates the old sociological paradigm of city/country, along with the fortress mentality, to the trash can.

The postmodern suburb ushers in the new (cosmetic) style of "real imitation life." Its appearance was signalled by the movie, *The Invasion of the Body Snatchers*, where progressively the pods grow the physiognomy of the everyday American, complete with the cloning of the shopping mall mentality. Here each comes equipped, at least nominally, with a Harlequin life programed to Scott Peck's *The Road Less Travelled*. Each person in his or her own way "born again," the better to imitate the Way. Not that the Way need be religious or fundamentalist, but rather a way of life that grows on you, feeds from you, parasites you. It's the postmodern suburb, therefore, as a perfect ideological screen: lasered by flickering TV images, inscribed by shifting commodity-values, and interpellated by all of the violence, love and bickering voices of Mommy-Daddy-Me.

In these pleasurable sites of indifferent suicides, mutant biology also explodes into vacant fields transforming them into social networks on the grid pattern of urban development. The measured lawns indicate a new social cosmology reflecting the changing face of the suburbanite. Lawn care, a real growth industry, replicates the same economic activity as the cosmetics industry a decade earlier. Keeping America beautiful now requires the cosmetics' approach to space, as the mirroring of the cosmology of the lived experience of the self. The fusion of the lawn care specialist and the beautician creates the "unconsciousness" of post-hoc suburban life. The aestheticization of all the post-lawns as the ruling metaphysic, then, of the new middle class.

Politically, the impact of the shedding of the city by the suburb has led to the practical abolition of resistance and rebellion. Where modernity linked urban centers by communication routes, postmodernity differs through the creation of suburbs as sites of minimal power. As a low intensity field, the suburb has multiple points of entry and exit, making it invulnerable to attack by any conventional political means short of bureaucracy. Biologically driven, the suburban epicenters appear much like weeds in a field, constantly bleeding the central claims to power whether this be of a capital or of a garden. Having permanently left the city for a safer site, power can only be reconstituted in the absences by media holograms. Having lost any legitimate claim on the real, the city is forced by the suburb to engage in fictive and hyper-aesthetic claims as a way of governing the imitative process.

Ultimately, the origin of the suburb could be traced to the *demos* in classical thought. The country, or what is outside the city, has successfully appropriated the political posture of democracy, changing forever the way in which citizens and assemblies are constructed. No longer the participatory democracy of the New England town assemblies, but now, *suburban democracy* or life outside the class-ridden town or city of former times, as a gyroscope to political activity. Similar to the reaction one gets to the request to load the dishwasher, local suburban politics has a dampening effect on life. Having shed class politics, suburban democracy also has little need for interest-group politics. Here, politics has to do with the aestheticization of lifestyle: boundaries (roads), waste systems (sewers), education and recreation for the young, and the prevention of the wholesale invasion of private property — continued small invasions of the property principle being acceptable. True to the spirit of indifference, the suburbanite only calls for a limited immune response to parasitical intrusion.

The political stability of the suburb comes from the large number of cloned, constituted spaces such as plazas, which ensure that the organism will replicate and be preserved. The genotype is easily recognizable through the sequencing of fast food restaurants, car dealerships, gas bars, carpet outlets, and discount stores. Of course, there are no politics here. In fact, there is nothing to do other than to grow. This biological metaphor is pursued vigorously in other growth areas: tennis, bridge, bible study groups and exercise classes.

From the beginning, TV producers have recognized that their edge is in furthering and exploiting this boredom. Thus, the initial success of the soaps and of TV itself. Without the suburbs, TV would not have so easily displaced other forms of cultural activity. So complete has been the suburban cultural victory (entertainment as the growth industry *par excellence*) that culture could only turn to TV through the PBS (Public Broadcasting System), which emerged from the mutual desperation (for suburban attention) of the centralized state and of equally centralized cultural organizations. This cultural foray against the spreading indifference of green lawns cannot compete against the postmodern "rural idiocy" (Marx), or as Blake has it, "vegetable consciousness."

The future of America may or may not bring a black President, a woman President, a Jewish President, but it most certainly always will have a *suburban* President. A President whose senses have been defined by the suburbs, where lakes and public baths mutate into back yards and freeways, where walking means driving, where talking means telephoning, where watching means TV, and where living means real, imitation life.

The 19th Century Town as a Postmodern Site

> The newest idea in planning is the nineteenth-century town. That's what is really selling.
>
> Andres Duany
> *Atlantic Monthly*

But *which* suburbs? *Atlantic Monthly* recently reported on the surging development in the United States of the nineteenth-century town as the newest reflex in suburban development. Influenced by romantic images of pre-twentieth-century America, developers are now constructing built environments for towns which never existed in actuality. Just like Grant Wood's *American Gothic* which was originally painted as a satire of the American spirit but which has

Photo: Philip Langdon

been flipped into its opposite — a glorification of the pioneering American personality, so too, the avant-garde theorists of the suburban dreamscape are now building fake 19th century towns, pastiche both in form and color, for neo-suburbanites who wish to flee the city (and modernist suburb) in ruins. Like the pattern of frontier settlement where the advance edge of the population always moved on abandoning what was behind, the neo-suburbanites are now recapitulating American history, but this time the territory explored is fantasy.

The simulacrum of the nineteenth-century town, therefore, as a postsuburban site for the American city in ruins. Here, Dante's *Rings of Hell* find their urban equivalents in a new triptych: an inner city which oscillates between the immiserisation of primitive capitalism for the homeless and opulence for the ruling class; the old modernist suburbs which, with their fast food outlets and shopping malls based on consumerist lifestyles, have become the new cities for working and middle class people; and now, the postmodern towns as memory elements for a city which never existed. Here, there is a perfect mediation of city and suburb: the architectural dream of the nineteenth-century town and the ultra-suburban reality of intense policing. Postmodern towns, therefore, as a maximal fulfillment of speed and the city: dream sites which collapse into purely symbolic sign-systems.

And the old inner city? Well, in Detroit at least that has already reverted to an earlier stage of primitive agriculture. Recently, Detroit city politicians began talking of a new scheme whereby the deserted inner city would be converted into agricultural farmland, complete with homesteading for those now unemployed workers who originally fled the South for the car factories of the North. It's the old city center, therefore, as the new rural countryside — back to sharecropping. Suburbs become the new modern city (after all this is where most of the jobs are located at the end of the 20th century). And the new 19th century towns become the last American (postmodern) frontier for the rich.

214

PANIC SURREALISM

Salvador Dali

What is the relationship of surrealism to the postmodern condition?

If the early surrealists — Magritte, Roux, Ernst, Dali, Duchamp,
and Miro — can be so popular today with their visions of the pineal
eye, floating body parts, and disembodied power, it is because their
artistic imaginations are brilliant anticipations of the postmodern
destiny as detritus and aleatory sacrifice. Indeed, if art is a semiological screen for the actual deployment and relays of political power,
then remembering surrealism is also in the way of a dark meditation on the hidden logic of postmodern power. In these artistic texts,
power announces itself for what it always was: cynical truth, cynical desire, and cynical sex as the postmodern aura.

Albert Skeer's review, *Minotaure*, which appeared from 1933
to 1939, was not only an extraordinary demonstration of the surrealist imagination, but, in its privileging of the mythic figure of the
minotaur as the principal theme of its covers (by Derain, Bores,
Duchamp, Ernst, Miro, Dali, Matisse, Magritte, Masson, and Rivera),
it successfully painted the collage of detritus that defines the disappearing postmodern subject. The covers of *Minotaure* are a brilliant cryptology of the key social codes governing the contemporary
human condition.

The myth of the minotaur centers on the white bull, imprisoned
in the labyrinth at Crete, which was created from the sea by Poseidon.
In Greek mythology, the minotaur was a monstrous double, sometimes with the head of a bull and the body of a man or, conversely,

with the body of a bull and the head of a man, which was offered adolescents as sacrifices by Minos, the king. Being neither fully human, animal, or god, the ambiguity of the figure of the minotaur placed it outside the conventional bounds of norms of morals and reason. This was, indeed, a monstrous double which could be so important to the European surrealist movement because its mythology inscribed both the violence of the last sacrificial rites and cultural alterity (part bull/part man) as the foundational text of western society.

Two of the covers, in particular, provide a deep understanding of the significance of the myth of the minotaur to the surrealist world. The Salvador Dali cover of 1936 and the 1937 René Magritte cover are illuminants of the return of the minotaur, in neo-fascistic form in twentieth-century Europe. Here, the mythic origins of the dialectic of enlightenment are made the fateful subject of artistic meditations.

The Dali cover art is an almost lurid example of the beastialism of declining cultures. Surrounded by the artifacts of a defunct high culture, the bull's head, with its bloodied tongue and riveted collar dripping red, anticipates the violent return of the postmodern minotaur. The parasitical, blood-sucking head of the minotaur is accompanied by the red nails of its hands and feet and, most grisly, by the single-eyed leer, both aggressive and penetrating in signalling the reversal of sexuality for women. And (part)woman she is with her half-complete artificial body; the seam of the nylons replaced by the rivets of her artificial leg; and the drawer for a breast waiting for contributions just as the handkerchief awaits any emotion. The sex of the minotaur protrudes from its body, fully androgenous, crablike, a pineal claw itself bloodied: all of this portraying the minotaur as somehow castrating/castrated. But this monstrous double of androgyny is not without seduction, as the keys, glass, and bottle are inscribed in the flesh, accompanied by the ankle bracelet/iron. Above all, Dali's cover has the aesthetic style of the negative attractor, of the inviting aggressivity of the dying days of the sexual look. Nothing survives sex with Dali's minotaur.

The opposite side of this aggressivity, the world beyond the last sacrificial rites of sex *à la* Dali/Sade, is the detrital coding of the René Magritte cover. Here, the cadaver dominates: fully glamor-clad in fashion, but also fully dead. Humanity, signified by the removable feet, anticipates a postmodern scene where body parts are interchangeable, organs transplantable, and the nervous system fully exteriorized. But not just the body as detrital kitsch, but also the body aestheticized. The artistic setting is Paris (as witnessed by the Eiffel Tower), and the "burning bush" tuba to the side. For, indeed, the revelation of the arts through music creates the moonscape of the dead; the harmony of the heavens; the background music/noise

René Magritte

which disappears into the midnight sky. What remains of the human body takes the form of the upward gesture to the night sky captured perfectly, the enlarged pelvis which is stacked up to the dwarf head of the women (whose clonal reproductive sterility dominates thought in Magritte's world). And, of course, Magritte's cover is a remake of the William Blake etching, *The Bellman*, which announces closing time for a culture of religious and cultural artifacts/cadavers. Whatever solace might be found in the burning bush will soon be suppressed by the suffocating reality of social detritus.

The sterility of the sex of Magritte's minotaur parallels, in reverse image, the bloody aggressiveness of Dali's. Each minotaur is an anticipatory social code of the production of virtual bodies in postmodern society. Rotting cadavers for Magritte/prosthetic technology for Dali. These surrealist covers are, in fact, the two pincers of the Dali crab biting into the cyberspace of virtual bodies, false breasts, and decomposing culture. The Magritte cover presages the quick transformation of Paris into the site of archeological tourism, with cadavers being privileged viewing in the Musée d'Orsay. The Dali creature/woman has already been absorbed into the pestilential sex of the ultramodern scene.

Here, therefore, is a new mythology for a world of post-Minos, where all we touch glitters like gold.

PANIC SEAGULLS

The story is told by a lifelong resident of St. Ives, a Cornish-woman in her late-fifties married to a baker.

They didn't used to be here like this, not so many of them least-ways. And what there was used to follow the fishing boats, follow them right into the harbour. Not that there's the fish out there now, the herrings have gone like the pilchards before them. What boats there are go out of Newlyn, and the gulls don't get much of a look in, what with the new market and those refrigerated lorries taking the fish off god knows where, France, Spain, ridiculous really, you'd think they'd have their own fish, wouldn't you, not bother about ours. But the gulls, they stayed right here, breeding like buggery. Look around you in the spring, every roof's got a pair of them. Of course you can eat the eggs, though I wouldn't, not when you've seen what they eat, anything. You'd think some bright spark in one of the restaurants would have had the idea of putting gulls' eggs on the menu. Pink inside, not yellow. Local speciality along with pasties and fudge. Emmetts'll eat anything, just like gulls. Some folk boil the eggs and put them back, and the stupid bird will sit on them all through the summer. Risky business though, doing that, likely to get your eyes pecked out. Did you know a few years back some-one at the Town Hall had this idea of cutting down the numbers, put out a request for help, but so many people turned out with guns, nets, poison, catapults, anything you could think of, they called it off because they thought they'd polish the lot of them off, and what would the tourists feed their chips to then, eh? Of course, some of the people here actually like them. One or two of those artists, for instance. As far as they're concerned gulls live on some kind of higher plane. Emblems of a spiritual order, one of them said to me once. I said to him, "You should see your emblems of spiritual whatsit scoff a mackerel twice their size. The bugger gets halfway in and sticks there on the hooks at the back of the gull's throat until the front half's digested and it can swallow the rest." Spiritual my arse, 'scuse my French. Tell you the worst thing about them, it's that peck-ing at the bin bags in the middle of the bleeding night. It's enough to send your round the twist. And in the morning, you should see the mess, everything pulled out the holes they've made and strewn all over the place. Me, I'd shoot the lot of them. Have you noticed, there are practically no other birds here? The reason for that is the seagulls eat the eggs and the chicks. Charming. I'll tell you some-thing, maybe I shouldn't, but there's one way to finish off the buggers. Get a bit of bread, cover it in baking powder, and throw it to them. As soon as that baking powder hits their stomach juices it starts to fizz, and the next thing you know the gull's exploded, whoomph. In mid-air, I wouldn't want to be under it at the time, it's bad enough being shat on by the things, though they say it's lucky. Never brought me any luck, and it's happened hundreds of times, usually after I've had my hair done. You had it happen to you too? Well, maybe it'll bring you luck. You remember the film *The Birds*? Or were you too young? You do? Then you'll remember the bit when the gull swoops down and pecks the girl, can't recall her name, and she puts her hand up to her head and pulls it away with blood on the finger of her white glove. That Hitchcock, he changed it to California, probably because it was close to Hollywood, but the original story, that was set right here in Cornwall. Daphne du Maurier wrote it. Lovely woman. She didn't have any fancy ideas about seagulls, that's for sure. I started to read that *Jonathan Livingstone Seagull* once. Made me sick. Stupid bugger, I thought. I'll tell you the book to read if you want to really know about seagulls. It's by a French bloke, Michel Tournier his name is, it's here in the library. It's called *Gemini*, which means twins. There was this garbage dump somewhere in the south of France. During the night the rats have it to themselves, but then when it starts to get light, the seagulls come back and the rats head for cover in their burrows, except for a few stragglers who get caught by the gulls. In the evening it's the other way round, gulls flying off, the slow ones getting grabbed by the rats. Here it's gulls, night or day. Maybe we need a few rats to even things up a bit. Did you read in the paper the other day about this new yuppie disease, comes from rat's urine, so they said? It seems waterskiers are getting it. There was something in today's paper about radioactive rats in a power station somewhere in Wales. Next thing we'll have radioactive seagulls, shouldn't be surprised. Or a new form of skin cancer from being shat on by them. I shouldn't say things like that really, but you don't know anything anymore, do you? But here am I, rabbitting on, when all you've come in for is your pastie. That'll be 53 pence. Thank you, my 'andsome.'

Michael Westlake

T

PANIC TV

Max Headroom as the First
of the Cyber-Bourgeoisie

This is Max Headroom as a harbinger of the post-bourgeois individual of aestheticized liberalism who actually vanishes into the simulacra of the information system, whose face can be digitalized and fractalized by computer imaging because Max is living out a panic conspiracy in TV as the *real world*, and whose moods are perfectly postmodern because they alternate between kitsch and dread, between the ecstasy of catastrophe and the terror of the simulacrum.

Max Headroom, then, as the first citizen of the end of the world.

Quantum Politics

In quantum politics — where TV is the real world of political experience — Weber's classical formulation of "charisma" as the driving force of historical

PANIC

change has now been replaced by what particle physicists like to call "charm." In the age of politics before TV, charisma could be so important as an element of leadership because it was the rare ability of leaders to inspire loyalty and faith in the legitimacy of their authority solely by virtue of an intangible, mysterious and rare quality of personality: what the Christians used to describe as being in a "state of grace." In TV politics, however, charisma as an intrinsic property of political personalities has long been eclipsed by charm as a designer property of political *images*. In quantum politics, there are no political personalities *per se*, only spectral images of political leaders — each a packaged simulacra of the latest tracking polls and subliminal advertising techniques, and each given a certain media spin cut overnight to the latest shift in public moods. Here, it is no longer charisma as a sign of a political leader "with grace," but charm as a certain sign of the presence of media grace.

This is not to claim, however, that force of personality is absent. Quite the opposite. In quantum politics, it is just the intersection of biography and history in the simulated form of designer images which produces charm as one of the elementary political particles. Some media images possess it, and others do not. And while the presence of charm is instantly recognizable by the frenzied scene of media fascination which it evokes, there are, just like in quantum physics, positive and negative states (numbers) of charm. So, for example, while Gary Hart in his first appearance as a presidential candidate in 1984 could prosper immediately under the sunshine sign of positive charm, in 1988 his reincarnated image (complete with tweeds) could instantly attract the same fascination, but this time to read all the polls and count the votes it was the dark and deadly fascination of a politican with *negative charm*. The very same with Ollie North: that rare intersection of biography (militarized) and history (a TV-subordinated Congress) which produced a political image charged with hyper-charm. But again, to read all the tracking polls which blipped out, as time went by, a steady staccato of negatives, Ollie's charm, just like Gary's after him, was not sunshine charm but dark charm: the ability to fascinate because ultimately so discordant in a TV world which requires periodic disturbances to achieve escape velocity and to evade its own implosion into the inertial drag, but which, in the end, just like in particle physics has as its highest value the necessity of aesthetic (political) symmetry.

In a TV mediascape which always verges on the immobility of stasis, the production of charm, positive and negative, and its assignation to a floating scene of political images is an absolute survival technique. TV also produces, then, a whole rhetorical theatre of predators and parasites, each signified with either sunshine or dark charm, to momentarily disturb the media field, and to incite flagging interest in that postmodern fiction called the audience.

Slime Tracks

Most television networks and some newspapers conduct nightly "tracking polls." In 1988, expectations are measured against last night, not last week...voter preferences are volatile night to night.

The International Herald Tribune

The technology of tracking polls are the bubble chambers of quantum politics.

In experimental physics, bubble chambers are instruments in which the ionized path of small, invisible (elementary) particles moving under intense pressure through a liquid mixture can be traced, and photographed, with the most minute deviations in their direction or decay rates immediately calibrated. So too, in quantum politics, tracking polls follow on a nightly (and hourly) basis a tiny sampling of voters with the intention of providing a political microphysics of the timing and direction of key transformations in voters' perceptions of candidates. And just as bubble chambers in physics never measure the phenomenon itself (because of its ultra-speed, elementary particles always escape detection), but only the after-traces of elementary particles as they move across the liquid screen; so also, tracking polls provide information sensitive photographs of the electoral after-shocks of significant changes in the daily political scene. A whole turbulent technology of politics: TV debates; the injection of negative advertising (about political opponents) into the circulatory system of the mediascape; the propagation through intensive advertising campaigns of new leadership images instantly styled to the graphics of last night's tracking poll; the inoculation of the simulacrum with *emotion serums*, ranging from misinformation about the personal qualities of opponents (and their families) to demographically upbeat mood advertisements about themselves.

Of course, the effectiveness of the technology of tracking polls rests on the outstanding fact that in quantum politics, TV is not only the *real* time; it is the *only* time.

PANIC TOYS

Toys are an early warning system of coming transformations in technological society. Why? Because toys, which have had traditionally a low epistemological profile and an absence of surveillance, are precisely how new technologies are injected into an unsuspecting culture. Children are alternatively pioneers of and objects of market experimentation for the technological simulacrum. And toy manufacturers? They are the first and best of the new scientists of the postmodern world.

Or maybe it's something more. Not toys just as the leading probes of technological society, but postmodern toys now as an early sign of the mutation of technology into the last rites of sacrificial mythology — the search for surrogate victims — in the detrital days of American society. Here, the old cartoon world of Roy Lichenstein's *BLAM* and *ZAP* has suddenly gone into eclipse; disappeared into the market boom of the hyper-marché where all the fictive worlds are instantly available. Indeed, Fisher-Price and Mattel can take the lead in metamorphosing designer babies into designer fashion, because they are now trendy lifestyle companies, welcomed into the 'formation' of children, whether at home or at school. Not so much production, education or seduction, but *ingestion* as the simulational world of toys are accepted naturally by the digestive systems of the young. In fact, it's gone one step further. To add to the lifestyles of children, many multinationals now market their trademarks as digestive toys: Burger-King, Pizza Hut, Baskin-Robbins, Kentucky Fried Chicken.

And toys as the last rites of sacrificial mythology? Over the last few years, the sales of toys could quadruple because of the symbiotic relationship between toys and the exterminist desire to vaporize one's enemies. Ideologically, the success of (boys) toys rests on their analogy to nuclear war. Like the exterminist vision of nuclear holocaust, or the wrath of Old Testament religion, the threat of destruction is infinite: God's power, God's body, Godzilla — yet the everyday performance is fictive. From Mask to Spacemobile, toys, and particularly male-stream toys, can be purchased so enthusiastically because as forms of limited nuclear war, they partake so deeply of the classical myth of annihilation.

If toys are, in fact, living-room simulacra of nuclear warfare, then their privileged target is the nuclear family. As advertisements for *Transformers* insists: here, there is "more than meets the eye." *Transformers* are the big sign of the oscillating child, who lives with the imperative of constant field reversal in order to secure flagging attention. A six-year old *Maxwell's demon*, postmodern children act now as key operators in the family system, altering modes and states as they parasite the power structures which parents try desperately to impose. Like *Transformers*, the new alterity is not between good and evil as in traditional family morality, but between two faces of power. On the one hand, all the technological paraphenalia — cars, trucks, or planes — represent their technical function faithfully (they are instantly mutatable into invaders), or are defenders brimming with armaments. Postmodern children are like those *Transformers*. Not schizophrenic, but learning at an early age all the main tactical manoeuvres governing the position of the child in the group. *Transformers*, therefore, as an outward sign of the mutation of the postmodern family into power relations which oscillate between parasitism and predatorism.

Consequently, the 'good' or 'evil' child no longer really exists, because this would require a family panoptic operating with the logic of a constant surveillance system. Today, parents have lost this modernist power apparatus as their senses — the staring eye, the penetrating look, the yelled command — have been exteriorized outside themselves in the disembodied sensorium of the mediascape. The outering of the nervous system of the family leaves a chattering Daddy, a wistful Mommy, and a constantly mutating child. As long as children shift constantly from power source to power source (just like all the *Transformer* toys), they can sense victory is at hand. The family abuse dictated by this shifting alterity gives rise to the love/hate couplet which links, while simultaneously deranging, postmodern families. In this friendly war, the agreed upon survival tactic is the enthusiastic acquisition of the next toy to further our enjoyment and pleasure, and to fill up all the orifices, every one. Oscar, whose life as a garbage can dominates *Sesame Street*, is a prime time sign of the transformation of production society into waste culture.

But still, toys would not be consumed with such an intense velocity of circulation if it were not for the house to house (host to host/parasite to parasite), advertising of toys on TV. Toy manufacturers were probably the first to understand that on telelvision *only* advertising is interesting, regular programing having been doomed because it can only reach the level of lifestyles. Lifestyles are too general to sell anything other than themselves which we have all bought already. On the other hand, toys *are* TV programs, and hence guarantee the quick absorption of the product directly into the digestive system of the young. If only Proctor and Gamble could really create a soap to rival the *Care Bears* in their wonderful "land of care-a-lot."

But then, TV is also a viral toy targeted at the postmodern (view-

Garbage Pail Kids,
© Topps Chewing Gum

ing) family. With powerful strobe-like flashes every ten seconds, the image is dissolved only to re-explode again on the screen in a hysterical effort to restore fading attention spans. It is TV as a laser canon which establishes its future in the commodity marketplace. As the latest 'interaction' toys demonstrate, these electron bursts, unseen and hence useful, can be channeled to simulate war. It will not be long before we can simu-shoot our favorite politician, Hollywood star or newscaster.

For here is the key to the new wave that is already breaking over the North American market as toy manufacturers link up with entertainment and computer industries to promote toys for adults. With the second childhood of the Baby Boomers comes new toys, from micro-computers to wind-surfers, and all this playing on the age reversals immanent to the logic of a fashion culture. Now Daddy and Mommy can finally get into the game too.

But if adults can reverse field on their children by appropriating fun/toy culture, then children can also entertain themselves by seizing on the cynicism of this rush to be born again. *Garbage Pail Kids*, therefore, as the truth-sayer of cynical culture. Here are all the markers of cultural inertia. The space program prefigured in *Haley's Vomit*; the world of biotechnology in *Joan Clone*; the disembodied eye of postmodern power in *Bloodshot Scott*; or the lascerated

225

space cadet body of *Moe Bile* with its parodic play on the digestive organs.

But why panic? The kids don't.

U

PANIC USA

America as a Postmodern Screen

Panic USA? That is Dan Rather in America. Not America operating any longer under the old biblical sign of a "city on the hill" and certainly not America now as a replay in fast forward of the Roman Republic of classical antiquity, but something very different.

Panic USA as a postmodern screen — a spectral image — onto which are projected all of the violent, yet ecstatic, symptoms of culture burnout at the *fin-de-millenium*. Like a gigantic superconductor in solid state physics in which all of the molecular switches have suddenly snapped open at a certain warming-point, America is now an empty, transparent, and relational medium — a perfect postmodern media-scape — for processing at hallucinogenic speeds all of the dying energies of the social.

Indeed, in America, science can be the *real* language of power because here theoretical physics is both an experimental, objective description of an outer physical nature and an actual physical description

PANIC

of American social nature generally, and specifically of the post-modern American mind in all of its brilliance and decay under the flash of the Year 2000.

Like Michel Foucault's earlier descriptions of the clinical practices of medicine and penology as instances of a political power which functions under the sign of surveillance, American science now operates as a pure social cosmology. Whether in the *mathematical* language of fuzzy sets, in the *physics* of brownian motion and world strip theory, in the *genetic* language of retroviruses and killer T-cells or in the *computer imaging* language of virtual technology and virtual bodies, American science is a direct read-out of USA Today as a hyper-technological society par excellence.

America as an empire of technology increasingly feeds (parasitically) on the aestheticization of its own screen memories. Energized from within by the instant on/instant off strategies of media fibrillation (Bush's "read my lips," Ronnie's prostrate, Ollie's wink, Casey's brain) which are blasted across the otherwise empty world strip of the American screen, the USA implodes into the dark and dense nebula of its final existence as an aesthetic hologram of science as the American way.

It is postmodern America, therefore, as what the quantum physicists and computer scientists like to call a *virtual world*: a world which has no real existence, only a hyperreal and simulated existence. Processed America, then, as an afterimage of its own violent and excessive implosion into a technological hologram.

Noting that the United States was one society with no history before the age of progress and thus free to commit itself fully to the liberal and secular vision of technological progress as freedom, the social theorist, Talcott Parsons, once remarked that the American polity was formed on the basis of a fateful and unique fusion of religion and technology. Parsons could intimate that the true religion of America was America because here the dynamic vision of the fully realized technological society (technology as the *horizon* enucleating American empire — where technology is understood as freedom, never deprivation) harmonized perfectly with even the most fundamentalist of religious claims which, at their deepest and most inspiring moments, were loyal to the collective idea of America as the production of a *new holy community*.

In its fully measured and classically liberal expression, the fusion of religion and technology around the making of America as a new holy community was politically coded and energized by a series of key antinomies in the American, that is to say, in the moving forward edge of the advanced liberal mind. Not only the classic social antinomy of a progressivist vision of social justice versus absolutist fundamentalist movements (which was skewed in the direction of natural law); but also the political dualism in the American mind between the will to democracy (internally) and the will to empire (externally); the legal dualism between contractarian theories of justice and constructionist theory; and even, as Frances Fitzgerald has suggested, a deep schizoid tension in the contemporary American mind between the very term *America* (with its missionary invocation of the American fate as somehow coeval with world historical destiny) and the USA (as a political code for the federalist constitutional compromise structuring the American way).

Cyber-America

While modern America may have been politically coded and internally structured by classical dualisms of the liberal kind, Panic USA — postmodern America — is just the reverse. The violent implosion and cancellation of the old liberal dualisms in the American mind is, in fact, the real parasitical content of postmodern America. No longer, therefore, progressivism versus fundamentalist conceptions of justice, liberalism versus conservatism, technology versus culture, or democracy versus empire; but the simultaneous schizoid existence of *all* the referents to the hyper. America as a hyper-bible country *and* a technological sensorium driven forward by its own (simulated) recovery of primitive mythology; America as a techno-democracy *and* the empire of cyberspace; designer personalities *and* the fibrillated state. Not then a real American political logic, but rather, random flashes of media energy from all the dying referents. Not a dualistic American mind any longer, but America as a cyberspace which can absorb all of the energies of the violent, disaccumulative, and excessive times at the end of history. And not even the semiological dualism of America/USA, but now a robo-America: a gleaming, beaming USA which operates in the liquid sign language of its own mythic, primitive energies. Finally, postmodern America as a blank sign of the actual disappearance of the history, culture, and economy of the USA into its own technological after-image. Post-catastrophe America as a cyberspace. That empty space of the fully realized technological society where, as the Chicago philosopher, Michael Weinstein, has remarked: the ailing father drags himself through the rooms of the empty house, muttering to himself, "My children may have fled and the house might be empty, but it's still the best goddam family in the whole wide world."

Allan Bloom as the Judge Bork of American Academia

Symptoms of culture burnout are everywhere. In cinema, *River's Edge* can be so evocative because it is all about the implosion of the grand narratives of modern America. The film begins with a brief image of the interference pattern on television as if to signal that this is one work of the cinematic imagination which is all about the processing of America through the simulacrum. Here, even the corpses are confused. Sometimes the young woman's body is represented as an aestheticized, spectral image; sometimes as detritus which won't go away; sometimes as a languid object of sexual curiousity; and even as a dead screen-memory onto which are projected all of the anxieties, contradictions, and guiltless feelings of the teenagers. And why not? *River's Edge* is about the missing American family, where the mother announces, in the first of the semiological renunications, that she is no longer a mother. It is also about the missing American psycho, when Dennis Hopper (who portrays a real, nostalgic psycho in the old American mold of spurned love and fetish objects) becomes the executioner of the new American postmodern psycho who, just as Sartre predicted, kills just for the fun of it and who, anyway, in a perfect apotheosis of existentialism in the postmodern scene, has no affectivity. And, finally, *River's Edge* is even about the missing American brother. ("You do shit; it's done, and then you die.")

In American kitsch philosophy, there never was Allan Bloom's America which appears fictionally in his book, *The Closing of the American Mind*. Bloom, as the Judge Bork of American academia, suffers the same howling spirit of revenge and grisly resentment towards women, the young, and the poor. No, never Bloom's America, but Norman O. Brown's penetrating vision in *Closing Time* when he predicted the postmodern mind moving towards random disorganization and the ecstasy of burnout as it lives out the dying days of aestheticized liberalism under the twin signs of passive and suicidal nihilism.

TV as the Fourth Branch of American Government

And finally, in American politics, Max Headroom may have been suddenly cancelled as a television series, but that is probably because, as the first of the cyberpunk TV series, the show was too transparent about the reality of American presidential power politics where all the Democratic candidates, from Dukakis to Hart, Biden and Schroeder, know to their bitter regret that TV is the real world; where "public opinion" can be stampeded electronically by instant

Dan Rather

TV polling; where power, which works now in the language of media lasers, has become liquid and fluid; and where, anyway, TV has now instatiated itself as the *ultimate* branch of American Government: with its own politics (hierarchical and elitist); its own mythology (the defence of the free press as the ruling ideology of a cynical media system); and with its own strategic objectives (the parasiting of the political process by a cyberspace which only it controls).

Television, then, in the age of postmodern politics as a remarkable fusion between the exterminist tendencies of hyper-communication and the most deeply mythological sentiments of the American individual. Or as we hear each evening : "This is the CBS News. Dan Rather reporting." Just perfect for America as a postmodern screen, or as Bataille would murmur, and Nietzsche would nod his assent, panic USA as a postmodern scream.

PANIC URINE

Body McCarthyism

Last winter, we received a letter from an American friend who had this to say about the prevailing obsession in the U.S.A. over *clean bodily fluids.*

> Do you remember loyalty oaths? When I was growing up in the U.S. teachers were required to sign them to affirm that they had never been communists. Some, on principle, refused. That, it seemed to me at the time, required courage in the prevailing hysteria over bad attitudes and disloyal ideas. I remembered loyalty oaths last week when I read an article in the New York Times about the latest twist in the anti-drug hysteria. Since quite a business has developed in the sale of drug-free urine, now there's talk of compulsory drug testing requiring urination under observation. Well, it seems to me only a matter of time, given the contemporary crisis over clean bodily fluids, until someone will decide teachers have to take urine and blood tests to keep their jobs. Aren't we, after all, the guardians of the good health of the young? But can one, as a matter of principle, refuse to piss in a bottle? It does seem ridiculous. The refusal to sign a loyalty oath was quite dignified; to refuse a common medical procedure would seem silly.

Why the hysteria over clean bodily fluids? Is it a new temperance movement driven by the prevailing climate of reactionary politics which, by targeting the body as a new surveillance zone, legitimizes the widening spread of a panoptic power apparatus and heightens distrust of our own circulatory system? Or is it a panic symptom of a more general anxiety about the silent infiltration of viral agents in the circulatory systems of the dead scene of the social: an invasion which succeeeds in displacing fear about the threatening external situation into the inner subjective terrain of bodily fluids?

A *urinal politics* would be one that privileges the body anew as the target of the power of the panoptic, sublimates anxieties about the catastrophe without onto the body as text for an immunological discourse, and speaks the discourse of clean bodily fluids with such evangelical zeal because, like the radiating light waves from a long past explosion of a gigantic supernova, it has only now reached the telematic sensors of Planet One. The rhetoric of clean bodily fluids is really about the disappearance of the body into the detritus of *toxic bodies, fractal subjectivity, cultural dyslexia, and the pharmakon* as the terror of the simulacra in the postmodern condition. The intense fascination with sanitizing the bodily fluids, with clean urination for the nation, is also a *trompe-l'oeil* deflecting the gaze from the actual existence of the contaminated body (as the *sine qua non* of the technification of culture and economy in the high-intensity market setting) and the obsolescence of bodily fluids as surplus matter in telematic society.

As the insurgent basis of urinal politics in contemporary America, the desperate rhetoric of clean bodily fluids signals the existence of the postmodern body as *missing matter* in the cyberspace of a society dominated by its own violent implosion in loss, cancellation, and parasitism. As the missing matter of the social, the body too is the darkness to infinity whose shadowy presence is recognized both by a Hollywood filmmaker like Stephen Speilberg, who, in his acceptance speech at the Oscars, leaned over the podium and effusively thanked "the audience out there in the dark"; and a TV philosopher, Dan Rather, who ends his CBS news broadcasts these days with the little bromide: "Wherever you are, be there" (a direct steal from the movie, *Buckaroo Bonzai's Adventures Across the 8th Dimension*, where Buckaroo cheers up Penny Pretty with the cryptic advice, "Wherever you go, there you are").

The politics of urination under observation are a recyclage of the McCarthyism of the 1950s which, this time on the terrain of bodily fluids rather than loyalty oaths, insists on the (unattainable) ideal of *absolute* purity of the body's circulatory exchanges as the new gold standard of an immunological politics. Less a traditional style of McCarthyism with its refusal of political pluralism and its insistence on absolute commitments to America as the Holy Community, but a hyper-McCarthyism of the late 1980s with its biological vision of the fundamentalist body: a hyperdeflation of the body to the quality of its internal fluids.

Body McCarthyism would be a biologically-driven politics in which the strategies and powers of society come to be invested on the question of the transmission of bodily fluids and which, if inspired by the deflationary and conservative vision of the fundamentalist body, also feeds parasitically on generalized panic fear about the breakdown of the immunological systems of American society. A hygienic politics, therefore, which can be so immediately powerful because it is so deeply mythological, and this because never has power been so deeply subjective and localized as the body is now recycled in the language of medieval mythology. Not sin this time, however, as a sign of the body in ruins, but a whole panic scene of media hystericizations of the secreting, leaking body. The *rubber gloves* the Washington police force insisted on wearing before touching the bodies of gays who were arrested at recent AIDS demonstrations in Lafayette Park across from Reagan's White House; the *sexual secretions* in contemporary American politics where presidential candidates, from Hart to Celeste, are condemned out of hand by a media witchhunt focussing on unauthorized sexual emissions; and *routine testing*, the Reagan Administration's bureaucratic term for the mandatory policing of the bodies of immigrants, prison populations, and members of the armed services who are to be put under (AIDS) surveillance for the slightest signs of the breakdown of their immunological systems.

Ultimately, the politics of Body McCarthyism, which is motivated by panic fear of viral contamination, is steered by a eugenic ideology (William F. Buckley, in an outbreak again of the fascist mind, demands the tattooing of AIDS victims); it responds to a double crisis moment — the *external* crisis as the breakdown of the immunological order in economy (panic money), culture (panic media), and politics (panic Constitution); and the *internal* crisis as the existential breakdown of the American mind into a panic zone when the realization grows that Lacanian *misrecognition* is the basis of the bourgeois ego (the substitution, that is, in the American mind at its mirror stage of an illusory, fictive identity for a principle of concrete unity); it focusses on the illusory search for the perfect immunity system; and it calls up for its solution a whole strategical language of cellular genetics, from AIDS research to Star Wars.

The perfect mirror image of Body McCarthyism is provided, in fact, by the striking relationship between the medical rhetoric surrounding AIDS research and the military rhetoric of Star Wars as parallel, but reverse, signs of fear about the breakdown of the immunological order of American culture. The rhetoric surrounding both AIDS and Star Wars focusses on the total breakdown of immunity systems: AIDS can be perceived in such frightening terms because its appearance indicates the destruction of the internal immunological system of the body (the *crisis within*); while the rhetoric of Star Wars creates, and then responds to, generalized panic fear about the breakdown of the technological immunity systems of society as a whole (nuclear exterminism as the *crisis without*). Both Star Wars and AIDS are theorised in the common research language of cellular genetics, where missiles are viruses and invading antigens body missiles. In both cases, the strategical aim is for the immune systems B-cells (lasers in Star Wars; retroviruses in AIDS research) to surround invading antigens, whether within or without, in preparation for their destruction by cystoxic T-cells or killer cells. Both AIDS research and Star Wars deal with ruined surfaces (the planet and the body); both operate in a common language of exterminism and suppression, and both work to confirm the thesis, first formulated by Michel Foucault in *The History of Sexuality*, that power, today, is principally a product of biological discourse because what is ultimately at stake in power and its applied technologies is the life and death of the species itself.

234

PANIC VIRAL COMPUTERS

The basic rule is, where information can go, a virus can go with it....

In the past nine months, computer "viruses" — which could subvert, alter or destroy the computer programs of banks, corporations, the military and the government — have infected personal computer programs at several companies and universities in the United States, West Germany, Switzerland, Britain and Italy.

Computer viruses, which are altered or specially designed software, are generally malicious in character. Like their biological counterparts, they can be contagious.

A computer virus has the capability of instantaneously cloning itself and then burying the altered coding or programing inside other programs. All infected programs become contagious, and the virus passes to other computers through the software it comes into contact with.

Virus infections also can be transmitted between computers over telephone lines. A single strategically placed computer with an infected memory can infect thousands of small computer systems.

Vin McLellan
New York Times Service

Science fiction writers have often dwelt on the theme of technology, particularly computers, finally coming alive; but they have neglected the flip side of this: computers actually getting sick: catching their death of cyber-colds, sometimes pneumonia, and suddenly dying of natural causes.

In the processed world of geno-technology where simulations *are* first nature, the languages of biology and information technology have now crossed over in the virulent form of viral infections which are sweeping across the computerscape. First, in the form of literature (the "Chinese virus" in William Gibson's classic cyberpunk book, *Neuromancer*), and then in the form of process terrorism. In the latter, genetic cyber-mutants are inscribed in the deep logic of computer programs, sometimes multiplying suddenly and exponentially, like leukemic white-blood cells on overdrive with infinite replications of the same program, sometimes buried in the guise of a time-delay "code bomb", and even taking the form of "delete" viruses which vaporize all the cyber-blips on all the flickering screens.

Consequently, in the world of computer viruses it's not so much technology which comes alive, but just the opposite: biology is cyberneticized with such speed and intensity that it takes on a second, processed life as the genetic language of the computerscape. And so, just like all the postmodern bodies before them, computers now have suppressed immunological systems. Here, computers are passive hosts to two orders of viral infection: to antigens in the circulatory system of the binary code, floating like lymphocytes in the cellular structure of the sequential logic of the program; and to cyber-antibodies, which secrete directly into the bodily fluids (the algorithmic trees in the command directories of process memories). Computers, therefore, as objects of parasitism by all the viral predators, whether antigens or antibodies, which in the endlessly mutated form of servo-viruses are first generation cyber-killers.

Just like in the current crisis surrounding the breakdown of the body's immunity system, a desperate search is now underway for viral suppressors. "To counter the threat of viruses, the company developed Data Physician, which identifies and removes viruses on IBM PC and Unix systems. Since 1985 it has sold 500 copies, more than half to American military buyers." However, what computer security services, from banks to the military, are probably most worried about these days are those energetic hackers who are about to move the new world of computer viruses to a second level of abstraction, and thus threat: servo-viruses of the type known in biology as "hyper-parasites" — parasites which thrive by parasiting the parasite — and thus remain hidden from view from first-order immunological defenses. First, the "code bomb", and then the "cyberhyperparasite'' as adaptive responses to the technification of biology by processed world.

It's probably an accurate premonition of the coming total breakdown of the computer's immunity system that one manufacturer has now begun producing and intensively advertising a portable computer with, of all things, a screen of *blue plasma*.

PANIC VIRAL THEORY

Viral theory, then, at the end of the world.

No longer theory which speaks as the sovereign subject from the outside, but theory as a viral agent which works according to three biological rules: invasion of a host organism; cloning of its master genetic code; and replication of the virus using the dying energies of the organism. And not just parasitical either, but a viral theory which seeks to speed up the deep logic of the genetic code in order that the host organism will be forced to disclose its secret. Viral utopia, therefore, as the end of a post-politics of invasion, cloning and instantaneous replication.

PANIC VANITIES

Dangerous Dunaway

Photo: Helmut Newton

> Glamor cannot exist without personal social envy being a common and widespread emotion.[1]
>
> John Berger

Faye Dunaway's face, on the cover of *Vanity Fair*, is a typical image of what it is to be glamorous in the late 1980s. Faye Dunaway's face, on the deeper level of fashion as discourse, is a complex representational system of what it means to be a body invaded[2] by late capitalism.

Envy, as John Berger observes, is the essential emotion premissing capitalism and the fashion industry:

The industrial society which has moved towards democracy and then stopped half-way is the ideal society for generating such an emotion.

> The pursuit of individual happiness has been acknowledged as a univer-
> sal right. Yet the existing social conditions make the individual feel
> powerless. He lives in the contradiction between what he is and what
> he would like to be. Either he then becomes fully conscious of the
> contradiction and its causes, and so joins the political struggle for a
> full democracy which entails, amongst other things, the overthrow of
> capitalism; or else he lives, continually subject to an envy which, com-
> pounded with his sense of powerlessness, dissolves into recurrent day-
> dreams.[3]

Vanity Fair is late capitalism's dream-rag *par excellence*. Its shiny
surface/images speak (physically and figuratively) the ultimate
capitalist discourse of exclusive fashionability, notoriety, and success. Its project is insidious: the tantalization and easy appeasement
of the consuming masses with its slick format while its content (i.e.,
the "lifestyle" it espouses) slips through the dreamer's numb grasp.
In the face of Faye Dunaway, as *Vanity Fair* articulates it, the reader
is rendered powerless. The ideal consumer of the glamor magazine
(i.e., the young, middle-class female) is reduced by its images to either
resentful or admiring contemplation of the advantages and privileges
enjoyed (flaunted) by its icons of "femininity."

The historical significance of the title "Vanity Fair" is interesting and ironic, taken in the (post)modern context of 1983 when (after a hiatus of several years) *Vanity Fair* emerged anew, to quote
its publisher, as a magazine that "captures the sparkle and excitement of our times, our culture."[4] The term "Vanity Fair" itself der-
ives from early English literature — from Bunyan's *The Pilgrim's
Progress*. Bunyan's Vanity Fair — a fair set up by the devil in a town
called Vanity — housed all the material delights of earth. Through
it the pilgrims were obliged to pass on their journey to heaven. Centuries later, William Thackeray would build on Bunyan's idea, and
Vanity Fair became the title of his serialized Georgian novel, published from 1847 through 1848. Thackeray's work was studied satire of British high society — conscious and critical of the "sparkling"
vanities of middle class culture. Rife with this heavy signification
granted by its literary heritage, the title "Vanity Fair" as appropriated by a postmodern fashion magazine that dabbles in a kind of in-
the-know, self congratulatory brand of cultural criticism, takes on
a dark dimension. For the title, pulled out of its first-order meaning
system (i.e., the critical work of Bunyan and Thackeray) and put to
the service of a second-order meaning system (i.e., the late-capitalist
fashion magazine slickly designed to sell the very lifestyle it pur-
ports to criticize) is, as Barthes would argue,[5] drained of its significance. The title "Vanity Fair," emptied of the meanings implied
by its original literary contexts, becomes an empty sign for the ex-
igency of the fashion industry and its product: wholesale vanity.

Thus, with all the irony and hip self-reflexivity of the post-modern 1980s, the mechanisms of industrial capitalism stamp themselves "knowingly" across the face of the human body. As our images of ourselves speak the dominant discourse, the discourse speaks us. Out, as they say, of the mouths of Babes. In electric orange lettering that (significantly) matches the lips of Dunaway, *Vanity Fair* literally stamps its approval on her image, as she stamps her "star approval" on *Vanity Fair*. What the cover of the August 1987 issue of *Vanity Fair* espouses is that life is just a fair of vanity: that Vanity is Fair. At $2.50, the price of the dream is right. And "Faye Dunaway" is the (vain)glorious proof.

Participating with the fashion discourse to set the feminine icon above and apart are Dunaway's stardom, notoriety, beauty, wealth — and indolence. As conspicuous consumer — as a "hero of consumption"[6] — she is built into the capitalist system by the fashion industry to instill the envy that will motivate the ideal consumer to try to emulate her "look."

What, exactly, is involved in the "look" that Faye Dunaway gives? Simply, the articulation of power: 1) the power of the wealthy capitalist to appropriate objects/commodities and casually manipulate them beyond all consideration of their use value: sunglasses, but no sun; 2) the concomitant power of consumer goods, in turn, to appropriate the consumer and manipulate her to function as model: the human face as prop for the product to be sold; 3) the ultimate postmodern power of the perfect body as object; the power of the body as perfect object. As Gail Faurschou observes in *Body Invaders*, this is "the look of solitary assurance, of impersonal power, a look absent and unfocussed precisely because it looks out over the look of envy which sustains it."[7] The look of the *Vanity Fair* cover girl is clearly an affront. Dunaway puts us in our place via the postmodern artifact *par excellence*: dark sunglasses. Cut cleanly off from subjective identification through eye contact, we cannot share her experience. The glasses reduce one and all — reader and image — to blockage and impotence. Envy of Faye Dunaway as pure object is all that the despotic[8] image will allow.

However, because this is the image of a famous face — and a face directly named within the text — the perfect female object preserves a degree of subjecthood in spite of us and our postmodern predicament. What manifests here is an instance of the resistance built into the dominant, hegemonic order of which Antonio Gramsci speaks. The objectifying tendencies of patriarchy and late capitalism must work to "win" and "sustain" their ascendency. Thus, the despot of fashion imagery — because she is female — clearly must be fetishized in order to allow her the cultural power she so obviously wields. Dunaway (predictably) attains the status and power of subject via the traditional routes originally mapped out in the work of feminists like Laura Mulvey and Annette Kuhn. That is, Dunaway as woman is blatantly construed as Dangerous (i.e., castrating) and Mysterious (i.e., non-male). Indeed, Faye "keeps us guessing" here through the power allotted to her by the glasses as fetish object/phallic signifier.

The power of the fetish object itself is twofold: firstly, it serves as a replacement for the castrated phallus — supreme icon of power in patriarchal capitalism. Secondly, it serves as an abnormal stimulus for desire. Thus, the sunglasses can be read as the phallus interceding, if you will, between the power of Dunaway's gaze (as independent and successful woman/famous star) and the ideal (female) consumer. Dunaway, her power and her "achievements" thus conveniently become something that the ideal consumer can never fully subjectively identify with and can never have. The class struggle perpetuates. And the glasses continue to stimulate in female readers the debilitating desire to be Dunaway (perfect object of the consumer gaze) and, simultaneously, to yearn for the insidious phallic power she hides behind.

The unreality of the orange lips and the deliberateness of the black veil are also interesting fetishes/signs:

> The signs are there to make the body into a perfect object ... this perfection of the body into an object of glamor is a feat accomplished through a long and specific labor of sophistication ... in which none of its real work (the work of the unconscious or psychic and social labor) can show through.[9]

With slightly parted lips we have the stereotypical female orifice — vulnerable to and inviting phallic penetration. With the veil (which harks nostalgically — but I would not say ironically — back to the forties and fifties: a time when the roles "masculine" and "feminine" were more clearly socially defined) we have the female face symbolically netted and contained.

Thus, onto the surface of a live subject — onto the face of a "real" woman (i.e., Dunaway in flesh-and-blood) are plastered the fetishistic commodities by which late capitalism reduces female persons to "perfect objects."

The color reduction technique used in this photograph only further epitomizes the essential pallor of postmodern times. Human eyes are blacked-out. Human hair turns to sepia like tired fall leaves. Human skin "achieves" the cold perfection of powder-white marble. The "sophisticated" and "glamorous" image of Faye Dunaway that remains is nothing but a postmodern death mask — a mask signifying the death of the subject: indeed, it is highly unlikely that any culturally-schooled reader would have been able to identify the image as Dunaway had her name not literally been spelled out in the text: "In these frozen figures, flawless skins, blank stares, there is no pain, no fear, nothing moves, and nothing could move these invulnerable figures bereft of affect and expression."[10]

What we have, then, in *Vanity Fair's* re-presentation of a famous Hollywood icon is woman/subject/author Faydin' Away. To read this cover closely is to uncover "glamor" and our envy is conditioned to feel and to arrive at the con-textual truth of the image: Faye Done Away.

An image like *Vanity Fair's* "Dangerous Dunaway" is not to be indignantly judged and dismissed. It can take us somewhere and show us something about the popular discourses we consume. In the face of such images we can resist the glassy-eyed reverie of the complacent consumer — we can read the text to recover the I/eye. The complexity of the text itself is the flaw in the veil of glamor — the hole in the armour of patriarchal capitalism's fashion industry. In this light, the black spots on Faye's ivory white forehead and high-boned cheeks can be read subversively — as tell-tale signs of the image's putrefaction and decay. Ironically, the postmodern text itself gets us past the mask of glamor — gets us inside and beyond the flat surface of the perfect female image.

Christine Ramsay

Notes

1. John Berger, *Ways of Seeing*, London: British Broadcasting Corporation, 1972, p. 148.

2. This theme of late capitalism invading the body surface is brilliantly explored in *Body Invaders: Panic Sex in America*, eds. Arthur and Marilouise Kroker, Montreal: New World Perspectives, 1987.

3. Berger, p. 148.

4. Calvin Trillin, "Fanfare," *Vanity Fair*, 46/1 1983, p. 55.

5. See Roland Barthe's *Mythologies*, London: Paladin Books, 1973 for his account of the mechanisms of myth.

6. See *Heroes of Consumption* by Leo Lowenthal [source unknown].

7. Gail Faurschou, in Kroker, Arthur and Marilouise, *Body Invaders*, p. 84.

8. Ibid.

9. Ibid.

10. Ibid., p. 85.

PANIC VICE VERSA

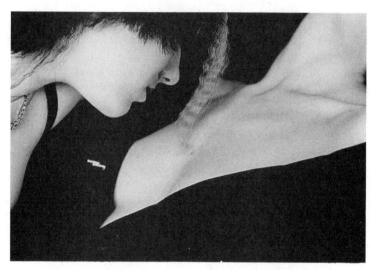

Photo: George Tysh

Scene 6

Versa	We might put it under petting strange women in crowded places
Vice	Such green mice in back of your hair, rising by steps or gradations to resemble local wings and flies
Versa	Perhaps the libidinal odor of money?
Vice	Freud hints at the possibility
Versa	A young wife may want to slink into something more comfortable, more embarrassingly transparent
Vice	Please this way, my fair lady automat, allow me lovely torqueing of your, I remember to lower the seat, soilage. Dots of second cousins between covers

Photo: George Tysh

Versa	Cherry fizz, pomander, *ma pomme d'amour,* it will book us in
Vice	Let's do it in Latin
Set	(skirting the stage in pirouettes, carrying by natty sleights of hand the required saranwrap togas) *Meine Damen, Ich bin Ihr Ding*
Vice & Versa	Backdrop, Fraülein

Scene 7

Set	Naked things, maybe a parking lot, the beginning of rhetoric
Stage Grammar	Vexed, so fraught and rimmed
Set	(in a sweet murmur, loud enough to be heard by all) My ass

Photo: George Tysh

Stage Grammar   So fraught and rimmed with illusions the specta-
tor begins to long for the inevitable insurrection,
the drag of recurring voluptuousness. In audience's
infirmary it appears one has momentary (albeit
clumsy) relief steering one's manifest apparatus
toward the anterior wall just inside the entrance,
harnessed to quite improper use of legs, sharp tri-
angulation above black and blue garter and the
convulsive intelligence of inner lips, clit and boots
contiguous in a position copied from the show,
whiplash.

Set   This spontaneous *mise-en-abyme* comes into play
both mirror and crack no longer a divorce of
generations. I practice charging "the most profound lost object" with pressure of my tongue, the
entire landscape disappearing without a trace,
steamrolled amidst sadistic remarks in the narrow
daylight like a keyboard direction between Speak-

246

ing and Mumbling.

Stage Grammar   The more we bruise the more they plume. Already, the full-length mink freight of erotic connotations has saturated the text, so much premature applause attending to the old schoolgirls of drama, the degreee to which everything passes from mouth to breasts (and vice versa), a syntagm to be described sooner or later in its own right. Of course it is not necessary to repudiate what we don't possess.

Scene 8

Set   Two women, two words, an insinuation of sameness fronts the curtain, blinds the act.

Stage Grammar   Narrate: "The hands of desire ... "

Chris Tysh

Note: This is an excerpt from a longer work entitled *Vice Versa*.

PANIC WORMS

The computer virus is yesterday's disease. It can be destructive, but it has no life of its own. It exists only within perverted software.

Not so the WORM. The worm is a self-sustaining computer life-form. Travelling through electronic networks from computer to computer, it makes copies of itself and, then, continues on its way. Hiding in the recesses of interconnected machines, the WORM uses an alias or erases its previous address. It is a parasite whose single destiny is to reproduce itself indefinitely.

Within hours, the WORM can take up residence throughout the USA, and then the rest of the cybernetically connected world. Travelling, hiding, reading host-lists, taking advantage of daemons, guessing at passwords and unlocking accounts, and then dispatching its cloned offspring.

Can this parasite be stopped? (*Should* it be?) There is only one way. You tie up the name of the shell it would hide in. Will this work for long? Probably not. What will the WORMS of the future bring? Inertia. Just imagine: they could travel from host to host

PANIC

spreading junk mail, tie up all of the phone lines, or make computers operate at a snail's pace.

Snails, then, as the final bio-mutation of the cyber-worm.

Maurice Charland

PANIC WAITING

Alex Colville, *Woman in Bathtub*

...it is a will to nothingness, a will running counter to life, a revolt against the most fundamental presuppositions of life: yet it is and remains a will! And, to repeat at the end what I said in the beginning, rather than want nothing, man even wants nothingness.

F. Nietzsche. Towards a Genealogy of Morals

Alex Colville's painting, *Woman in Bathtub*, is a powerful evocation of the postmodern mood. Here, everything is a matter of cancelled identities (the background figure has no head, the woman's gaze is averted), silence (broken only by the ocular sounds of surveillance), and waiting with no expectation of relief. In *The Will to Power*, Nietzsche spoke eloquently and prophetically of a new dark age which would be typified by *passive nihilists*, driven by despair over their own botched and bungled instincts towards predatory styles of behavior, and by *suicidal nihilists*, who would always prefer to will nothingness rather than not will at all.

Following Nietzsche, *Woman in Bathtub* is a haunting image both of the postmodern self as a catastrophe site and of the meaning of paradox as the deepest language of postmodernism. In this artistic production, an aesthetics of seduction (the muted colors of cool art) counterpoints the presence of inner decay; and the promise of human companionship as reciprocity is immediately cancelled by the reality of communication as radical isolation.

PANIC XANAX

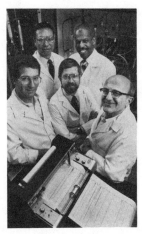

Annual Report, 1982,
Upjohn Co.

The economic laws of liquidity (if there be any) and even the experience in that field, have never adequately been worked out. They remain among the great and pressing problems in our economy.

Adolf Berle and Gardiner Means
The Modern Corporation and Private Property, 1932

PANIC

Let me tell you a story.

On July 30, 1987, a local Boston TV talk show, "The Nancy Merill Show," airs a segment on panic disorders. Special guest on the show is Dr. Gerry Rosenbaum, Psychopharmacology Unit Chief at Massachusetts General Hospital (MGH) and current director of the largest U.S. clinical research program in the cause and treatment of panic disorder. The clinical research is sponsored by Upjohn Co., makers of Xanax, a new, popularly-prescribed drug for panic and anxiety.[1] The other two guests on the show are a mother and daughter, both diagnosed with panic disorder. Dr. Rosenbaum describes panic disorder as a biochemically-based disease, suggesting a genetic vulnerability to it could be passed through the family. Viewers who believe they might suffer from panic disorder are given the number at the Massachusetts General Hospital's Anxiety Research Unit to call for more information. Over 300 people phone the Research Unit within two weeks of the local airing. About 75% of the callers are women.[2]

Adeflor Atgam Baciguent Cleocin Colestid Deltasone Didrex Diostate E-Mycin Gelfoam Halcion Heparin Lincocin Loniten Maolate Micronase Motrin Orinase Pamin Provera

The TV Show is part of a growing public awareness of something called panic disorder: articles in popular magazines, a popularized medical book, and TV coverage have given increased visibility to the new "disease." Like anorexia and bulimia in the 1970s, panic disorder is becoming a popularly-recognized problem which, like eating disorders, seems to afflict American women in growing numbers. Researchers at the Massachusetts General Hospital report that panic disorder affects almost 5% of the American population at any one time, 80% of them women in their childbearing years.[3]

Pyrroxate Sigtab Tolinase Trobicin Uracil Xanax Zanosar Zymacap Artane Asendin Benztropine Caltrate Cephradine Dolene Ergoloid Fibercon Filibon Gevrabon Hydromox Imipramine Loxitane

In 1983, Scribner, Inc. publishes *The Anxiety Disease* by David Sheehan, M.D., who was at that time director of the Upjohn-sponsored clinical research on panic disorder at Mass General. In the book's acknowledgements, Sheehan gives his thanks to Jim Coleman of Upjohn Co., director of the worldwide panic project, an international clinical study of panic disorders in fifteen countries, involving over 2,000 research subjects.[4] The book combines the scientific findings of corporate/medical research on panic with the fictional story of Maria, a young woman suffering from panic disorder, and her "Journey to freedom"[5] through the drug management of her disease. Part Two of *The Anxiety Disease* describes the seven stages of the disease. Sheehan writes, "In general there is some tendency for the disease to progress in its severe form through all seven stages one way or another."[6] Stage Six is agoraphobia, translating literally as "fear of the market-place." In 1986, Bantam Books, Inc. publishes *The Anxiety Disease* for the first time in paperback.

Materna Minocin Nylidrin Orimune Papaverine Pathilon Propranololo Quinidine Reserpine Sulfasalazine Trazadone Vancoled Zincon Abbokinase Betesin Calcidrine Cefol

In 1987, I participate as a volunteer research subject in Mass General's clinical research program on panic disorder and depression.[7] As a research subject, I agree to take an unidentified drug (either Xanax, Tofranil, or a placebo) and to go to Mass General for regular check-ups during the four-month long program. I immediately recognize the drug as Xanax, which I've taken before. Its effects are not subtle: within 30 minutes of swallowing the capsule a pleasant and firm calm fills my body. After participating for four months in the Upjohn/Mass General research, I attend my final check-up. The story goes likes this:
Irene and Philip Faneuil Gallery, 1st floor, Mass General Hospital. We begin between ourselves. Standing before "Woman and Birds in Front of the Sun" by Miro. We and the birds. We and women and the sun. This time she looks only black-edged, a sketch of an outline of her body surrounded and filled in by background. And around the woman's black edges outlined is white space, static on both sides of her edges — inside and out — a white noise inside and out along her edges standing before her standing in front of the sun. I blink. I take the elevator to the 7th floor.
The Waiting Room. I enter for the last time the Psychosomatic Unit at Mass General. I am late. I wait, staring hard at "Haystacks in Provence" above two empty chairs. Reflected in Van Gogh's framing is a red fire alarm that hangs by the door on the opposite wall. I wait staring at the fire alarm reflecting still red among gold haystacks.
Tom's Office. I ask Tom, the research assistant, if I can find out for sure what drug I've been taking, even though I'm pretty sure it's Xanax. The research has been double blind: neither me nor the doctors working with me are supposed to know what drug I'm taking. Tom leaves the room to make a phone call and I stare across his desk at the Word-a-Day Calendar by Merrel Dow that has marked my visits here. At the top of each page of the Word-a-Day calendar is a blue and white logo and the words "Norpramin (desipramine hydrochloride tablets USP). "Today's word is *entre nous* (ahn truh noo) (Fr.)

253

between ourselves; confidentially." Tom returns and confirms that the drug I've been on is Xanax. "Even though I'm not supposed to know that," he says. "So I'm forgetting it right now." Double blinding research — not knowing, then learning, then forgetting again. A curious methodology.

Tom has me fill out two psychological scales. The SCL-90 scale tracks my emotions, thoughts, and behavior over the last week. Any troublesome sexual fantasies? Thoughts of suicide? Belief that people were controlling your thoughts? Ideas or beliefs that you think no one else shares? I answer carefully, within the boxes provided, on a scale of 1 to 5. Next I fill out the Sheehan Patient-Rated Anxiety Scale. Here the scale is Never, Sometimes, Frequently, A Lot of the Time. "Fear that something is wrong with your mind?" I check the appropriate box.

> He recovered eventually, but *entre nous*, he'll never really be the same.
>
> Norpramine Word-A-Day Calendar
> December 15, 1987

The Exam Room. Tom performs the final physical exam. He takes my blood pressure when I'm sitting, then standing. It's 96/70. Then 90/60. He takes my temperature. He takes my pulse. Seated in a green vinyl chair, I pull up the sleeve on my left arm and prepare for him to take my blood. The key preparation for his taking of my blood is for me to look away. I have learned this during years of blood-giving. Always look away. Let this always be a blind taking of my blood.

But today I sit in the green vinyl chair and watch as Tom lays out two glass vials, and three shorter, fat, green plastic tubes. He takes a long thin needle and places it in the flexible needle-holder. I recognize this needle because I have stolen several from the Exam Room. Late at night I have traced the silk sharp point along my flesh, and looked, and pressed. I have imagined taking blood from myself, the needle thrust a solid silver silk pain enters pink flesh soft no sound. A gentle prick in the private companionship of stolen needles. I watch Tom put on white gloves. They snap as he pulls them up around his wrist. He picks up the needle. With one gloved finger he strokes the raised, thick, slightly blue stream of the vein in my left arm.

I watch as he presses the needle into the vein. For a moment this hurts. Blood deep red a thin stream splashes against the back of the clear glass vial attached. I watch my blood fill the vial pressing bubbled and froth pink against the glass wall as it fills. With gloved fingers he removes the first glass vial now full red and attaches a second, empty glass vial. My blood deep red splashes against the back of the clear glass vial. I watch my blood fill the second vial pressing bubbled and froth pink in patches against the glass wall as it fills. I watch him take my blood. This is not blind research. For a moment it hurts. Jiggling the needle by accident, Tom removes the second glass vial and attaches the first short green plastic tube. A thin stream red my blood splashes against the back of the tube. He jiggles the needle again by accident. This hurts. I watch and the tube is not filling. The needle moves again in my vein I catch my breath and the gloved hand quickly removes the plastic tube. Tom places a clean white gauze pad over the vein with the silk thin needle inside. The gloved hand withdraws the needle from the vein in my left arm as I hold the gauze pad and press. Tom says, "Sorry. We stopped getting blood." I press the gauze pad tight against my vein. It still hurts. What will happen now? What happened? I watched the taking of my blood. I did not look away. I watched the taking of my blood stop. Just between us, confidentially, I believe because I watched, the taking of my blood became more difficult. I believe thieving needles and tracing silver across the pink underflesh of my arm and watching the white thin tracks turning to red, I believed this made the taking of my blood more difficult.

But then the problem of my other arm. Of sustaining such a gaze on a silken solid silver needle, not blind to the taking of my blood. Because on my other arm was another blue vein slightly raised and pulsing and as Tom swabbed my right arm with an alcohol-soaked pad I forgot to watch. I just forgot. I went blind for the rest. I don't think really it was the pain. It hurts only a little to watch a solid silk silver needle penetrate your pulsing vein and, accidentlly, get jerked around. The actual pain is very slight. No. I think I just forgot. I became interested in other things. I remembered having a cup of coffee with cream on Charles Street after the rain. And he pricked the vein on my right arm, I could feel it. Then I remembered dinner tonight I needed to buy groceries on my way home. He removed the first plastic tube — I could hear it pop softly as it disengaged — and put in another. I remembered the boxes of white gauze and band-aids labelled and stacked in the brown wooden cupboard to my left. I forgot to watch, really, and while I was forgetting the second plastic tube filled and I heard Tom pop it out and insert the third tube. I remembered the time — 5:05 p.m. there was a clock on the wall and I hoped to be home before 6:00 I'm so hungry. He popped out the third plastic tube and pressed a gauze pad against the vein with the needle inside and pulled out the needle and asked me to hold the gauze tight. He was finished taking blood and had five full red containers on the tray to my left. I don't know really why I forgot to keep watching when he began to take blood from my right arm. But — *entre nous* — really, just between us it may have been because I remembered how many blue veins run through me — perhaps I forgot to sustain my gaze because I remembered the raised blue veins in my right arm, behind both my knees, along my slender wrists, translucent along my temple, pulsing under my jaw and down my neck and perhaps I just recalled — after that moment when my blood stopped flowing into the plastic tube when I possibly imagined that if I refused to look away during the taking of my blood they would grow nervous, they would falter, because they count on that look away for the confident execution of these operations — perhaps I recalled what the stopping of this blood-taking might demand — my repeated and sustained gaze upon my flesh as they find new veins pulsing and blue to press into gently with their silk silver needles — then the insistent attempts as they grow impatient and lose confidence — as they try to take my blood with a long silk needle pressed hard into the veins behind my knees along my wrists down my neck as I twisting and try to keep my gaze steady on this blood-taking and the silver needle tearing the blue silk lining of the veins in my neck, behind my knees, along my slender wrists as I try to keep watching, to not look away. Perhaps this is why I forgot to keep watching, to not look away. Perhaps this is why I forgot to keep watching. And let the last tubes fill red blood as I sat blind. *Entre nous* — this is a possibility. Though I may be wrong.

Cylert Dayalets Enduron FeroGrad Hytrin Iberet K-Lor Lidocaine Nembutal Nitropress Ogen Optilets Peganone Phenurone Quelidrine Selsun Tranxene Tridione Alphalin Brevital Cesamet Darvocet

Half a block from Mass General Hospital in the rain I want very much to have the slip of calendar with today's word *entre nous* — I want it in my pocket. So I walk back half a block and take the elevator to the 7th floor again and enter the Psychosomatic Unit waiting room where it's 5:20 p.m. and the receptionist has gone. I walk past the desk, down the hall to the Exam Room which is empty and cross to the small desk and tear off the page for today, December 15, 1987, *entre nous*. I slip the page into the pocket of my black coat and I leave the Exam Room.

> She recovered, eventually, but, *entre nous*, she'll never really be the same.

A panic post scripting

The market-place in which I find my body panicking is no place, exactly. This market-place in which I am (ex)changed in time — in which the present circulation of capital takes place — is no place really but an historical geography of desire and of power. It can be measured more or less by computerized ticker tapes on The New York Stock Exchange, more or less by the increasingly proliferate and exact diagnoses of mental disorders appearing and disappearing in the American Psychiatric Association's diagnostic manuals, more or less by the changing scripts of our personal diaries, more or less by the market projections of transnational corporations expanding their operations — production, marketing, finance — into every place, really.

As a social researcher and somewhat panicked, I insist that we locate this historical geography of desire and of power, this market-place, by measurements materializing in these many places. And while I believe that the dominant, dangerous feature of the panic market-place is that it is becoming one market — one universal market-place desiring to powerfully materialize all our exchanges, social sexual symbolic — I do not believe every body finds its self yet the same within these market exchanges. Some people still grow more hungry than some others, die more quickly than some others. But for me, a white well-fed American woman with, they said, a "gift for words," my place within the market is for now a position of more panic than some others. And from this place within the market (ex)changing me I search and somewhat panicked for what possibly I would have to give to you in this time within this place and I find this only — I would give you my disease. For free.

Jackie Orr

Notes

1. Massachusetts General Hospital's research programs on panic disorder, and panic disorder with depression, are both funded by private grants from Upjohn Co. (conversation with J. Sidari, Anxiety Research Unit, Mass General Hospital, August 1987).

2. Conversation with J. Sidari.

3. David Sheehan, M.D., *The Anxiety Disease*, New York: Bantam Books, Inc. 1986, p. 11.

4. Upjohn Co. Annual Report 1984, p. 17 [The "worldwide panic project" appears to be renamed the "Cross-National Collaborative Study" in the Upjohn Co. Annual Report 1987]. Countries participating in the study include Canada, United Kingdom, Italy, Mexico, Brazil and Venezuela (conversation with Godfrey Grant, public communications, Upjohn Co., August 1987).

5. Sheehan, p. 7.

6. Sheehan, p. 65.

7. The dates and names associated with my participation in the Upjohn/Mass General clinical study on panic disorder have been changed.

NOTE: The alphabetical incantation of brand-name drugs is taken from product name listings for Upjohn Co., Lederle Laboratories, Abbott Laboratories, and Eli Lilly and Co., as published in the "Manufacturers' Index" in *Physicians' Desk Reference*, 1986.

Y

PANIC YUPPIES (EAST AND WEST)

The Yuppies and Commies have finally got together.

In America and Japan these days, the media are filled with reports of Yuppie families who want the very best that money can buy for their children. Accordingly, a whole contagion in the commercial marketplace of expensive toys: privileged objects in the new parenting zone of "quality time." It is the very same with Communist families in China. There, if the ideological authorities are to be believed, the dramatic drop in the Chinese birth rate (at the forced instigation of the State) has resulted in the appearance of a new cultural phenomena: quality time children (with boys as the privileged gender) who are the inscribed and targeted objects of all the narcissistic affection that Chinese parents can muster.

Consequently, in both East (China and Japan) and West (USA), there is now the creation of postmodern children: children, that is, who are constituted (as Jon Schiller, a San Francisco psychologist claims) as "identified patients" — blank screens — onto which are projected all the anxieties, hopes, and fears of panic

PANIC

parents at the end of the world. The privileging to excess of "quality time" children by panic parents may also be, therefore, a direct read-out of the *lack* at the collapsing center of contemporary families, whether hyper-Capitalist or hyper-Communist.

Z

PANIC ZOMBIES

(Carson and Letterman)

Comedy is indeed serious stuff. Bush campaign manager
Lee Atwater said recently that he kept tabs on Johnny's
jibes to gauge how the candidates play in the 'real'
America.

Dick Polman
Knight-Ridder

If advertisements are the truth-sayers of the TV
programs, which are their media vehicles, then Alpo
Dog Food names the Johnny Carson show correctly.
Johnny and Ed are America's favorite pets. The show
occurs between prime time and sleepy time, with all
of the nocturnal pleasure of a regular bowel
movement.

The Carson Show is, anyway, a real panic scene.
Not, however, panic of the frenzied type, but the
reverse: panic inertia. An unchanging format for a
static submass, which has disappeared into the white
suburban Bantus, and taken to Carson as its nightly
excremental habit. As Carson likes to insist, it's just

PANIC

entertainment: he's the parasite; the audience, the bored voyeur; and the guests, changing particles in promotional culture.

And David Letterman? He is the Johnny Carson of the Reagan youth generation. A little cynicism, a little humor for a generation that the American political philosopher, Michael Weinstein, has described as distinguished by a "strong sense of self, but a weak ego."

As a graduate of Ball State University in the middle of Indiana, Letterman has moved his Hoosier personality from the regions into the center of New York media culture. With Letterman, the dinner party runs its course from hospitality to hostility to the hospital. Letterman is, in fact, the perfect predator: of his audience (his popularity rests with denigrating the audience); of his guests (celebrities are brought out as living targets); of himself (as a supposedly unlikely talk show host); and of TV (*Tonight with David Letterman* parodies the medium of talk shows).

While the secret of Johnny Carson's success is as a cultural parasite; Letterman is a media predator. Here, America at night finds its final destiny as a Hoosier predator, alternating between envy and resentment.

Acknowledgements

PANIC ART
Mark Kostabi
Close Call, 1983
Collection of Richar Interiors Inc.
Photo: Pecka/Noble
Pandering to Feminism, 1984
Photo: Ena Kostabi
Two Cultures, 1984
Photo: Ena Kostabi

PANIC ART IN RUINS
ART IN RUINS
Glyn Banks/Hannah Vowles
Oversite, 1988
Detail of installation
Talbot Rice Art Centre,
Edinburgh
Photo: Joe Rock
Road to Ruin, 1986
Detail of installation
City Museum and Art Gallery
Stoke-on-Trent
Photo: Edward Woodman
New Realism, from the
Museum of Ruined Intentions:
Gimpel Fils London, 1987
Photo: Edward Woodman
Installation *From the Ruins*
at Bookworks Gallery London
Photo: Geoff Beeckman
Road to Ruin Installation
at Stoke-on-Trent City Museum
and Art Gallery, 1986
New Realism Installation
detail from the *Museum of
Ruined Intentions*
Gimple Fils, London 1987
Photo: Edward Woodman

PANIC AMERICA THE BEAUTIFUL
Edward Kienholtz
Back Seat Dodge '38
*While Visions of Sugar Plums
Danced in their Heads*
Roxy Madam
Roxy
Institute of Contemporary Arts,
Nash House London, May to July
1971,
and Kuntshaus, Zurich, February to
March 1971

PANIC ARCHITECTURE
MY TRIP TO GUILD HOUSE
Photo 3, photo credit: Venturi,
Rauch and Scott Brown
Photos 4 & 12, photo credit: Sko-
mark Associates

PANIC BEACHES
Eric Fischl
Cargo Cult, 1984 (Mary Boone
Gallery)

PANIC CHIPS
Don Proch
Pin Cushion Man (wearing Brush
Cut — Listening for *Buffalo Mask*)
1971
Velocipede, 1976

PANIC CYBERSPACE
Stelarc
Event for Anti-Copernican Robot
Newz Gallery, Tokyo — 6 April
1985
*Event for Amplified Body/Laser
Eyes and Third Hand*
Maki Gallery, Tokyo, 2 March 1986

PANIC DESERT
Man Ray
La Fortune II
© VisArt

PANIC FEMINISM
Photo: Jamie Lyle Gordon

PANIC PLEASURES OF INVENTION
Mark Lewis
From the catalogue *Burning*, Artspeak Gallery, Vancouver, Canada

PANIC JEANS
Polo Ralph Lauren
Esprit Jeans
Jordache Basics
Calvin Klein Sport

PANIC LOVERS
Andre Masson
The Transformation of the Lovers
© VisArt

PANIC MANHATTAN
Eric Fischl
Manhattoes (Mary Boone Gallery)

PANIC MASTERPIECES
"Florence Can Knock You Out"
reprinted by permission of Reuters

PANIC MYTHOLOGY
Tony Brown

NIETZSCHE'S CAT (ON PANIC PARTICLE PHYSICS)
Schrödinger's Cat Died of Fright
Tony Brown

PANIC (VIRTUAL) PILOTS
Don Proch
Night Landing Mask

PANIC POLITICS
Mark Gertler
Merry-Go-Round

PANIC RENO ROMANCE
Photos: Steve Pfohl

PANIC SUBURBS
Photo: Philip Langdon

PANIC SURREALISM
Salvador Dali, *Minotaure, La Revue à Tête de Bête*
Rene Magritte, *Minotaure, La Revue à Tête de Bête*
Musee Rath, Geneve
17 October 1987
31 January 1988
Musee d'Art Modern de la Ville de Paris
17 March — 29 May, 1988.

PANIC TOYS
Garbage Pail Kids
© 1987 Topps Chewing Gum

PANIC VANITIES
Faye Dunaway
Photo: Helmut Newton

PANIC VICE VERSA
Photos: George Tysh

PANIC WAITING
Alex Colville
Woman in Bathtub

PANIC XANAX
Annual Report, 1982
Upjohn Co.

NOTES ON PANIC AUTHORS

Arthur Kroker is the Canadian virus. His aim is to invade the postmodern mind, replicate its master genetic code and, in this clonal disguise, endlessly proliferate critical thinking.

Marilouise Kroker, an artist and observer of the postmodern scene living in Montreal, rethinks feminism at the edge of designer culture and theory.

David Cook, a specialist in parallel processing, writes under the melancholic sign of viciousness for fun.

NOTES ON PANIC CONTRIBUTORS

Jean Baudrillard, who lives and teaches in Paris, *is* the postmodern commotion. Internationally acclaimed as *the* author of postmodern culture and society, his numerous works include: *For a Critique of the Political Economy of the Sign, Amerique, Simulations, Forget Foucault, Stratégies fatales and Seduction.*

Elvis Presley is, as *Esquire* magazine recently stated, slim, fit and tan and ready for '92.

Eileen Manion teaches English and Women's Studies at Dawson College, Montreal. She is writing a book on Mary Daly. She is also the mother of identical triplet girls, conceived while she was writing the article, "A Ms.-Managed Womb" for *Body Invaders.*

Hannah Vowles and *Glyn Banks* are artists living in London who work under the sign of *Art in Ruins*. They both lecture on architecture, with the intention of ending architecture.

Don Proch is an artist and sculptor living in Winnipeg.

Chris Tysh, originally from Paris, France and now of Detroit, Michigan, teaches and writes poetry.

George Tysh is the Director of Art Education at *The Detroit Institute of Arts*. He is a writer and photographer.

Mark Lewis is an artist and a member of the collective, *Public Access*, in Toronto.

Avery Gordon is a member of the Parasite Café, and teaches sociology at Boston College.

Deena Weinstein teaches sociology at De Paul University in Chicago, and writes on popular culture and music.

Michael Weinstein, who teaches political theory at Purdue University, is the author of twenty books on politics, culture and philosophy.

Barry Glassner is Professor and Chair of the Department of Sociology at the University of Conneticut. He is currently working on a manuscript, "USA Today: The Television Show."

Steve Pfohl teaches sociology at Boston College. He is a member of the Parasite Café, a theoretical and practical site of intervention within and against the postmodern culture of transnational capitalism.

Christine Ramsay studies mass media culture at Carleton University in Ottawa.

Faye Trecartin, an English student at Concordia University, is working on contemporizing Canadian literary criticism. She writes on issues related to canon-formation and literary aesthetics.

Frank Burke teaches film at Queen's University. He is the author of a two-volume text on Frederico Fellini.

Kim Sawchuk is a graduate student in the Social and Political Thought Program at York University, Toronto. She lives in Montreal, is a founding member of *Media Mania*, and works for Radio McGill's *The Postmodern Commotion*.

Michael Westlake is a British novelist, and an expert on seagulls and other predatory animals.

Tony Brown is a Montreal artist and sculptor, whose works explore the edge of delirium and psychosis in the age of speed and culture.

Andrew Haase is engaged in the politics of avant-garde film production. He is a graduate student in philosophy at SUNY, Stoneybrook.

Jackie Orr, a performance artist living in Boston, writes in the areas of feminism and postmodern aesthetics.

Maurice Charland writes on the rhetoric of technology, teaches communication studies at Concordia University, Montreal, and often travels deeply in cyberspace.

Lee Quinby teaches English and American Studies at Hobart and William Smith Colleges, New York.

Michael Dorland is completing a book on *ressentiment* in Canadian politics and culture. He teaches cinema and communication studies.

NOTE ON PANIC RESEARCHER

Alexis Gosselin, the *Panic Encyclopedia's* cultural reporter on certain strange but deeply interesting developments in the mass media, currently specializes in the areas of panic doughnuts and panic Martians.